THE WRITER'S PLACE

The contribution of the McKnight Foundation
to the general program of the University of Minnesota Press,
of which the publication of this book is a part,
is gratefully acknowledged

THE WRITER'S PLACE
Interviews on the Literary Situation in Contemporary Britain

Edited by PETER FIRCHOW

UNIVERSITY OF MINNESOTA PRESS, Minneapolis

Library of Congress Catalog Card Number: 74-22835
ISBN 0-8166-0735-4

For John Enck,
Who Loved Books and Talk

Preface

As far as i know, this series of talks with writers and literary figures is unique in that it was carried out during a limited period (three months), concentrated on a relatively limited subject — the writer's relation to his society — and elicited the views exclusively of such people as are or were at some time principally concerned with the profession of letters. If the book is successful, it should convey to the educated but uninitiated reader a real sense of what it is like to be a writer in contemporary Britain, of the difficulties of making a reputation, and of the difficulties of having made one. I say "a writer" here because "the writer," as any reader will soon discover, does not exist. Though the framework is limited, the response is manifold, with as many views as there are voices. For the categorizing literary sociologist or historian this may be regrettable, but to others such variety will probably seem an indication of the continuing vitality of British intellectual life. The writer's place is not merely in the garret or the ivory tower, it is also in the university and the bank and the hairdresser's shop. It is wherever he can pause and take literary stock of his surroundings.

Permission to publish has been granted in all cases by the persons interviewed and is herewith gratefully acknowledged.

Contents

THE WRITER'S PLACE

Introduction

IF POETS had written less on the subject of love, La Roche-foucauld wryly observed some three centuries ago, it would be an emotion practically unknown to the general run of mankind. Nature, as another famous aphorist put it, imitates art—or, to be more precise, not so much nature as society. The poet, like a kind of Shelleyan unacknowledged legislator, makes laws which the less perceptive and original reader obeys. The myths of society, those supreme fictions by which it lives because they alone provide its ultimate purpose and justification, are the creations of poets.

Or are they? And if so, what is the relationship of a "poet" like Hitler—a man obsessed by his fictions if ever there was one—to more conventionally defined poets like Uhland, Wagner, and Nietzsche? How much were the fictions of Nazism the fictions of a society and a culture and a literature, and how much of a single man? Or, for that matter, can even an insight like La Rochefoucauld's—so forceful at first glance—withstand closer analysis? Was it the poets who first induced people to fall romantically in love or was it, as C. S. Lewis has maintained, a massive and inexplicable change of consciousness abetted by a feudal order which placed talented and ambitious young men at the service (and mercy) of powerful women? Do the poets, in other words, have the society they deserve, or does the society have the poets it deserves? Nowadays, in the technologically advanced countries at least, the tendency is to choose the latter alternative. La Rochefoucauld, in the modern view, is dead

3

wrong. In "expressing themselves" poets express their society, whether it be a society in love, in indifference, or in revolution. The mirror which the poet holds up to society is of society's own manufacture; the poet is merely the medium and society itself is the message.

That is the prevailing orthodoxy. But like all orthodoxies, it deserves to be treated with some degree of skepticism. Mirrors notoriously distort and reflect only what they are allowed to see. Stendhal's famous comparison of the novel to a mirror traveling down life's highway is unacceptable unless that mirror is held up in all directions simultaneously and unless it reflects accurately even at the edges. But that condition is optically and novelistically—even with the novel at its most experimental—impossible.

It is the writer who chooses, consciously or unconsciously, the mirror which we call his style, and who chooses as well the moment and place at which to hold it up: his content. Even if society, both directly and indirectly, influences those choices, so too does the individual personality of the poet. Otherwise it would be impossible to account for the multiplicity and variety of reflections. Tradition must be made up of individual talents. There has always been a conflict between the writer attempting to impose his vision on society (where it was possible for the writer to express himself freely) and the society attempting to impose its views on the writer. There always will be.

Nevertheless, the writer is perhaps the most social manifestation of Aristotle's social animal. The act of writing is always a social act, since it seeks to communicate, if not a point of view, then at least a view. No matter how deeply the writer may withdraw into a real or figurative desert, he never escapes his reader who continues to peer over his shoulder. Argus-like, the writer always keeps a third eye open and on the lookout for him, even if only in posterity. For without the reader, the writer does not exist; and only through him is he resurrected after death. Taking a cue from Vaihinger's *Philosophy of As If*, it is arguable that Descartes's "cogito ergo sum" should be extended into "scribo ergo sumus"—or even more boldly into "scribo ergo ero."

4

Introduction

The question of the writer's relation to his society is a difficult one, not unlike the problematical relation of the chicken to the egg. Which to take as the point of departure? Should one define the chicken from the point of view of the egg, or vice versa? The only satisfactory solution, perhaps, is to define both from both, and from all the intervening stages as well. The child is father of the man, but so is the adolescent, so (after Freud) is the infant. And the man is father of the child, not only physically but spiritually as well, for only in manhood can he become truly aware of what he was: see Wordsworth's *Prelude* for extended proof.

Reflections on the place of the writer in his society go back almost to the beginning of history. In *The Republic* Plato expelled a whole class of writers from his ideal community, a class whom we would today identify, for want of a better word, with "creative writers": the poets, the fictionalists, the irrational mythmakers. Plato based his decision on "reason," though paradoxically that decision was formulated in a work of the imagination. The state, so far as Plato was concerned, must have a monopoly on fictions and myths. For him the final meaning of the allegory of the cave was that there is only one truth, which it is man's task to discover, serve, and communicate.

So begins the long and dreary journey of the artist as propagandist, culminating in our century in the service of the truths of Goebbels, Zhdanov, and a variety of detergents and toothpastes. This is the point at which society and the writer become most closely intertwined, locked in a materialistic embrace which threatens to suffocate both. In its most extreme form, this condition may be observed in the Soviet Union, where the utterance of competing truths by writers like Solzhenitsyn is rendered virtually impossible. The exit from the allegorical cave is by way of the propaganda ministry. The full illumination of the man-eating, truth-dealing sun, however, comes only when, as in Orwell's *1984*, the ministry of propaganda becomes the ministry of truth. The longest journey, the marriage of artist and state, ends in Room 101 under O'Brien's tutelage. "I kiss the hand of the father who punished me," said the composer Shostakovich after being warned by Stalin to toe the line.

But even propaganda cannot be simply dismissed out of hand. Propaganda *can* be art of a kind, if the official truth is sincerely enough believed in. The rich history of liturgical art bears ample witness to this fact. But significantly this is propaganda for an otherworldly state, for a sun we will only see when we emerge from the allegorical cave of life. Propaganda for this-worldly truths, on the other hand, rarely seems capable of transcending the artistic level of the "Marseilleise."

Are we to conclude, then, that art and politics do not mix? No, probably not. "Politics in a work of literature are like a pistol-shot in the middle of a concert," wrote Stendhal in that powerful and very political work of literature *The Charterhouse of Parma*, "something loud and vulgar and yet a thing to which it is not possible to refuse one's attention." One could cite innumerable instances of the accuracy of this perception, from *Antigone* to *The Aeneid* to *The Divine Comedy* to *Hamlet* to *The Possessed* to *Major Barbara*. Great literature is not necessarily a sociopolitical vacuum, no matter what the art-for-art's-sakers and their disciples, the "New Critics," may have argued to the contrary. Indeed, as Aldous Huxley said, vulgarity—which, by a Stendhalian extension, may be said to include politics—is a prerequisite for great writing.

Perhaps this is merely another way of putting Horace's hoary dictum that art must instruct as well as please and that such instruction must inevitably be in part social and political, man being the social and political animal he is. To argue that this is truistic is in itself a truism, but it is worth pausing to reflect why it should have become so. George Eliot's equation of a literature that is merely amusing with "spiritual gin" is perhaps too severely Victorian, but it makes a point which has its application to modern times as well. Drinking—whether spiritual or physical—is a social act, even when solitary, for it prevents and at times produces behavior disruptive of social harmony. When the mid–twentieth-century equivalent of Eliot's spiritual gin, the television, fails, the consequences are ominous, as in the famous New York electrical blackout.

Spiritual gin versus the nectar of the gods, high style versus low, popular versus serious literature—it is a dichotomy which has plagued writer and reader alike since the beginnings of critical thought. Erich Auerbach's classic study of the representation of reality in the West, *Mimesis*, seeks to trace the history of this separation of styles from Homer's *Odyssey* to Joyce's *Ulysses*, concluding that the progressive fusion, or confusion, of high and low literary styles reflects a progressive blurring of social class lines. Whether this is in fact the case may be doubted by less optimistic observers, but what is indubitable is that, starting with the invention of the printing press, this separation took on an entirely new meaning. The example cited elsewhere by Auerbach of Pliny the Younger meeting his audience in a section of the circus reserved exclusively for the use of the aristocracy—an example which continued to hold true, generally speaking, throughout the Middle Ages, with the substitution of the clergy for the aristocracy—was no longer quite so valid after Gutenberg. By Shakespeare's day, the audience was in the pit as well as in the stalls, and literacy was no longer the virtual monopoly of a single social class. But it was not until the nineteenth century that the literary situation really ceased to be, as Richard Altick has observed, "a dialogue of equals—well educated, socially superior writers addressing well educated, socially superior readers."* Not that, as we shall see, the make-up of writers changed significantly: the change was all on the side of the readers.

This is not the place to trace the development of improved education and mass book production, with their consequent effécts on the state of British letters. Some of this area has in any event already been explored and partly mapped by such critics as Tillyard, Sutherland, Q. D. Leavis, and Richard Altick. The last-named's *English Common Reader*, especially, is an exemplary study of the writer's presuppositions about his audience in the

*"The Sociology of Authorship," *BNYPL*, 66 (1962), 403.

nineteenth century. For the twentieth century and for Britain, however, information is rather less easy to come by, at least "hard" information providing facts and figures. There have been, to be sure, interesting studies of best sellers, detective and spy stories, and popular magazines (with George Orwell's brilliant essays leading the way in most cases), but there has been no coherent synthesis. The closest approximation to one, *The Sociology of Literature* by Diana Laurenson and Alan Swingewood, is more in the nature of a general overview, and where it does touch on the condition of the modern writer as such (as in the chapter entitled "The Writer in the Present Century") it does not advance appreciably on Richard Findlater's pioneering pamphlets of the sixties. On the other hand, the last twenty or thirty years have seen a real flowering of speculative criticism about the relations of the writer to his society. Much of this has been sparked by the Marxist criticism of Georg Lukacs, whose analysis of the writer's situation after the abortive revolutions of 1848 is particularly valuable, despite occasional and spectacular dialectical somersaults. How strong Lukacs's influence has been in Britain is apparent even in the work of critics, such as George Steiner, who are very lukewarm toward Marxism.

On the basis of the small amount of hard information that exists, the only generalization it seems safe to make now is that the background of the writer, both material and spiritual, has changed little during the last century and a half. The main change, not surprisingly, is in quantity: during the period from 1881 to 1931, the number of people in Britain who, for census purposes, declared themselves to be authors rose more than threefold, from 6,111 to 20,599 (the figure for 1951 was 23,822).* But otherwise it was business as usual. Placing the first thirty-five years of this century over against the comparable period one hundred years earlier, the proportion of women to men in the profession was 20.9 percent for the former period, 22 percent for

*These and most subsequent statistics are drawn from Altick's article and from Richard Findlater's *What Are Writers Worth?* (London, 1963) and *The Book Writers, Who Are They?* (London, 1965).

the latter, or a negligible increase of slightly more than 1 percent. In terms of social class (as defined by the origin of the father) the percentages for the two periods were as follows: upper class, 12.7 percent and 10 percent; middle class, 83.9 percent and 84.2 percent; and lower class, 3.4 percent and 5.8 percent—again a fairly negligible change, though with a hint of a possibly significant development in the last category. More dramatic is the drop in the percentage of writers with little or no educational background, from 11.3 percent to 7.2 percent, and the corresponding increase of university trained writers, jumping from 52.5 percent to 73.3 percent and thereby providing tangible proof that modern literature is intellectually more sophisticated than that of the nineteenth century, as well as more dominated by an elite.

The change, however, which has the most profound consequences for the writer's situation—as for the human condition as a whole—is in technology. The modern writer, as John Wain nostalgically observes in his interview, has been pushed off center by radio, film, and television; his audience, unlike the audience of the Victorian or Edwardian period, has shriveled up once again into a minority. That Wain is not alone in this awareness is borne witness to in many of the other interviews, though he perhaps feels the loss of the mass audience more acutely than, say, V. S. Pritchett or Margaret Drabble do. The serious writer of fiction has become unpopular almost by definition, unless he consents to trim his wares for consumption by film or television. (William Trevor consciously converts his stories into TV plays, though admittedly only for the BBC's Third Programme.) How wide an audience even mass-production novelists like Harold Robbins reach is open to question, since no one has yet examined carefully what part of their books is actually read by the public. The only genuinely popular fictional genres today seem to be the detective story (or its variant, the spy thriller) and the science fiction fantasy. Significantly, Kingsley Amis has tried his hand at variants of both.

As an inevitable consequence, the modern writer of serious

The Writer's Place

fiction finds it difficult, if not impossible, to make a living by his pen. And rather than improving, the situation seems to be growing worse. "In 1938 a young aspiring writer without dependents," Richard Findlater observes in *What Are Writers Worth?* "without influence and with only his talent for capital, could get by on £4 a week. This was enough for a furnished bed-sitter in central London, for keeping in touch with films and plays, and for a weekly meal out in Soho; and it could be earned with relative ease on the fringe of the literary world so that he had time for his own writing. By 1952, however, a young man living in that way would have needed at least £9 a week; while by 1962 the minimum was £12 a week, for a Spartan existence without much to spare for playgoing (or smoking)." That Findlater is not merely blowing here into the trumpet of the Society of Authors is apparent when we compare his figures with those stipulated by Virginia Woolf in 1929 (£500 per annum and a room of one's own, or the equivalent of £10 a week) and George Orwell in 1946 (£1000 a year).* Bill Hopkins even goes so far as to suggest in his interview that a literary movement like the Angries would be impossible today because of the high price of tea and coffee in places where writers are likely to meet (though beer or even pot sounds more realisitc for the seventies).

Not surprisingly, then, for many writers and perhaps even for most, writing is more of a sideline than anything else. The writer may be an editor like Anthony Thwaite or Ian Hamilton, or a publisher's reader like Giles Gordon, or a librarian like Angus Wilson, or a lawyer like Roy Fuller, or a hairdresser like Maurice Callard. Only a relatively small number of writers ever shed the protective chrysalis of a second job: of the writers just mentioned only Angus Wilson has done so and even he teaches intermittently at the University of East Anglia (though not entirely for financial reasons). The poets, of course, are the hardest pressed, conscious as they are of the obstacles to be overcome in even reaching an audience, much less in making that

*In answer to a questionnaire put out by *Horizon*.

Introduction

audience pay (both Fuller and Gordon speak to this point in their interviews). At present the only practical alternative to starvation or to a nonwriting job seems to be a grant from the British Arts Council. Alan Burns, for instance, had just been awarded one at the time I interviewed him.

This kind of situation is, of course, not new, except perhaps in the degree of hardship it imposes on the writer. What is new, however, seems to be the concentration of writers into a relatively few professions, especially publishing and teaching. Inevitably such a development threatens to bring with it the mandarinization of literature. Cyril Connolly was lamenting this tendency in British letters as long ago as the late forties, implying that it led to inbreeding and literary stagnation.* Judged by the resurgence of literary vitality in the fifties, that analysis seemed for a time badly mistaken, but perhaps it was only badly timed. Although even now the British literary scene is not characterized, as it is in the United States, by the marriage of academic and writer, the day, as Wilson, Amis, and Pamela Hansford Johnson suggest in their interviews, may not be far off when it will be. A number of dons, to be sure, do figure prominently in modern British letters—one thinks, for instance, of Pater, Housman, and Tolkien—but these are exceptions rather than the rule and they were never exposed to the peculiar dangers of teaching "creative writing." Furthermore, the nineteenth-century tradition of academic sinecures or of positions in government and the clergy has decayed, with such jobs either disappearing or ceasing to be sinecures. Without the assistance of the British Arts Council, of the literary pages of the Sunday papers, of enterprising publishers like John Calder, and of the occasional lucrative visit to an American university, the lot of the British man of letters would be even less happy than it is. "If Britain's authors had to depend for a living *on their books alone*," Findlater concludes in *The Book Writers, Who Are They?* "most of them would be on National Assistance."

*In his *Horizon* "London Letter" for April 1949.

11

The Writer's Place

This is not to say that many writers have no reservations about external support, especially when it comes from the state. Not long after the Arts Council came into being, partly through the agency of John Maynard Keynes, George Bernard Shaw argued that writers would be best served by being assigned routine jobs with shorter working hours. That would save them "from being the feckless nuisances they now often are, living in an imaginary world and ignorant of the real one."* In the present volume, another sometime socialist, Kingsley Amis, comes close to making the same point. But reservations about the role of the Arts Council are not the prerogative of the political right or the establishment. Alan Burns, for example, feels intensely the pull of the metaphysical strings which are attached to accepting a grant from the state.

Even so, one can agree with Charles Osborne, the literary director of the British Arts Council, that a growth which is valuable and which can no longer flourish unaided in a state of nature ought not to be allowed to die. A hothouse plant is preferable, in the final analysis, to no plant at all. It is the Arts Council which therefore, in many respects, lies at the heart of the contemporary literary situation—perhaps it has even become the heart (however artificial), pumping the financial lifeblood not merely to individual writers, but to publishers and little presses and magazines and literary organizations alike. It has assumed the burden of literary patronage, largely abandoned by the aristocracy in the eighteenth century.

State support of literature is one of the major themes running through this collection of interviews. Some of the other themes concern the system—or lack thereof—of reviewing books, the threat of competing media like film and television, the ways in which literary reputations are made, the groupings of literary people, the "internationalization" of literature and the consequent disappearance of the typically and recognizably English man of letters, as well as the growing influence of the

*"Art Workers and the State," *Atlantic Monthly*, 180 (November 1947), 124.

universities, both as places to work in and as audiences to write for. As one might expect, there is no uniformity of response to any of these questions, nor should there be. What I have hoped to elicit here is a spectrum of informed opinion which would be wide enough to provide the reader with a sense of what it is like to be a professional, serious writer in Britain today. The stress here falls on the word *sense*, since obviously a collection like this one is not and cannot be exhaustive. Without statistics and without adhering to a rigid and approved sociological strategy, this book—coming as it does, so to speak, straight from the horse's mouth—represents ultimately a series of impressions: its effects are best appreciated from a certain aesthetic distance rather than close up.

Insofar as it was conscious, my intention was to gather together writers of various age groups, of differing degrees of critical and financial success, and—within the broad limits of poetry and the novel—of various types: experimental and traditional, elitist and (while still remaining serious) popular, along with as many of the intermediary shadings as possible. I have attempted, too, to secure the views of persons who are intimately and professionally involved in literary life, without perhaps being writers themselves; that is, publishers, editors, and officials from the Society of Authors and the British Arts Council. But beyond these general guidelines, I have avoided following a set procedure, bearing in mind Wordsworth's advice that dissection is preceded by murder (or else that vivisection poses a moral demand for anesthetization). Despite its socio-literary flavor, this book belongs to the category of the arts rather than that of the sciences—even "soft" ones. Hence, although the bulk of interviews deals with the writer's social role and although in the earlier interviews especially I used a prepared set of questions, I never hesitated to pursue other topics, even quite unrelated ones, when these came up spontaneously and promised to be of interest.

All the interviews were made in the spring and summer of 1969 (with the exception of George Osborne's which dates from

The Writer's Place

September 1973). They have all been edited from the original tapes, and the transcripts were remitted for further revision. That revision was, for some of the interviews, radical, though almost always in the direction of cutting rather than changing or adding. L. P. Hartley unfortunately died before I was able to get the transcribed interview to him.

I am much indebted to all of these very busy literary people who so kindly and patiently put their time, experience, and frequently their hospitality at the disposal of yet another American come knocking at their door. I want also to thank Arthur Koestler, Iris Murdoch, Harry Patterson, and Julian Shackborough for allowing me to interview them, even though their interviews unfortunately could not be included in this collection. Finally I want to extend thanks to Robert Wickenheiser, now of Princeton University, for helping me to set up this project, to the MacMillan Fund for paying my travel expenses, and to the Office of International Programs and the Graduate School of the University of Minnesota for help in paying for typing and clerical assistance.

Peter Firchow

Edinburgh
October 1973

Kingsley Amis

KINGSLEY AMIS was born in 1922 in London and educated at the City of London School and at St. John's College, Oxford. He served in the British Army in the Second World War, taught English at University College, Swansea (1949–61), and at Peterhouse, Cambridge (1961–63). He has been married twice, to Hilary Ann Bradwell and to Elizabeth Jane Howard, and has three children. His long list of publications includes various collections of poems, the latest being *A Look around the Estate* (1967); a book of short stories, *My Enemy's Enemy* (1962); and eight novels, among them *Lucky Jim* (1954)—which brought him fame—*Take a Girl Like You* (1960), and *The Green Man* (1969). He is also an incisive and at times highly unconventional critic, as one can see from those two remarkable "pop" books, *New Maps of Hell* (1960), devoted to an analysis of science fiction, and *The James Bond Dossier* (1965), a study of Ian Fleming's thrillers.

The interview took place at Amis's club, Traveller's, where he appeared dressed in a gray flannel suit, bowler hat, umbrella, luminescent pink socks, and matching tie.

Q: It was the chance of receiving a legacy that provided you with the leisure to write *Lucky Jim*. Would you say that was somehow the equivalent of a British Arts Council bursary? Not awarded by an official agency but by an act of God.

Amis: Well, to begin with, the bursaries are never enough. I don't

15

think any government on earth could or should afford the money to set writers up. Because how would anybody have judged me? I hadn't done anything. Here's a chap who says he'd like to be a writer and he wants somebody to subsidize his writing. So, we'll buy houseroom. And there must be a million people in Great Britain who'd like to be a writer. If only they had the leisure or the money.

Q: On the other hand, don't you think it would have been easier for you if you had, for example, received such a bursary?

Amis: A bit, yes, but it wouldn't have been long enough. That's to say, that the time I could have bought wouldn't have been long enough to enable me to write a whole novel.

Q: A year?

Amis: Well, a year's quite expensive for anybody if he has a wife and children. I think what would have happened if my wife hadn't had this legacy is that I should have had to wait a bit longer, before starting. Another couple of years, when I got onto a more favorable part of the salary scale, then I'd have been able to afford something comparable.

Q: Do you think your career would have been similar—that *Lucky Jim* would have been written two years later?

Amis: Well, two years or a year because I think there comes a point when the writer, however badly placed in his circumstances, can't go on blaming those circumstances indefinitely. I think I would have got to that stage. It doesn't matter that the only place I have to write is the children's bedroom. I'd have to find a cupboard at the university library where I could go and write. I think I would have got there, and I think most writers finally do that—make some sort of accommodation in that way.

Q: So you'd say that if a writer really wants to write and has something to write about, he will do it no matter what the governmental agencies?

16

Amis: I would like to think that. I think that having something to write is very arguable, because what it takes in one's character to decide to be a writer and become one is very important. When I say what it takes in one's character I don't necessarily mean good things. George Orwell was helpful on this. Remember his essay on "Why I Write." Motive number one, as I remember, was the desire to be thought clever. To be talked about by people you've never met, to be famous, to have your name in the newspapers. And most human beings, I think, are such that this is important to them, in varying degrees—vanity, conceit. All those things, plus energy. But as I say, having something to write about, we can only see that later, if we ever do. I think that talent is often being found in combination with this kind of determination. But not exclusively, certainly not always. But I think that the literary career is what Cyril Connolly called it, the most disappointing profession in the world. It's fine for people who make it and so on, but it does need tremendous patience and ability to put up with rebuffs. Again you can call that ability, faith in oneself, or toughness. You can also call it conceit. You *know* you're good. The fact that nobody agrees with you can be disposed of in a matter of time.

Q: Would you say then that talent, like murder, will out; that there's nothing that can stop it?

Amis: No, I wouldn't say that. Because obviously we only know about the people who have emerged. I'm a great disbeliever in the garret existence as an essential prelude to producing worthwhile work. I think it's possible that persistence and perseverance are required not only at the beginning of a literary career, but throughout. It's always much easier not to write a book than to write a book—however much you want to do it and however important it may be to you economically. And so I think that anybody who has produced a large body of work by definition must have this persistence. And it's not as if there weren't plenty of examples of writers who've done well to start with, perhaps found it easy to start, produced two or three books, were well

The Writer's Place

regarded—and then faded away. Perhaps they didn't have the essential sense of perseverance. Perhaps it wasn't needed earlier in their career, and when it was needed later, they didn't have it.

Q: What features of the English literary scene, say, including the British Arts Council, would you change? If, that is, you were suddenly put into the English equivalent of Malraux's shoes.

Amis: I think I'd do away with the Arts Council. I don't like the notion of the state handing out bursaries and awards to favored writers. I don't mean that the writers who've had such awards in England have been defenders of the system or pro-establishment figures in any sense, but I think it's a bad principle. And I think it encourages what I would call—from a lofty pinnacle—an undesirable attitude. I would rather have a writer whose strategy was as mine was and all the people of my generation, the people who preceded me and some of the people who've come later: he should say to himself, "I've got a wife, I've got a family, and so I'll have to get some money from somewhere." Well, he should get it from work, I think. There are plenty of allied trades—journalism, the academic world, anything in which writing is necessary. Television, even commercials and so on. It's not difficult now—perhaps this is different from what it was like twenty years ago—but it's certainly not difficult now if you can hold a pen to make quite a decent living in London. I'm not at all sure about the relationship between experience and final literary output, but I would guess that somebody who had had to teach in a school or had had to work in an advertising agency or in the BBC, etc., in the most straightforward literal-minded way has accumulated much more experience, has met more sorts of people, than someone who says, "Well, I'm twenty-three and I want to write an epic poem, and I haven't got any money so I think the Arts Council ought to give me an award." I'd rather have the first type of person. I think there may be no relation between these things, between quantity and variety of experience and the end product, but if there is, it's clearly going to go the way I suggest.

18

Q: What do you think of countries like the Soviet Union, or less extreme examples like, say Austria, where culture, or what's called culture, for example, theater, opera, whatever, are very heavily subsidized by the state and, in fact, the quality of an orchestra like the Vienna Symphony Orchestra can only be maintained by very heavy subsidies from the state?

Amis: That's a different thing. About the Soviet Union, of course, that certainly is a country in which every writer, if he continues to function, is an employee of the state. Or is somebody who doesn't offend the state—somebody who has to write what is expected of him in some way or other. But as regards subsidies of arts like opera, ballet, and classical music—this is certainly necessary. These are arts that can't pay their way. And there has been a controversy here about the opera house at Covent Garden and shouldn't we make people pay an economic price for their seats or more than an economic price for their seats so as to set this against the enormously heavy subsidy that they receive at the moment. I don't know about that, but I think literature is a paying proposition. More and more so. I don't say that it's a good thing, but it clearly is paying—through television and so on. But the performing arts are in quite a different position. Any decent country has *got* to have a national ballet company, a national opera company, and not just two or three but a couple of dozen good orchestras. I know we are certainly far behind the Austrians and the Germans on these matters. You have to put money in, and this is where you have to be a little authoritarian. People say, "But what am I getting out of it? I live in the middle of the Yorkshire moors. And so why is it right for me to subsidize the Covent Garden ballet?" Tough. Here's the answer: we hope you can come to London once in a while and go to Covent Garden.

Q: You say that literature is a paying proposition. Would you say that of literature as a whole or only of a certain kind of literature? That everybody should write that kind of literature, because it pays?

Amis: One should never write anything because it pays. I don't

think that there's much literature that's being written o
certainly, that we remember that was written because it pays.
doesn't last. If it's written merely to pay, it won't be any goo
Nobody can sit down and say, "I'm going to write a West En
stage success." If you're very lucky, the play that you believ
passionately in turns out to be that. But at the moment, here i
London, I don't think it's ever been so easy to get work publishe
in magazines and in book form as it is now. This may change, bu
for the most part, standards are in such a chaotic state, it's n
longer—I hope I don't sound as though I were complaining—bu
I think it's merely true that standards are all shot to hell, s
nobody knows whether anything futuristic or modernistic is goo
or not. So you can get away with anything, and anything tha
seems to be merely new in some way or other, that's to say, it hasn'
been done for the last eighteen months, is certain of a reception, i
certain to be published, and—not certain—but very likely to be
put on the stage. I think that this thing may be reversed when
American publication methods become more widespread here
That is to say, you drop the book that will only sell two thousand
copies. You cut down the extent of your list, and you concentrate
on the big selling lines, which I understand is happening a great
deal in America. And, of course, that's the schedule we'll be
following here too. But the only kind of work—oddly
enough—that might be difficult nowadays to place with a
publisher or get put on the stage is something that is in the
tradition: novels with long descriptive passages in which the
reader is never in any doubt about what's happening; plays that
have a coherent Act 1, Act 2, Act 3 structure. That may be, but I
think there are still enough readers and people in the audience
who are old-fashioned enough to expect a story from a novel and
a series of clear dramatic situations from a play.

Q: Isn't there a contradiction when you say that somehow Covent
Garden, for example, can put on *Wozzek*, which is certainly not a
popular opera, and yet a publishing company ought not to
publish something that is unpopular, that does not sell over a

ertain number of copies, that one segment of the arts ought to be operated on a kind of socialist system and the other on a strictly apitalist enterprise system?

mis: Well, I think one's got to treat these things on their merits nd try to be empirical about it. To try to work out a eneralization that would incorporate one's whole attitude oward all the arts would be impossible. I don't think we really ught to do that. You can treat the whole of the book trade and he writing trade as one problem, and then you have to change ver to a different philosophy when you come to the performing rts, which are in this very odd state and which have never lourished except when there was a tremendous amount of private money about. In the eighteenth century, when every tiny ourt had to have its court composer, its court orchestra, it was omparatively easy. This doesn't happen now. So the public aymaster has got to step in. But I would like to see more private noney—that is to say money from corporations and firms—being used. There are some firms who have done this already. Guinness, for example, made a start. They put quite a lot of noney into the visual arts, though I don't know what they get out of it—in any sense. Of course, I don't see how you can force people to do it.

Q: What do you think of the modern equivalent of this kind of eighteenth-century literary patronage, namely the universities?

Amis: I feel that the interests of the young writer ought to be considered. I've got a soft spot for that, having been through that stage. I think that if it's a scholarship with no duties or a fellowship with no duties which allows a poet to be on campus, it's a very good thing. I wouldn't want to discourage that at all. But I'm a little suspicious of any closer ties between the academic setup and the literary setup. I think that, on the whole, a lot of people have had their lives made easier and that as a result a lot more books have got turned out, in the United States. And because there is all this and because it's not difficult to get a year or more on campus

21

and all you have to do is to talk to an occasional student and get o
with your novel or your poems, that's very nice in one way. But
produces a very inbred kind of literary society, and this I think i
going, or has gone, beyond just starting to change the kind o
literature you get at the end of the line. For example, mos
novelists or at least a hell of a lot of novelists are teachers o
English literature.

Q: Is this true of England as well?

Amis: Not so much yet, because we haven't got the money.

Q: But you see it coming?

Amis: I see it coming, and I certainly see it in the States. They're
either teaching it, or they were teaching it, or they've been invited
back to be under the wing of the English department for their sta
on campus. So, the novels are written by that sort of person, and
the people who review the novels are people who are teaching in
English departments, or were teaching in English departments
or have been invited back under the wing of the English
department to be critic on campus. And an immense number of
the final copies of the book sold will be sold to English literature
students who are being taught by members of the English
department who have perhaps written the books, or their friends
and brothers have.

Q: And will be required in their courses.

Amis: Yes. I'm not going to mention any names, but there are
novels that seem to get written for an audience of academics. I
don't mean they're academic novels in the sense that they're
mandarin and coated with style or anything like that, but they'll
be interesting material for university discussion. I'd much
rather—I think it's healthier to have someone like Harold
Robbins or Grace Metallious, who, whatever you can say about
them, what you can't say against them is that they are writing to
appeal to campus classes and discussion groups. This happened
with poetry in England about . . . oh, in the fifties. All the people

writing it were dons, and all the people who were reviewing it were dons, and all the people who were reading it were dons, and so on. So you've got a kind of donnish poetry. I think it was very good because I was one of them, you see.

Q: You don't think this is the case anymore?

Amis: I think that's all gone now. But it may return. All those people have now gone away. They're no longer teaching at the university, with one or two exceptions, and so that sort of campus nexus was broken up. But I certainly see it in fiction. You see: "Here's a novel by somebody. Who's he? Oh, you know, he's at Columbia." And here's somebody reviewing him: "Mr. Fortiscue is head of English Studies at the University of What-Not." So it's all, paradoxically, a rather small circle.

Q: Your own first novel, at least the novel that made you famous, *Lucky Jim*, also deals with the university. And *One Fat Englishman* deals, at least tangentially, with the same subject. (*Amis:* "Very much so, yes.") In a way, one might say the same of *I Like It Here*. Would you say that it's almost inevitable for the serious literary man nowadays in England to come up through the university and inevitably draw on his experience of the university? Your own career has only gradually moved away from the academic life.

Amis: I think this must happen. And as more and more people go to universities and the demand for an expanded teaching force grows and grows, it becomes a tremendous temptation. I don't say it's a bad temptation, but it's there for anybody who has done at all well at a university to stay on or go to another university and teach there. So there's bound to be—I don't know if it's reached its full expansion yet, perhaps it has—but there's bound to be a very close connection there. This is another reason why we have a tie-up between the academic world and the literary world. I think that—branching off for a moment—financial success and financial independence, or a modicum of that, are easier in both our countries than they've ever been before. It's easy for me to say so from my position, but I think it may be a bad thing because

23

when you become a full-time writer you cease to be anything else, and you only meet people because they're your neighbors, and you're going to meet them anyway. But if you meet people as anything you meet them as a writer. It's the opposite from having a job. I think that's enormously valuable—to meet people who don't know that you're a writer. I don't mean to say that if they know you're a writer they'll change how they behave to you, but you change how you behave to them. To have colleagues, people that you work with and so on—that you're participating with on a completely equal basis. They're doing the job and so are you. When he gets home, he tends his garden or looks after his pigeons; and when you get home you write your book. But while you're in the job, you're exactly the same sort of person he is. I think that retirement, in the sense of not having a job, is delicious, of course, but I think it's very debilitating to one's talents. It's something I miss, something that one can't get in any other way. It can't be done artificially. You can't get the same experience by, let's say, joining a charitable organization or joining a political organization. These are good things to do, but they're different, they're sort of diluted—and in a way unreal. I think that if one were going to make a hostile diagnosis, as I might do if I had the time, of American fiction nowadays, I'd say that this is part of it. I'm not saying that success spoils people. You can't tell what it's going to do to them until they've got it, and in many ways, as Somerset Maugham pointed out, success is good for the soul. You become much more tolerant and much more kindly, and all that, because you haven't got a chip on your shoulder. To be a success at twenty-three and never have to work any more, and have the *New Yorker* magazine on the other end of the telephone, I think that's bad for the soul. I don't know what you can do about it; I'm sure you can do nothing about it. But it interests me that so many American writers have written marvelous books to start with—a few examples: *The Naked and the Dead*, a splendid book; *The Caine Mutiny*, a splendid book; *Catcher in the Rye*, a splendid book. No doubt there are others that I can't think of. But something has happened to all those writers. Partly it's through becoming a public person, but partly, I think, also through being taken out of the kind of life that the books were part of. Two of them were war novels, so perhaps one can't say that. Nobody voluntarily takes part in that sort of thing. But ordinarily, when I say involvement I don't mean it to sound grand—I don't mean commitment—but being, whether you like it or not, involved with boss and colleagues and junior people is much healthier for a writer than going up to his summer place with his typewriter. What's he going to write about when he gets there?

Q: But does this kind of thing not apply to England? Are writers here not spoiled by their first great success?

Amis: As always, we'll get there given time. We're about five or ten years behind you. But I can see that, since the day of the small independent publisher, for example, is very much drawing to a close, in five or ten years there will be four or five large groups, something which is financially very good for the writer. But at the same time I get uneasy when I think of that and the book being conceived of not as the output of a human intelligence but a selling line. Perhaps my optimism is quite misplaced there. I feel very divided about that.

Q: Earlier you were mentioning as nonuniversity writers people like Metallious or Harold Robbins. These people obviously make good incomes from writing, just looking at the number of paperbacks sold of something like *The Carpetbaggers*, the film rights, and so forth. You yourself have had, for some of your books, enormous sales and also film rights. Would you say that it's possible for the writer of fiction still to make a good living?

Amis: I'd say so, yes. Enormous is probably a little too complimentary a word to use about my sales. They go on selling very nicely, thank you, over the years. And they even accumulate a certain amount of revenue by being taught, you know, required and everything. To keep at it is the thing. People tend to drop out. Ken Kesey, who was talked about with a tremendous roll of drums, now has declared his intention of stopping being a writer any more. I don't lament this exactly, but writing is perhaps ceasing to be a sort of way of life. It has become just part of the scene or of one's own scene. Like being a poet has certainly become that sort of thing. It's like taking trips and riding in boxcars and riding a motorbike. One-tenth of the time you might write a poem, if you get round to it. I think perhaps the novelist, as a profession or as a way of life, is possibly on the way out.

Q: What would you say is replacing it?

Amis: Well, doing everything perhaps. One would have to wait another ten years to see what's going to happen to the younger people who are now starting off—whether they'll stay at the job.

Q: What do you think of people like Mailer, who are becoming more and more interested in the film, and who suddenly realize that with the new technological innovations they can make films in almost the same way they used to write novels? Do you consider this merely a fluke or a fad, or does it portend that the novelist will indeed be replaced by the film maker?

Amis: Well, that might happen, but it would, of course, mean even more that the good but potentially unpopular writer—perhaps forever unpopular—would not get a look-in. It's what I suggested as the coming situation in publishing. It's the big selling lines that get the attention or get published at all. It's that picture written a thousand times larger. Because at least a book doesn't take ten million dollars to be published and sent around. So you'll be left again with half a dozen or a dozen big names—if this ever comes to pass—who will be all over our screens. I suppose until recently I'd have welcomed the idea of a more direct relationship between the writer and films, because a writer's cinema is something that has never been tried yet. They keep telling us it has. Apart from *Rosemary's Baby*, which I believe was, so to speak, shot straight out of the novel, and to my mind was a total disaster, and *Decline and Fall of a Birdwatcher*, we really haven't had that.

Q: Faulkner and Hemingway and Huxley, for example, have written film scripts.

Amis: Yes, but in those days it was filtered through an immense amount of front office and the star system and so on, which again one ought to deplore. But I must say I've got tremendous respect for the talent that Mailer used to have. If it were the Mailer of *The Naked and the Dead* who were going to do this, fine. But if it's the Mailer of *An American Dream* doing it, then I'm going to stay at home and watch television.

Q: Do film or television as media attract you as possible substitutes for presenting your ideas?

Amis: I was born too early for that. For me it could never be anything but a tremendously interesting thing to do afterwards. I would always regard writing a film script or a television script as something else to do. My main job is writing fiction. If I have what you might call a second-rate idea, an idea that fascinates me but that I don't think is really important: marvelous! If I can obtain the backing, let me make a film out of that, or a television play out of that. But if it's something that I really care about, for me it's got to be a book. I'm sure people ten years younger than myself would feel differently about that. But I belong between hard covers.

Q: And yet when you think of it, a film or a television program reaches an audience, at least at the moment of its showing, that is much greater, usually, than almost any book of fiction will ever reach.

Amis: Well, certainly. But then they're going to be doing something else next week, and they'll have forgotten you. I think it's essential—I'm talking about myself now—that if you're going to write for anybody (in the first place you're writing for yourself, of course), it should be a small audience which you hope has read the other things you've written and has some regard for them. In the first place, I think it's disaster to say, "I used to sell ten thousand copies—next year I'm going to sell 200,000 copies, and I'm going to ensure that by the kind of thing I write." John O'Hara is the classic example of that. He started off in *Butterfield*

Eight, Hope of Heaven, and so on—and *Appointment in Samara*—as a marvelous, straightforward minority novelist. Oh, he was difficult, but he was writing for people who cared about books. Then he came to *A Rage to Live*, which I picked up with enormous enthusiasm. Not a book of 120 pages like John O'Hara normally writes, but 360 pages. Wonderful! And I couldn't finish it because here was a case, I thought, of a writer who's deliberately broadening his field of fire and thereby lowering his sights—it's not too neat an image. So I think that there might be a split in the literary consciousness, your million copy sale book that could equally well be a movie or television series, and your serious literary effort that will sell five thousand copies, ten thousand copies, if of course there's the publication machinery. We might even go back to the way of the sixteenth or seventeenth centuries when serious work was circulated in manuscript. It could certainly happen with poetry, I think, which seems to react more quickly to change.

Q: One of the changes—though, of course, nothing really new—is literary collaboration. Your collaboration with Robert Conquest, for instance. How did that come about?

Amis: Well, we collaborated on editing science fiction anthologies and on writing the introductions to these, which are not really collaborations. You know, "I'm bloody well not going to do it this time, it's your turn" kind of collaboration. We did collaborate on a novel, but that was not collaboration in any full sense. Conquest showed me the draft, and I said, "One of these years when I'm going on holiday I'll do it. It's a marvelous idea that you have here, a marvelous structure. But I don't feel that it's been properly fleshed out. Well, I'll do that." So I took it to Spain one year and did most of it there. It was a collaboration totally the opposite of—certainly not word by word. He's done it all and then I went through and did it all, and then he went through it again and said, "I don't like this; and what about doing this?" and so there we were. But again I would not accept a collaboration on anything that I thought was really important. This was a light novel which we both got a lot of fun out of, and it's not totally unserious by any means, but it's a sort of holiday job. I don't see any particular future in that.

Q: You don't see the collaborated novel with a group of specialists, in the style of the film, as something that would interest you? A kind of collective?

Amis: I think that one of two things would happen in such a case. Either one person would drive out the others, who would physically or morally depart. Or the end product would be totally tasteless—flavorless. There have been attempts to do this in the past—there have been attempts to do everything in the past. A detective novel, *The Floating Admiral* I think it was called, was written by fourteen or fifteen detective story writers, each taking a chapter. Well, that's fun for them, I think. But it wasn't a satisfactory detective novel.

Q: It makes it a kind of folk poem, though, doesn't it?

Amis: Yes, I suppose. But all the transmission in the passage of 500 years would make a bit of difference.

Q: But is writing fiction of any kind really a serious occupation? What do you think, for instance, of Ortega y Gasset's notion that the desire to read novels is actually a juvenile throwback— something that appeals primarily to the child's love for stories which survives as a "barbarous residue" in the adult?

Amis: There's a half-truth in that. But I think he gets it wrong. Certainly the idea that adventures appeal to a child ought to be a reason for including them, not for leaving them out. There's been a lot of talk about maturity recently, how we ought to be mature, especially in sexual matters and so on. Well, I think that maturity is good, but a mature person to my mind is somebody who incorporates all the best parts of being a child and being an adolescent and being a grown-up man. By definition, a grown-up man who leaves out his adolescent self and his childish self isn't a grown-up man. So I think that the child's love of surprises and

The Writer's Place

also his love of not being surprised, of getting what he expects, and his interest in shocks and violent action—when I say violence I don't mean punishing, I mean abrupt changes of scene and of incident—is a very important constituent of novels. It's no accident that it's children who like stories more than most people. This should all go in, I think. Adolescent pedantry, adolescent eroticism, also ought to go in. The adolescent, if the adolescent admitted it, also desires to be thrilled. That should be there. Old Gasset, as you might expect—not a prolific novelist, I think?—leaves that out. You know, this bring up James Bond and all that stuff. One of the interesting things is that the child and adolescent parts of the reader of serious fiction aren't being catered to, as they were catered to by serious novelists a hundred or more years ago. Dickens, for example, got a lot of child and adolescent into his books. I don't mean just his characters, though that's important too, or his way of looking at things, but as covering the kind of appeal he made: trying to horrify you, trying to thrill you, trying to make you feel afraid, trying to divert you even at the most superficial level. One of the reasons why he's better than most of the people around is that the high-brow novel hadn't emerged yet. It *all* went in. So this really is a split which took place long ago. The action novel, the thriller, the ghost story, science fiction, the western, the stories of espionage and private eyes, and all that kind of thing: all separate little streams. And then there's another stream which is the serious novel where the writer is sort of letting the side down a bit, if he includes something from the other streams. And I think this is lamentable.

Q: Aldous Huxley once observed that the kind of novel Joyce was writing or even Lawrence was writing, was not modern. That theirs was really very primitive stuff which had been done before; that, in fact, in the most barbaric civilizations this was the kind of thing you found. And what was really modern was the very minute and psychological analysis of people.

Amis: I suppose it depends whether one's using modern as a term of abuse or a term of description. Yes, I think that's so, but it's all become much more minute in the sense that in Hardy, for example, one gets some splendid psychological portraits. But largely done in terms of externals, which is much harder and also much more interesting. I would rather read at any time about what a character did than about how he felt. If a novelist is really good, as in Hardy's case and Dickens's case, you know how he felt because of what he did. When I say what he did, I don't mean jumping onto horses and galloping away, but his actions, even perhaps quite minute actions. For example, to take a tiny case in *Martin Chuzzlewit* when Jonas Chuzzlewit comes back after the murder, I think it is, and enters his house and can't face anybody, and wants to enter it unseen and unheard, and wants somebody to say, "Are you there?" and somebody to come to him! Dickens doesn't go very much into how he felt, except in a quite removable way, but that picture of how Jonas behaved when he got back to his house after committing this crime is much more informative than pages and pages of analysis of exactly how he felt. This is very hard to do but when it comes off it's better than any analyzing.

Q: Would you say that this empirical way of letting the reader know the motives is the kind of thing you try to do in your novels?

Amis: That's what I'd like to be seen or thought of as doing, certainly.

Q: What do you think, by the way, of L. E. Sissman's essay on you—did you see it?—which was published in the *New Yorker*?

Amis: Oh that. Very interesting, and very complimentary a lot of the time, but it seemed to me to be written from a quite well-concealed sociological or political standpoint. That Amis had let the workers down was what it ended up as. That I used to write about ordinary people and that that was marvelous, because those were the people I understood. It was the ranks of them from among which I sprang. "But now that he's written a book

31

about the rich, this really won't do because . . ." The only really naive remark was there aren't really very many rich people, and most of us don't know them, so why write about them?

Q: Strange for the *New Yorker* to publish that sort of statement.

Amis: Well to compare great things with small: what would have happened if somebody had said to Shakespeare, "Now look, this Danish royal family. I mean, have you ever met a Dane? How many princes and kings do *you* know? And how many of the audience have ever seen one? Now, don't do that. Write about a lower middle class family in Stratford. *That's* the stuff." I think that it really doesn't matter where you turn your attention.

Q: Do your novels, at least your earlier ones, consciously aim at bringing about some kind of social change?

Amis: There was never anything social about my novels, except to a very small degree. That's to say, I think—though of course I've been put right many a time on this—they were novels and continue to be novels about human beings as they've always been. That's to say, ambition and lechery and drunkenness and irresponsibility and despair always exist wherever you are. But, of course, if you're setting a novel in England in 1954, then out of professional pride, if you like, or competence, you say, "We've got to get it right. There's no use talking about the busses in this part of town, busses stopped in 1903." Merely on the crudest detail, one's got to get that right. Furthermore, of course, the novel being such an elastic form, a ragbag in which you can put anything, and novelists being human, the novel is a platform from which they can deal out digs and unpleasant remarks and little bits of satire lasting a paragraph or two at a time, because there's room for that. We hope the reader's being carried along and he's going to say, "Now stop a minute, while I tell you this one about what the conservative MP said to me the other day," and the story can go on. But I don't think that I'm a social novelist or a sociological novelist any more than anybody else has ever been. Or a satirist even.

Q: Do you conceive of yourself, at any moment, as someone who has enabled somebody to sleep better, has enabled someone to become a better person? Do you think your novels, in other words, perform some kind of moral, ethical function, of seeing a situation more acutely, more subtly, of understanding other people more deeply—of becoming a better person in that sense?

Amis: It's almost impossible to answer that question, apart from a flat no, without seeming pretentious. So you'll have to sort of lay off that. (*Q:* "Sorry.") No, I'm not reprehending you, I'm merely defending myself in advance. Well, yes, certainly.

I said a minute ago that one writes for oneself, and that's perfectly true. But I think that if you can do that, if you can make people mind things less, that it's a good thing to do. I don't say that it's necessarily a part of one's literary function. It may be, but I haven't thought about that. But if you can help people to laugh at things that they would otherwise cry about or feel despairing about, merely by saying, perhaps, "Well, this has happened to me too." I've found this a comfort in reading fiction: you say, "Well I've felt like that. But this situation has made me feel much worse. This man doesn't seem to mind. Perhaps I was taking myself too seriously or taking the situation too seriously before. Next time, perhaps, I'll be able to smile a bit instead of groaning."

To take a specific case of this, in one of my books I described a feeling of hysterical tension that I think is called depersonalization by psychologists—when the self that you are observing and the self that is doing the observing become separated under conditions of tension and which can give you a sort of panic. Well, I used to suffer from this in the past, so I put it into a novel. It happens to one of the characters and I got an express air mail letter from a girl in the United States that said, "I've just read this. Has this happened to you or are you making it up? I should very much like to know." So I express air mailed a letter back saying, "Yes, it is, and I'll tell you what the psychologist I went to told me about it. And I can tell you that I'm all right now, and if I'm not all right this week I know very well I'll be all right next week." And so she replied saying, you've helped me a lot. Well, of course, one ought to do this, but that's a sort of extreme example. I was very pleased for weeks that I had helped this girl who I knew nothing of before I got her letter. The idea that unpleasant shocks are therapeutic—this is the other side of what you're talking about—is one I don't really hold to. Of the two, it's better to buttress somebody in their complacency, really, than to offend them.

Q: Is this why you would say that you're not a satirist? Or not primarily a satirist?

Amis: It may not be connected with that. Perhaps you could say on the satirist thing: it's no more than saying, gently, this sort of person is perhaps not quite as admirable as you thought. But I would put that as part of a general task—if it's a task—of gently trying to propel the reader in the direction of more self-criticism and more criticism and looking at things twice, so to speak. Satire is supposedly the correction of vice and folly by ridicule. Well, I think that's rather a task. It's a bit grand for me. I certainly have very strong moral ideas, but only on individual issues really—"Here and now you should do this." I can't say we ought to have more tolerance, or less tolerance, because the moment you come to any particular question the case is altered.

Q: To come back to your remarks about British versus American fiction, and the differences in tradition and environment. Would you think of yourself, for example, as a peculiarly *English* novelist who could not be mistaken for anything else?

Amis: Oh, yes. I think so, very much. As the culture changes, and as differences get ironed out, and as Kent becomes more and more like California, then these differences will perhaps disappear. But on the other hand, these things tend to keep step, in the sense that, when America and England were really very different, because of the then cultural preponderance of England over the United States, American writers tended to write in an English way. So there wasn't much difference there. As the cultures become more similar, perhaps they'll write in different ways. I don't know.

Q: Would you call *One Fat Englishman* an American novel because it's set in America?

Amis: I don't think one can quite say that. It would be very difficult to say what Englishness and Americanness are. I think that one of the reasons why, according to me, the English novel has got it over the American novel at the moment is because of things like English snobbery, and English conservativism, and English class consciousness, and living in the past, and all that kind of thing. Because I think that all this so-called wave of modernism has hit the English novel less hard than any other kind of novel. It seems to me that, little as I know of it, thank God, the French novel is in smithereens now, because of that wave. And this perhaps is true also of certain kinds of American novels. And I don't think that any Englishman, again thank God, could have written *Portnoy's Complaint*, because that represents some sort of fragmentation of the novel that (since fragments are smaller than a whole) does less. It takes what used to be a small part of what the novel was trying to be and makes of it the whole—the individual voice, if you like. Well, any novel that's any good is the expression of an individual voice to some degree. When Graham Greene writes a novel it's Graham Greene, and you know by line three that it's Graham Greene talking because, even though he's not talking in his own person, and it's not dialogue, and it's not the author lecturing the reader, it's Graham Greene because that's the way he looks at things. Individuality has always been an ingredient. But in Roth's case, for example, the ingredient has become everything. It's *all* the tone of voice. So, going back to where I started, this is why I feel more at home in a stuffier kind of novel such as the English write, which looks very much like the sort of novel that was being written fifty years ago. And I think that it's doing more. I don't mean that it gets deeper in any sense, but that it's fulfilling more tasks.

The Writer's Place

Q: Do you see this kind of novel continuing to be the English novel of say the next twenty, thirty years?

Amis: Only among older chaps like myself. We'll go on writing narrative, if you like to call it that. I don't know about recruitment, but quite a lot of young people do seem to be writing novels that have passages of description and dialogue and drama and characters. Experiment has never really taken root in England—literary experiment.

Q: Except perhaps Virginia Woolf.

Amis: Well, that's all died down now. I think what's happened is what should have happened: namely that we've had an innovation. For example, *Paradise Lost* was, in its day, a tremendous innovation. And everything that came afterwards got a slight push out of true from that. Things would never have been quite the same if it had not been written. But then they swing back and all that influence is assimilated.

A very interesting writer who's virtually unheard of in America, Elizabeth Taylor, is a kind of heir of Virginia Woolf but she's absorbed it and then swung back towards the mainstream. There are passages of which you can certainly say with truth—and I'm sure that Mrs. Taylor would agree—that they could never have been written if Virginia Woolf had never existed. But these are merely a couple of new weapons in the huge armory that the novelist inherits. Occasionally there's a new one. Or an old one is repolished and refurbished. Elizabeth Taylor, though born—I don't know—thirty years after Virginia Woolf is more traditional than she is, though Virginia Woolf has left her mark on her.

Q: Do you do much reading of novels yourself? What do you think of writers like Joyce Cary or Francois Mauriac or Anthony Burgess, who are on record as preferring to the novel other kinds of reading like history and biography?

Amis: I can sympathize with some of that. I think that the reason why they're pretending they don't read novels is a novelist's

Kingsley Amis

reason. No, I don't think it's a novelist reason; I think it's a reader's reason. And the reason they don't read novels is the same reason why my aged mother-in-law doesn't read novels. Because she can't make them out. And she doesn't enjoy them. And I see what she means, even though she's twenty-seven years older than I am. It's not interesting any more, it doesn't deal with a recognizable world, and it doesn't deal with it in a recognizable way. So, here's a new biography of the Duke of Wellington—well, we know roughly what we're going to get and it's very interesting, and Wellington was a real man. And we understand his world better than we understand the world around us. So, we read that. Autobiography is the same thing. And again, genre-fiction hasn't done that because until we got to these corrupters like Len Deighton and John Le Carré, for instance, the genre-novel—the thriller and the espionage novel—retained the old-fashioned qualities of suspense, clarity, drama, and so on that in many cases the straight novel had lost. My recourse is not to biography or autobiography and history, but to George MacDonald and to science fiction. Science fiction isn't about a world we recognize, but then it's not supposed to be that. We're not constantly made aware of the fact that the writer understands what he's talking about and you don't. You're one with the writer because you're both equally prepared or unprepared to imagine what it's like in a hundred years' time. So one reads that. And I think, leaving Burgess out because he's a friend of mine, but those two, I'd expected them to be very pompous about it, to give a high-sounding literary reason why they didn't read novels any more. But I think it's the same for lots of people when they reach the age of fifty or so.

Q: Would you say this is by and large a condemnation of the novel as it's usually written?

Amis: I wouldn't call it a condemnation. I'm not nearly learned enough to say that, and I'm not interested enough, and I'm far too lazy to say it validly. All I can say is that taste is changing so much faster nowadays. The wave-falls of changing taste used to

37

be much further apart than they are now, but I feel that the modernist revolution, which I thought safely done with about 1940, has taken a long time. Here we have it again. Because people—and I think this *is* a novelty—people who are starting to write now no longer bother to read the works of their predecessors.

There's a poet in England who boasts of never having read a line of Shakespeare. That shocks me in a fuddy-duddy way but, I think, also in a quite legitimate way: you can't be expected to do much by putting pen to paper without having a rough idea of what your predecessors have done. I don't mean that you should consciously set out and say, "Ah, I see, we've got to set letter L now. Well, I'll provide letters M and N, and go on in that way." But I would have thought as a matter of mere professional curiosity, you'd want to do that. And you find the same thing in the visual arts. We're having Dadaism all over again, not because people think it has a new lease on life, but because people don't know. But it's all been done before. I think we might get a swing back perhaps to another stuffy kind of traditionalism when the thing blows over, if it ever does.

Q: George Eliot and Henry James?

Amis: George Eliot, yes.

Q: Thank you, Mr. Amis.

Victor Bonham-Carter

VICTOR BONHAM-CARTER was born in Bearsted, Kent, in 1913, and educated at Winchester and Magdalene College, Cambridge. Before becoming director of the Society of Authors, he worked in publishing and as secretary to the Royal Literary Fund. He is married to Aubrey Stogdon and has two sons. He has published extensively on biographical and historical subjects, including *The English Village* (1952) and *Surgeon in the Crimea* (1968).

The interview took place in the London premises of the Society of Authors.

Q: Could you say something about the history of the Society of Authors?

Bonham-Carter: Well, the Society was founded in 1884 at a time when the business relations between publishers and authors were chaotic. The moving spirit was Walter Besant, who was a popular writer and educator, a fighter for causes. He felt the time had come for authors to protect themselves by banding together; and he was, on the whole, remarkably successful. The Society got off to a pretty good start and received the support of most of the leading men. For example, Tennyson agreed to be the first president, and he was succeeded by George Meredith, Thomas Hardy, and men of that standing. Of course Besant and his colleagues had an uphill fight, but they managed to get themselves established in about ten years; and now we are coming up to our ninetieth birthday (1974). Our present membership is about thirty-five hundred.

In general the Society exists to defend the rights and to promote the interests of authors. In practice it takes three forms. First of all, every member gets free legal and similar advice on any problem connected with the business of authorship.

Q: What is the cost?

Bonham-Carter: The annual subscription is 10 pounds 50, a sum which would not go very far if one had to consult a lawyer. Of course, if it does come to a court case, or some highly specialized difficulty, and advice is needed beyond what our own staff can give (and we can give most things), we ourselves will call in, shall we say, a libel lawyer or someone of that sort. And we would pay the fee. If we decided that this was a matter to go to law about, and we've gone to law many, many times, then the Society would pay for it. That would be done as a matter of policy by the Management Committee. You may get a sense of how far the organization has come when I tell you that in the early 1900s, something like fifty or sixty or even more court cases would be taken on in a year. More than that even! I've been looking back through the archives, since I'm the historian here. But now court cases are rare. Matters are almost always settled before we get that far.

Q: How many of these cases were won?

Bonham-Carter: Practically every one. It was a jungle. Anyone who showed any fight, or got organized and did it in a businesslike way couldn't fail to win. Mostly insisting that an author retained his copyright and signed a fair contract with the publisher. Besant called copyright "literary property." In other words, copyright in a literary work was a piece of property that belonged to the author, who then licensed the publisher to give the work on certain conditions specified in the contract, more or less as now. Our members can have their contracts vetted, clause by clause, if they wish; that is part of the Society's service. The second thing we

40

do benefits authors as a whole, whether they belong to the Society or not; in other words, campaigns. Now the one I'm personally responsible for is Public Lending Right. This is, as you know, a campaign to obtain a lending payment for authors for the use of their books in libraries. After many, many years—over twenty years now—the government is at last taking notice of our claim. We have actually got a scheme in draft and are discussing it now. I predict that we will bring this off in about two years. It will take that time to work out the details and obtain ratification from Parliament. Authors, in general, benefit from other campaigns that the Society has fought. For instance, income tax concessions. Two or three of these have been obtained since the last war through successive Finance Acts. One, for example, allows you to spread your income back since the moment you started writing a book for the purposes of tax.

Q: Was this achieved through the courts?

Bonham-Carter: No, through representations to the Chancellor of Exchequer. Another concession concerned the sale of copyright—which we regard as a piece of capital property—we've always argued that its sale should not be taxed at all, because this is like selling your shop or your house. We've not won that battle completely, but we've gained a partial success. This applies particularly to old authors, who want to sell their copyrights and raise a large sum of money to buy a house or an annuity. Although the sale still counts as income, it can be spread over six years for purposes of tax. We've also done a great deal toward reforming censorship. We were entirely responsible, for instance, for the 1959 Obscene Publications Act, and since then have helped with subsequent legislation. And so it goes on.

We fight by putting pressure on MP's, on big organizations such as the BBC or the Publishers' Association—there's an old love-hate relationship between us and the publishers, as you can imagine: individually, when we argue about clauses in contracts and, generally, when we are both involved in matters of principle, for example, to stop the misuse of photocopying.

The Writer's Place

Q: Is the Labour party more responsive to your needs than the Conservatives?

Bonham-Carter: In some respects, yes, but one can't be politically biased oneself; one must take help from wherever it comes. If one party gets run out next year, I don't anticipate much trouble in carrying on with the other. On the whole, Labour spends more money for the arts, especially if they can show that they are helping the underdog. The Society's third main activity concerns specialized types of writing, for which we have set up groups. Translators, educational writers, children's writers, dramatists, radio writers are some of the special groups we have formed. Each group has a secretary of its own, that's to say, one of us on the staff. If you join a group, it doesn't cost you any more; it's all within your subscription. What happens really is that you get specialized attention. If you're a translator, we've a secretary who is an expert on all the translation clauses in contracts, rates for the job, and who helps organize a series of translation prizes (French, German, Italian) each year.

These are the three main ways in which we work. As far as income, that comes in from several sources—chiefly membership subscriptions and commissions on the handling of certain authors' estates. We aren't literary agents in the ordinary sense. In fact, we try very hard not to compete with the regular agents. But quite a number of authors, especially those nearing the end of their lives, say, "I would like you to look after my estate on behalf of my widow and my family for the term of copyright (fifty years after my death)." This happened with Bernard Shaw. So we have been designated, and generally have accepted, the responsibility of handling distinguished dead authors' estates or distinguished nearly dead authors, if I may use the phrase. Joyce and Eliot are other instances. That is an important section of the Society's work and of course also an important source of income for us. The third source is normal investments and reserves, which bring in a certain amount of income. We also handle a number of funds, mainly prizes, and one or two more charitable funds, for which we get management fees: the Somerset Maugham Award (for young authors), the Eric Gregory Award for Poets, and so forth.

Q: What percentage of working British authors do these four thousand represent?

Bonham-Carter: That's terribly hard to say. I know Richard Findlater, editor of our journal *The Author*, and an independent journalist, thinks probably there are about seven thousand (more or less) committed men and women, who really regard themselves as professional authors. So the Society has about two-thirds, something between a half and two-thirds, very likely. But you realize that authors are inclined to be loners and nonjoiners, so you would never get anywhere near 100 percent, not by voluntary methods at any rate.

Q: You exclude journalists, then?

Bonham-Carter: Journalists can be members and of course can be members of the National Union of Journalists (NUJ) at the same time, if they write books. But we're not principally a journalists' union. We do, however, have available confidential information about what rates are paid in the different journals. That is a service to our members who do that sort of thing along with writing books. Acceptance for membership in the Society depends ultimately on the Management Committee, whom they accept and whom they don't. Roughly speaking, you must have had at least one book published by a respectable publisher. It doesn't count if you pay for publication yourself, for example. In other words, publication must usually be in the hands of a member of the Publishers' Association, or its equivalent in other fields, such as radio scripts or plays.

Q: You would exclude poets, for example, who have not had a published volume of verse?

Bonham-Carter: Yes. But we would try and encourage particular cases, without bothering to insist on the rule in every instance.

There's elasticity here, and we regard that as true for the Society as a whole. I couldn't give you a hard and fast rule about that.

Q: Does the Society solicit members?

Bonham-Carter: Yes, it does. We now and again have recruitment campaigns, e.g., among academics. But most applications come in unsolicited. We get about three hundred applications a year without too much work on our part. Earlier this year we had a terrific burst of publicity on Public Lending Right; as a result, recruiting shot up vastly because our names were all over the papers. We lose about a hundred and fifty through resignations and deaths. So we're left with something like a hundred and fifty natural increase and that's the reason why we've been growing.

Q: Are most of the better-known writers, Graham Greene for instance, members of the Society?

Bonham-Carter: Yes. If you look at our Council list you'll see it's pretty impressive. Certainly most of the top-line names, but not everyone, because there are writers who never will join anything or who have fallen out with us. This happens in every field of human relations: people don't always get on. But we do have a great number of distinguished authors, novelists, playwrights, etc., and many others who are only well known in their special fields. For instance, we have a lot of good historians. Academic authors have particular problems. An academic author *must* get published in order to help his career along. That may mean he doesn't worry too much about what royalties he's going to get, if any, or rights, so long as he gets *published.* We point out that we quite understand the reason, but it does no good for writing as a whole if you accept bad terms from a publisher. It destroys the basis of negotiation for ordinary authors. We are ramming home that an academic author's contract must be as good as any other's. We've been working very hard on this. We are also grappling with the exploitation of copyright work by photocopying, private recording, and other new techniques. In another instance, an author is perhaps a member of a team and it's very difficult to sort

44

out what his position is and what rights he should have. We're working on all that too.

Q: Has the Society really helped in getting more money for authors?

Bonham-Carter: Yes of course, but it's a never-ending battle. We've helped enormously, since we started, to increase authors' incomes by improving (a) their royalty rates, and (b) their rights, namely the kind of returns they get from having a book utilized other than in volume form, e.g., by conversion into a film or a stage play. Not to mention all those rights that derive directly from publication: digests, anthologies, editions, etc. Originally the hardback publishers assumed that they would have paperback royalties fifty-fifty with the author; but now we insist on a minimum of sixty-forty in favor of the author.

Q: Have you enforced this sixty-forty arrangement?

Bonham-Carter: We've got it in most cases, and sometimes better terms still.

Q: How do you go about representing your case?

Bonham-Carter: Two ways. One is to tackle the Publishers' Association, which represents the great majority of publishers; and the other is to deal with individual publishers of the authors concerned. Often, if the author is a man whose book is wanted very badly for a paperback edition—and this is where a prominent author can help his fellows—he'd say, well, you can't have it unless I have sixty-forty or seventy-thirty written into the contract. Once you've got that established as a precedent, it's very much easier next time for someone else. This has been going on a lot. For instance, in Public Lending Right we've already established that, if it comes, the division of that royalty—the lending royalty—will be 75 percent to the authors and 25 percent to the publishers. That's been done in advance. We're also stating that we agree that publishers, as a matter of principle, should participate in Public Lending Right (PLR) because they are coproducers of work that is being lent. Nonetheless, it would be a very nice gesture on their part to set up a fund with their 25 percent for helping authorship in various ways!

Q: Have you a system of blacklisting publishers who don't cooperate?

Bonham-Carter: Not officially, but we certainly do informally, and occasionally we publish notice of warning in *The Author*, a very carefully worded one, of course. We have said in connection with a particular publisher whose methods we didn't care for that any author approached by the firm should communicate with the Society first, and we'll give him private information about the situation. That has worked very well indeed. When a publisher of that sort starts using threatening language, we say, well, please take us to court, we're delighted. He never does.

Q: How often have you been in court in the last year or two?

Bonham-Carter: Very rarely. Most disputes are settled out of court.

Q: How large is your legal staff?

Bonham-Carter: Our last general secretary was a qualified barrister, Miss Barber, and she remains as a consultant. Otherwise we have at least two members of the staff with legal experience; in addition we have several specialist lawyers available when wanted. One for libel, for example, another for tax matters.

Q: Most of your legal work then is connected with taxes rather than with more extreme cases?

Bonham-Carter: No, the general run of cases is much the same as in the past. Infringement of copyright, failure to pay royalties, libel, taxation, bankruptcy, and so on. Often the trouble is that an author comes to us too late. He gets into trouble and rushes to us to say, "Can I join and will you sort me out?" We have to say, "Look, we may be able to help you, but we're not going to promise to involve ourselves in something which you have probably lost

46

already." This is a human failing, as you know, to leave things until too late.

Q: Does the Society of Authors deal with film rights?

Bonham-Carter: Yes, usually as a subsidiary book right. But there's another organization, called the "Writers' Guild," which deals with film and television writers. That is their main concern. We look after radio writers (one of our specialist groups), but professional screenwriters we leave to the Guild, or individual agents.

Q: How about foreign rights?

Bonham-Carter: Well, we have a department dealing with that subject, and such rights are always checked in any contract submitted to us by a writer. In the case of a political protest—a foreign writer such as Solzhenitsyn, or of those imprisoned for their opinions, as in Greece—we don't regard that primarily as our function. We leave that usually to another organization, PEN. We are an organization for British writers first and foremost. There's really a limit to what we can do effectively.

Q: The Society, then, is primarily an economically and legally oriented organization, or do you envision it becoming an organization to foster meetings among literary people?

Bonham-Carter: The business of authorship is what we exist for. We're not interested in value judgments at all. You can write a Western or you can write a deep book of philosophy. As far as we're concerned it's a book, and you have to have a contract and you have to have your rights. We're not interested in its quality. Not in the least. If it's pornographic, then we're interested purely in its relation to the law on obscenity, that's all. We're involved in that sort of way. But we wouldn't say whether we thought it was a dirty book, or even a nice book.

Q: Do you ever institute meetings of authors?

Bonham-Carter: Oh, yes, very much so. But on specific subjects, such as censorship or access to government archives. I've had any number of meetings on Public Lending Right, and I go round talking not only to authors but to rotarians, women's clubs, librarians, and students. In the latter case about Public Lending Right or how an author makes a living. Most people—even in the book trade—are very ignorant about writing as a business; and yet without us there would be no trade. We also keep in contact with the Arts Council, which has a Literature Panel, on which I sit with publishers, librarians, and others. We all work together on various schemes for the encouragement of *literature*. The Arts Council asked us recently for a list of writers who might be interested in visits to schools and factories and we helped them on that.

Q: Do you envision the Society growing larger?

Bonham-Carter: Yes, I would think we can't fail to get larger, because there are so many more part-time writers now. The number of books, or titles anyway, is increasing. I would think the distribution of books is going to undergo a revolution shortly. Already you can get paperbacks in supermarkets and so on. This thing will expand enormously, and it will be very good for the book trade as a whole, even for existing booksellers. Through that expansion and through the increase in reading, we can't fail to increase as long as we keep our organization lively.

I'll give you a short definition of what we are: a de facto trade union but not de jure. The reason why we're not a de jure trade union is partly historical and partly because there's a great resistance among independent people, such as authors, against being organized in that way. We would lose a great many members if we decided to become a trade union. That's really different from the other writing organization—the Writers' Guild—because their members are mostly on some kind of contract with film companies or with television. It's a different setup. Whereas most of our people are literally independent. Principally, we give individual advice to authors who do not have agents, who prefer to operate on their own or aren't well known

Victor Bonham-Carter

enough to justify having an agent. What we do is simply to give them advice about their contracts and often their business problems, and say, well, do you want to have this, that, or the other? If so, make sure that the clauses concerned are properly worded, and we suggest the right phraseology. We don't actually act on their behalf (except in a court case); we advise them. But even where somebody has got an agent who normally does his selling for him, or contracts for him, he still comes to consult us. Often the agent comes too, because we're an outside body with ninety years experience in the hard craft of authorship.

Q: Thank you, Mr. Bonham-Carter.

Alan Burns

ALAN BURNS was born in 1929 in London and educated at the Merchant Taylors' School and the Inns of Court. He began a career as a barrister (1954–59), switching subsequently to journalism and later to fiction. He is married to Carol Lynn and has two children. His publications include *Buster* (1961), *Europe after the Rain* (1965), *Celebrations* (1967), and *Babel* (1969).

The interview took place in Burns's London apartment.

Q: Do you think of yourself as an English writer working in the tradition of the English novel? *Europe after the Rain*, for instance, seems removed from particular time and place.

Burns: The English novel and Englishness itself mean very little to me. I don't particularly like the English novel, and I don't read much of it. I'm more interested certainly in the European novel and in the Russian novel, insofar as those terms have any meaning at all; that is, the very rough line of development which I call the Dostoevsky-Kafka line is what interests me. There's another line which includes Tolstoy and Dickens; this disinterests me. I think of Tolstoy as very wide, particularly in terms of his historical understanding, and of Dostoevsky as very narrow. In general historical terms the English novel disinterests me rather, as such. There are, of course, individual books that I've enjoyed.

However, I entirely disagree with your estimate of *Europe after the Rain* being, as it were, removed from history. On the contrary, it is absolutely grounded in history, and one of my

Alan Burns

regrets about the book is—not that I'm going to talk about my work all the time—one of my regrets is my sense of dismay and guilt that I have taken too much from history, that particularly those aspects of the book that we'll call, say, the concentration camps, are not playing fair because the novelist has only got to use the word Auschwitz, or imply that experience, and he picks up such massive associations that his job is being done for him. I think there's a good deal of unscrupulous, sensational writing being done which battens on history, particularly on contemporary history.

Q: Of course this isn't specifically English but international history.

Burns: This novel in particular, as the title implies, is European history. But I would say that one of the things I'm trying to do as a novelist is to comprehend history. I'm concerned with understanding what is going on and in transmuting that understanding into art of one kind or another. I was going to say fiction, but I tread the borderline between fiction and poetry, particularly in my later work. And therefore my relations with history are very intimate, and often very agonizing. This is the great excitement in my work, as far as I'm concerned.

Q: But you're not interested in trying to capture a particular place, a particular scene, or, to come back to Tolstoy, in taking a particular battle and moving from this very particular place to larger generalizations?

Burns: Well, if I say I'm not interested in the kind of thing that Tolstoy did, that doesn't mean that I don't think he is a magnificent writer. When you talk about Tolstoy's description of a battle, that is incomparable writing and certainly beyond the powers of any contemporary writer. But I'm not interested in trying to do anything like that. And I don't think those contemporaries of mine whom I respect are interested either, for a number of reasons. First of all, I think that this is territory for sociologists, that's what you're really talking about: the

51

sociological or documentary novel of which there is a mass of examples in England at the moment, the John Braine kind of stuff, which is a terrible bore. Part of the reason why it is boring is that, as I was saying a moment ago, the sociologists have moved in on this territory so effectively and in literary terms often so grippingly that they've scooted the novelist out. And fiction comes a very poor second. Not only the sociological novel but TV and a certain style of film have effectively occupied this territory, and driven out the novelist. But I think it's to his benefit that he has been driven out, because he's being driven some place else and that's a rather good place to be. He's been driven, in fact, inside himself. That doesn't mean that the work—my work or the work I respect—is therefore remote, ivory-tower subjective stuff which you might conclude from my use of that phrase. To be sure, in desperation one can get driven that way, and there's a lot of very way-out hippy mystical rubbish that suffers from this defect. But I think the way to react to the occupation of that particular territory is very well summed up in Trocchi's phrase "the cosmonaut of inner space." That is to say, the novelist needs to explore his own imagination, to use his imagination as never before. He's got to plumb his own subconscious as never before. But if he gets stuck there and remains there, then his work becomes irrelevant subjective rubbish. One has somehow got to combine this concern with the exploration of one's unconscious with what I mentioned earlier, with a concern for history. One would think that once you're deep down there, you can't get out and make contact with history. The answer to this contradiction lies quite possibly, though I'm not sure about it, in the Jungian concept of the collective unconscious.

Q: What about Aristotle's notion that poetry is better than history because poetry is general and history is particular? Sociology in those terms is simply the particular explanation of a particular thing, whereas poetry would be not necessarily a general explanation, but the statement of a general, universal truth.

Burns: Yes, a poet needs to be concerned with the general. On the other hand, the reverse of that must be an intense preoccupation with the particular. Kafka, if anyone, generalizes about humanity. His work takes place in no particular place, no particular time. But he copes with what would otherwise be an impossible handicap by a most intense consideration of the particular. The detail in Kafka is absolutely riveting, and I share—well, I will take as read all the necessary apologies that go with linking one's own name with the greats—I share this Kafkaesque need to be particular, and, even more, to be physical in order to offset the general.

Q: Aren't you implying that the novelist is, so to speak, a prophetic historian who generalizes from the past to the future, and writes a Utopian or anti-Utopian fiction? Somebody who perceives the movement of history in himself and extrapolates from that?

Burns: Precisely. Though I would think that any historian is concerned with the future as well as the past.

Q: What about a book like, say, *1984* or *Brave New World*?

Burns: I don't like either of them very much. I don't like science fiction very much, not necessarily to equate the two, because they make this effort far too obviously, far too much from the top of the mind. They are not really imaginative works. They're clever, rational works, but they don't proceed from a point that really excites me. I think it's poetry I'm after, and the vision that is a poet's rather than the extremely interesting and intelligent ideas of intelligent men, as Orwell and Huxley were. But neither of them was a poet. And neither of them had the real vision.

Q: Are you using the word *poet* in a more general sense to include novelists as well?

Burns: Oh yes. But I would hate to have to try and explain the difference.

Q: Maybe we can go on to something else. When I began thinking about making some of these interviews I asked a considerable number of literary people if they would cooperate. And one of them wrote back and said, well, he didn't think that making a literary reputation was something that one actually studied; that everybody who deserved a reputation had one, or would get one. And in a way the thing for the literary historian to do was, like an astronomer, simply to measure the magnitude of the stars. And it was self-evident that these magnitudes were measurable. Do you agree with that? Do the literarily rich merely get richer?

Burns: Well, my immediate personal reaction to that guy is to respect him, certainly, though I detect an arrogance, a conceit behind this attitude nevertheless.

Q: So Pope is right in saying that whatever is, is right, and literary reputations are pretty much as they ought to be?

Burns: I'm not sure. Of course, it's self-evident that those whose work is of high quality and deserve to be known, but never do get known, we never know of. This must be so. Leaving that aside though, I think one needs to see literary reputation, like every other historical or sociological phenomenon, as a dialectical process. Which is to say, it exists in relation to society at a particular point in time and it will change as society's needs change. Therefore, there's no such thing as an absolute reputation that exists for all time. I also agree with the Marxists that, as a general rule, the cultural values of any particular society are created by the dominant class. They have the ability and the need to create the cultural standards of the day. And therefore one faces the problem that those standards will judge highly that work which corresponds to the need of the dominant class. But at any particular time there will also be produced a body of work that corresponds to the values of the dominated class. So that as in any two-class society, there will be two sets of values at war with each other, just as there are two classes at war with each other. If one's going to talk about literary reputation, one must ask Lenin's old question, "Who whom?"—and find out, as it were, "reputed by whom?" It may well be that very good stuff is not reputed very highly at one point in time. But as the class structure changes, its general estimates and general uses will change.

Q: Using this dichotomy, what works or what writers are shaping society? That is, what writers of the dominant class in England, would you say, are dominating?

Burns: I would hope to class myself with the radical element, which is to say the revolutionary element, the element that is wanting to change society. But it's immensely difficult, in relation to contemporary English literature, when one's asked to name names, because it's rather a wasteland. There's not much of value going on, unfortunately.

Q: How about some of the older writers?

Burns: One could mention one, almost a lone figure: William Golding. Now, he's a remarkable member of the older group of writers in his moral courage. Each book tends to be a breakthrough and an exploration. He's also a marvelous stylist, not flabby in the way that so many of the more discursive sociological novelists are. I would name him as the outstanding writer of his generation, of what I call the radical type. Of the more traditional novelists, I think Angus Wilson is excellent, so good a technician that he's good to read.

Q: What about the "amicable" kind of relation between writer and state that seems to exist in the USSR, where the writer becomes the paid employee of the state?

Burns: I think that would be murder. Just because it must inevitably lead to what it has led to in the Soviet Union, the monstrous situation of state-run arts, where one becomes a sort of extension of the Agitprop setup, or one starves, or one gets persecuted, prosecuted, or God knows what. What you bring into question here is the whole relation between the writer and the state. Well, I think today and in the foreseeable future the only possible relationship between a writer and the state must be a state of war. And if he's to do that, not because he wants to wave a flag, but because this is where the good work lies, then inevitably the state's not going to pay him to overthrow itself. So he's going to be faced with an intolerable choice. With a state as powerful and as all-embracing as the Soviet state, it must be a very terrifying situation to be in. Of course, the Western capitalist state has its own ways of buying writers. I've just now myself been bought for two thousand quid by the Arts Council, which I've accepted with immense gratitude but quite aware of the unseen strings attached. In America especially there is a highly sophisticated setup whereby writers are treated generously and I hope in due course to get treated equally generously myself if I don't cut my throat by speaking the way I'm now speaking. These are the means whereby in the West the ruling class attempts to buy and gag and generally run the writers, analogous to the much more brutal way it's done in the Soviet Union. The writer is by nature a dangerous man politically, and the state recognizes him as such. The Hungarian Revolution was partly set off by a writers' group called the Petöfi Circle, and writers have played an important role in Eastern European revolutions generally. A writer's a marked man. He's a dangerous man politically, and this is fine. But it means he's got to be on his guard against the various means that the state will use to neutralize him.

Q: Do you envision a state for which you could write without conflict?

Burns: Well, speaking quite personally, I'm in something of a political turmoil at the moment. I'm very hesitant about making political generalizations; at least I feel the need for constant qualification, and might very well change my mind tomorrow. But my ideas are tending these days very much in the direction of the libertarian or anarchist state with a small "a," which is to say not to the doctrinaire anarchist, who seems to me just one more brand of Trotskyist or something-or-otherist, with his own dogma. When I am asked therefore what kind of *state* I would write for, the answer is none. But if you ask me what kind of society would I write for, then I could only envisage the kind of stateless society that the anarchists envisage, but, quite frankly, I don't see that as a practical possibility in my lifetime.

Q: What sort of literature do you think this sort of society would have?

Burns: It is immensely difficult to envisage because I think what we are heading for is a historical break of the same importance and the same fundamental nature as that between, say, the Middle Ages and the Renaissance. In other words, it's rather like asking the medieval man to envisage the kind of art to be produced in the Renaissance. He'd be totally incapable of doing it, unless he was sufficiently prophetic to sense that it would be totally different. One's tempted to make over-simple generalizations, but one envisages a society without the contradictions and tensions that arise from class divisions. It's possible, therefore, that a great deal of the zing and excitement of art would go. It's rather like Picasso's great painting "War and Peace." Giant panels with war on one side and peace on the other. He painted it at the time of Korea. The war side contains the most ghoulish and dreadful Bosch-like, Breughel-like devils gnashing their teeth and hell-fire coming out on all sides. It's a brilliant painting, absolutely fascinating. I saw it in the big Picasso retrospective exhibition in Rome some years ago. When he came to paint peace, I can imagine him sort of scratching his head, saying what the hell can I do with peace? What we get is a series of rather feeble old men sitting on mounds playing the pipes of Pan, and some very unreal looking maidens dancing round. In other words, this is a long way round to answer your question about the sort of art that is appropriate to the lack of contradiction and tension. Peace, in other words, may very well be rather joyful and rather tedious, but I don't know.

Q: To backtrack for a moment: is literature really in England a kind of old boy network, even among the old boys who don't like to be known as old boys?

Burns: Undoubtedly. I don't say that, however, in an envious way, because it is also true that there are very considerable and growing resources, as it were, on the other side. I don't want to oversimplify and overemphasize this class war angle, but nevertheless I think it is fundamental to the situation, and it is what goes to the root of this kind of question. One of the surfaces on the social plane is this old boy network, and the need to have good manners, as they would say. You go to the right parties, and sleep in the right beds, and know the right folks, and say the right things. This is all true to an extent. But it isn't really good enough for an aspiring writer to say, well, I can't get in because it's dominated by them. Because I think that the situation is sufficiently fluid, and there are sufficient contradictions even within the so-called old boy network to make it quite possible for a person of ability to obtain recognition.

If there is any obvious physical manifestation of the ruling literary clique, I would have thought it was in the so-called literature panel of the Arts Council, which provides patronage and purports to run the show. I am a fairly uncompromising radical, and yet, as I say, they have treated me extremely generously. To that extent, what can I say? I don't consider myself part of the old boy network, but the old boys have treated me all right is what it comes to, and therefore I beware of oversimplifying in relation to them. Particularly the ones I've met are nice folks. This again is another very awkward characteristic of the British social-political scene: that our bourgeoisie, our tyrants, are such nice folks. They're nice to be with and they're so cultivated and so understanding, that it's difficult to hate them.

Q: So they absorb those who want to remove them from power?

Burns: Undoubtedly. This is the classic way of dealing with a rebel, isn't it? To convert him.

Q: The strings you were talking about before?

Burns: Yes. But as I say I wouldn't want to oversimplify this. It doesn't work in a simple way. I don't picture the ruling class sitting around a table and deciding what to do about Alan Burns. It doesn't work that way, I know. It's a very subtle process.

Q: What would you say about an outsider like D. H. Lawrence?

58

Alan Burns

Burns: Well, for a start he was not so much of an outsider. Of course, in his time this old boy network was much tighter and much more powerful than it is today. Reading his correspondence, one can see that he was hobnobbing with Lady this and Lord that. He was quite one of the boys, albeit a rebellious boy. But the club needs a few rebels too, to help make the scene.

Q: To move on to something technological rather than social: how do you react to the challenges against serious writing of any kind provided by television and film? In the United States, at least, a writer like Norman Mailer seems to be abandoning fiction in print for fiction on celluloid, and in France Robbe-Grillet is doing the same thing. Do you sense here a threat to your very existence as a writer?

Burns: This is a genuine anxiety in the minds of working novelists. I know that from my friends. Whereas it used to be said that all art aspires to the condition of music, it is now said that all art aspires to the condition of the film, because the film, damn it, is incomparable as a medium. It's got everything except one thing, which I'll mention in a minute. In sensual terms it appears to have everything: movement, color, pictures. Faced with the desperately old-fashioned, clanking typewriter, one may very well ask oneself, "What the hell am I messing about for? It's no good. I can't even hope to approximate the visual impact of the most amateur home movie maker." One of the reactions of the writer is to try to compete nevertheless: I do it myself. A picture in every line—I want to get a physical picture. I'm also immensely influenced by and tremendously interested in painting, partly because the experimentation of painting, especially in surrealism, excites me—especially the surrealism of American painters which can teach the writer a great deal.

A number of my friends are on the verge of packing it in, because of the counterattractions of the film. They write for television now, and for two reasons primarily: one is the far greater sensual impact of the film, but the other, equally important reason is the audience. If one makes a television film,

59

one talks in terms of millions: even if one makes an art movie, one probably talks in terms of tens of thousands, and if one gets on the circuits, it's international millions again. And unlike the novel, it's a captive audience and an attentive audience in this marvelous physical situation of darkness and warmth. All this would tend to make one feel, well, if the novel ain't dead now, then it never will be. Why does it survive? The one thing the novel has got that the film and television don't is the peculiarly intimate relationship over a period of time between writer and reader. The reader can read and reread; he can answer back, as it were. In other words, there's a genuine dialogue here. It's a democratic thing: you writing, motivating, moving, changing your reader in a way that television certainly and most films fail to do. Hence you can't achieve the same profundity in a film as you can in a novel. If, therefore, one can foresee a better society with leisured, cultured people, who won't merely absorb art in a passive way, then I see a great future for the book.

Having said all this, I'll say that, nevertheless, what I want to do now is make a film.

Q: Do you sense a reverse influence of the film—aside from the visual aspects—on the novel? Especially in a technical sense, say in structuring a novel?

Burns: Godard is very close to my method of working, which is one of fragmentation, of putting the pieces together in a mosaic. Reading something of Godard's methods and learning that the hotel room he lives in is usually knee-deep in snippets and little cuttings of magazines, I recognized immediately that this is the way I work. I also work, as he does, without any preconceived idea. I create a great mass of fragments, and then I search in and live with those fragments. As Picasso says, I do not seek, I find. I find in those fragments a pattern and build up from there. This is partly an extension of Burroughs' cut-up method, and there really is a great connection between Godard and the most interesting modern novelists.

60

Alan Burns

Q: Why do you use the novel, rather than poetry or drama, as your preferred mode of expression?

Burns: The great attraction of the novel lies in its search for form. The secret may lie in the word *novel* itself. If it's new, then it's novel. There was a great question about my last book as to whether to call it a novel or not. If by novel you mean the conventional novel with story, plot, and character, I'm not very interested. It's irrelevant and dated. None of the certainties and absolutes—God, progress, the family—which pertained in the heyday of the novel during the nineteenth century, pertain today. We're living in a desperate era of uncertainties, populated by absurd nightmares and phantoms, generally deriving from the abolition of the ultimate absolute, God, and fixated on the only absolute which still remains, death. It's therefore purely a historical accident that what I write is still called a novel. My recent book was composed of a series of almost completely disconnected paragraphs. Each paragraph might be called a novel in itself. Sometimes it's an aphorism, sometimes it's an anecdote, sometimes it's a simple picture. There is, in fact, an association between that which precedes and that which follows and the whole is informed by an elemental construction, but this is very far nevertheless from the conventional novel. It's only called a novel for the most practical reason of all, because of the publisher and because of the reviewers and librarians who feel compelled to categorize. So the answer is, no, I'm not interested in the novel, if by the novel you mean the traditional novel, I'm interested in something else that may be called the novel, in poetry, epic poetry.

Q: Then why don't you call it poetry and publish it as such?

Burns: Because I'm still concerned with trying to define the difference between poetry and prose, and I am not yet sufficiently certain of the answer to say one is one and one is the other. It's also so long and you can't call that a poem, because people say, well, that can't be a poem. So I say, OK, we'll call it

61

something else. This is all connected with the breakdown of categories, and some of the most interesting work is being done on the frontiers of the various media. I know, for example, a number of painters who are making what really are sculptures, but not quite.

Q: Thank you, Mr. Burns.

John Mackenzie Calder

JOHN MACKENZIE CALDER was born in 1927 and educated at Gillings Castle, Yorkshire; Bishops College School, Canada; Sir George William College; and McGill and Zurich universities. He served as director of Calders Ltd. (timber company) until 1957, when he resigned to devote himself fully to the publishing business he had founded originally as a hobby in 1950. His business talents have also found expression in the organization of literary conferences, such as those at the Edinburgh Festival in 1962 and 1963; and he has also stood (unsuccessfully) for Parliament as a Labour candidate. He has been married twice, to Mary Ann Simmonds and Bettina Jonic, and has two daughters. His publications include *A Samuel Beckett Reader* (1967).

The interview took place in the London offices of Calder & Boyars, Ltd.

Q: How do you go about choosing your authors?

Calder: Well, we choose our authors purely and simply by liking them. We get an enormous number of manuscripts. Once a week, when our editorial committee, which is normally four people, happens to be in London and on the spot, we sit down for about two hours and sift through manuscripts. Anything that looks absolutely hopeless goes straight back. Anything that looks possible gets put aside to be properly read.

Q: What are your criteria for hopeless manuscripts?

Calder: Something badly written. You judge this by reading the first page, by reading the last page, and by looking quickly through the book to see what the author's trying to do. If it seems below our standard, then we don't go any further. If there seems to be something interesting about the book, even if there's something about it we don't especially like, such as being very badly typed, or even handwritten as happens sometimes—against which we have an enormous prejudice—we put it aside to be read more carefully. Of the manuscripts put aside, probably twenty to thirty a week, we decide who is going to read them first. We have a panel of about ten readers.

Q: How did you choose the panel?

Calder: Well, most of them are people who write for us.

Q: The editorial committee is also made up of writers?

Calder: The editorial committee is made up entirely of people who work here on the premises and who do all sorts of different jobs, including editing books. We then divide the manuscripts up. That's to say, every week. I settle myself with seven or eight manuscripts, books which I think are interesting enough to be read by me. The others go to other readers. We know everybody's prejudices and preconceptions, and within the next two weeks, we turn in written reports. Eventually all these reports will go before an editorial meeting, and there we decide what we're going to publish. This is, of course, the procedure for manuscripts in the English language, including a great many coming from America. American publishers these days are publishing much less fiction than formerly.

Q: What percentage are American manuscripts?

Calder: Oh, perhaps only 2 or 3 percent of the great bulk that comes in, but of the ones that are seriously considered, it might be 10 percent. In other words, we tend to get a better American manuscript, and very often we accept a book that's been turned down by most American publishers, and then send it back to America a year or so later. Somebody like Gil Orlovitz was turned down all over New York, and we took on his novel *Milkbottle H*, a big massive novel, published it here, and it has been received very successfully. We sold it to Dell in America, who published him in both hard cover and paperback, reprinted him twice and that established Orlovitz, who was quite well known as a poet and literary editor, as a novelist. His second novel is coming out this year.

Q: Also through you?

Calder: Also through us. This happens with quite a number of other people from time to time. One way in which it works, of course, is that our writers go to give lectures, or do a tour in the States, or go over on some foundation grant. There they meet a number of writers whom they try to help get published by their publisher in this country. This happens quite often. Of course it works in reverse too, sometimes.

Q: You said earlier that you knew your readers' prejudices. What prejudices do you yourself have as a publisher?

Calder: Everybody has prejudices. My partner, Marion Boyars, has a rather different taste than myself. So certain books will go to her to be read, and certain books will come to me to be read, purely because I know that a certain kind of book I'm going to find myself not liking because of the subject matter or style or possibly because I met the author and didn't particularly like him. And vice versa. But at least half of our publishing consists of translations from other languages.

Q: Is that the money making end of it?

Calder: No, it isn't.

Q: Do you lose money on translations?

Calder: Well, we make more I think on untranslated materials than on translated. But some of our best and most prestigious authors are from other languages. I read French, German, Spanish, Italian, as well as Serbo-Croat and Russian. I trust myself completely in French and German, and to a certain extent in Italian. But when you get, say, into Polish or Dutch, we have to have specialized readers. And there we have to really be able to sniff if a book is worth following up and would pay getting specialized readers for. You do it partly by knowing the publisher's imprint, by knowing the publisher well enough to go carefully into his description of the book when he offers it to you to decide whether it's something you might really publish or not. Because you don't want to waste a lot of money on readers' reports for books that are completely impossible anyway. I tend to read all the French books that come in and some of the German ones. Marion Boyars, who was born in Germany, tends to read most of the German books that come in, some of the French ones, and since she also has some knowledge of Polish, the Polish ones, enough to be able to get an idea of a book, of whether it's worthwhile or not.

Q: Are these books simply sent to you or actively solicited?

Calder: Well, normally we actively solicit. We see perhaps twenty foreign publishers every week. They come here, or we go abroad. We go to the big book fairs, we meet them, we exchange information, we get their catalogues, we get their publicity. And we read reviews in international papers and magazines that deal in literature.

Q: How long have you been in the business?

Calder: Twenty years, twenty years this year.

Q: When you founded the company did you have a fixed editorial policy in mind?

Calder: Well, obviously one wanted to follow one's personal taste. We've always done that. But we started off very eclectically. I think we're still very eclectic publishers. But our list consists mainly of fiction; half of our books are fiction. We also do a lot of books on all the arts, particularly music, and on the social sciences and philosophy. Our list is, broadly speaking, an intellectual list,

John Mackenzie Calder

and we very seldom remainder a book. When we publish a book we expect to go on selling it for the next century. That is really our criterion. Is somebody going to want to read this book in ten years' time? We hope in a hundred, but certainly in ten years' time. If we don't see the book lasting ten years, our tendency is to say no. We don't want to publish it.

Q: Do you depend on library sales to break even?

Calder: Well, library sales eat up most of the hard-cover editions in this country at present, although our exports are quite strong too. We have two paperback series. One of them is large format, egghead sort of paperbacks. They were originally based on the first Evergreens, although we had the idea long before Grove Press even got started. But we kept on holding up paperback plans. And we held them up for five years because we were at one time distributors of Evergreens in Great Britain. We imported the first intellectual paperbacks into Britain and established them here. We felt we could only really begin launching our own—which meant big printings—once we had done that. Well, we've given up all the agencies now and we do our own. We also have a rather more popular paperback series called Jupiter Books, which are moderately priced and have authors such as Samuel Beckett, Ionesco, Heinrich Böll, Ivo Andrič, and international writers from Britain and America—books which have claims to be twentieth-century classics.

Q: Do you consider yourself to be a vanguard publisher who's willing to go out on a limb for experimental writing?

Calder: Well, up to now we have been. I think that the experiments which are coming on now are a little bit beyond us. Unless we can feel personally enthusiastic about something, we're not interested; we're not interested in following trends or fashions. It's better for some new, younger publisher that's on that particular wavelength to publish them. We don't try to publish books which we feel are tapping a new fashion which we don't particularly like ourselves. The generation of writers who

67

are twenty-five and under and are going into very anarchistic literary experiments; we really don't have very much interest in them. There are a few people here and there in whom we see a definite talent. We publish quite a lot of concrete poetry. But we feel that anything we publish has got to have meaning, and some of the things going on in France right now—the Tel Quel group—don't. We published Phillipe Sollers's books up to a certain point, but when I read his last novel five times and had no more idea what it was about the fifth time than the first, I just decided no—let somebody else do it. It might be a work of a genius, it might be the literature of the twenty-first century, but unless it in some way can appeal to me, I'm not going to be able to put it over to the public.

Q: I noticed that you have some repeats in publishing younger authors. If you published somebody the first time, does that mean you'll keep publishing him?

Calder: Oh yes. I mean once we take somebody on, we try very hard to keep on doing him. It's only if we really feel he's impossible that we don't. We don't think about commercial motives until after we have put the book into production. We don't worry about how it's going to sell, we worry about how we like it. Besides, if you're really enthusiastic about a book you can eventually find a way of making it sell. And most of our books do sell. We are completely opposed to any kind of computer approach to publishing, because this *must* be dependent on past experience. You can't judge a book that has no relation to any other previous book according to any kind of prearranged standards. How is it going to sell, who's going to want it? I mean there's no public for a book until you create the public; you've got to bring it into being. That's the publisher's job.

Q: Do you print the hard cover first and then the paperback? Or both simultaneously?

Calder: We're very flexible, but normally we have a gap of eighteen months, two years, sometimes up to five years between hard cover and paperback publishing. If the hard cover is selling well, we hold up the paper until we feel the thing's going to drop off. If the book is the type of book that's only going to appeal to a certain kind of buyer who's not going to buy a hard cover in any case, but might buy the paperback, we then sometimes publish simultaneously, or have a very short gap in order to tap that market when the book is still being talked about.

Q: Who do you think are the buyers of the first novels you publish?

Calder: I would say that there's a large number of people who read the Sunday reviews, the weekly paper reviews, and literary reviews of different kinds. (Every newspaper in Britain devotes a certain amount of space to reviewing books.) They read reviews fairly regularly and try to buy or borrow from the library books that have been reviewed in a way that attracts them. These people tend to be, very often, in universities. I think our market is very largely an academic one. To a certain extent, students, schoolteachers, professional people of all kinds, sometimes retired people, elderly people who've managed to keep surprisingly up to date in what they read. We get quite a correspondence from people reading our books who comment on what they've liked and what they haven't liked. I suspect that of the manuscripts we receive many of them come from people who are fans of our particular policy or some of the authors we publish. I think in this country the public tends to be rather more imprint-conscious than in the United States. There's a feeling that a book from a certain kind of publisher is a book they're going to want to read. If it comes from a completely different publisher, well, they're not going to be so certain.

Q: How large would a hard-cover printing be of a new novel?

Calder: Well, the most we've ever printed was forty thousand and the smallest quantity about two thousand. I would say that our average printing is between three and four thousand copies. The paperback is bound from the same sheets, so we don't bind up a whole edition. If it's a very doubtful quantity we probably bind a thousand and then wait to see what happens. If it goes on selling, we keep on binding until the thing slows down; and then bind the balance of our sheets in paperback. If the book gets extremely good reviews, but the sales are rather slow, we may bring out the paperback rather quickly, even if we still have a lot of hard-cover copies left. The hard cover does go on selling even when the paperback comes out, although of course more slowly.

Q: How many new fiction titles, not translated, do you publish every year?

Calder: Well, this year we're publishing forty-eight novels, of which twenty are probably first novels; this is the largest number we've ever done. We try not to publish more than two or three novels in the average month, but we have such a pileup at present that it was just necessary to bring them all out because authors were getting very unhappy about delays. We had some major censorship cases in the last two years that slowed us up, mostly over *Last Exit to Brooklyn*, which had three trials, very expensive trials. Fighting that took a lot of time and money.

Q: How long a period is there between acceptance and publication?

Calder: It normally takes six to twelve months between acceptance and publication. If it has to be translated, of course it's much longer.

Q: So you have a considerable backlog.

Calder: Well, we're publishing some books just now that we accepted five years ago, but that's not the rule. When things are going fairly well, we tend to put books into production that we know aren't going to do very well but which we feel we can't hold back any longer. If our financial position is very tight, then we tend to push forward the books we think are going to be more commercial.

70

Q: Do you think of yourself primarily as an "idealistic" rather than commercial publisher?

Calder: Well, I think the word "idealistic" is rather difficult to define here because I've always found that the book one really likes oneself is ultimately the book that one's going to live on in future years. If you don't trust your own taste, you shouldn't be in publishing. You really have to believe that you can make a book you believe in a best seller over a period of years. It might take a long time. When we first took on Beckett he was completely unsalable. Today Beckett is taught in universities. We've made a very nice revenue purely out of allowing people to quote from him in their own books. There are on the average five, six books coming out about Beckett every month, somewhere or other. There are always little fees for quoting this and quoting that.

Q: Do the universities play a crucial role in helping sales then?

Calder: Not in an official way. Beckett had a very large readership before the universities began to take him up. It's really individual enthusiasm of people teaching literature that finally got him into the universities as such. There's still a lot of prejudice against Beckett in academic circles. But he's very widely read, and he's read much more than he's taught. Beckett is somebody who helps us to live these days. I wasn't terribly hopeful when I first took him on that we were ever going to see our investment back, but I thought here was somebody we had to publish.

Q: In other words, you don't consciously use popular authors to offset more serious and less popular writers, as other publishers do?

Calder: Well, we do. But we don't plan it that way, and we're often agreeably surprised. We don't think somebody is going to sell very well and he does. Also, we're very good at selling subsidiary rights. Because we buy a lot of translations from other countries, we're good at selling our authors. I'm sure that more than any other publisher in this country, certainly more than any in

71

America, we're good at selling our authors to French, German, Scandinavian publishers and so on. Some of our authors who sell slowly but regularly here are in fact extremely well known in other countries. On the whole, serious writing is more commercial in countries like Germany than it is in English-speaking countries.

Q: If you were to close your doors tomorrow, do you think English literature would suffer thereby?

Calder: Well, it would, yes. I mean it would suffer if any publisher closed his doors. We at present are getting great pressure from other publishers' writers to take them on, partly because they feel their publishers don't present them properly or don't sell them well enough, or just for their lack of sympathy in what they're doing. In many cases, writers who have had two or three books published but haven't sold very well find that a publisher doesn't want to continue with them, so they come to us. Would we take them on? It's very difficult with extremely limited resources to go on doing what we're doing and also to take on people you would like to take on who suddenly find themselves free. We constantly have to make agonizing decisions.

Q: Would you compare yourself as a publisher to a company like Boni and Liveright in the twenties?

Calder: Yes, to some extent, I think so.

Q: Performing the same kind of function for English literature?

Calder: I don't think these days we consider ourselves as being very avant-garde because the avant-garde has gone in other directions. I think what we're publishing today is a book of solid worth and value in a market we know quite a lot about and which we're quite good at reaching.

Q: How do you go about advertising a book, getting it to the market?

Calder: Well, first of all, we spend a lot of time getting reviewers, literary editors, and other writers interested in a new writer that

72

we publish. We do quite a lot of entertaining and give quite a lot of parties.

Q: For what sort of person?

Calder: Well, we have about two or three parties a month, usually given in these offices; sometimes we have bigger ones outside, and we invite about a hundred to a hundred and fifty people who will be what you might call the literary establishment, and the journalists who are interested in new writing, for them to meet the writer, to get a certain excitement, to find out a bit about what the book's about. Everybody takes a book jacket away, but we don't let them take the book away. They get the review copy in the proper place. We do this purely to make the name known a bit. At the same time we try to get people who we think are going to review the book in the right sort of way, who are going to put their oar in to review it in the place where they normally review. This is not a difficult thing to do, but it does take time and quite a bit of thought. Beyond that, we advertise in the more serious papers. We don't do very much tombstone advertising in Sunday papers: that's to say, title, author, and a couple of quotes from what somebody said about it, and the price. We don't think this is particularly noted by the public. We try to make our advertisements read like review copy. We lay the advertising out differently. We try to have something eye-catching about it, to make people read on. Over the years I think our advertising has been very successful and is now being quite widely copied by other publishers. It's time for us to do something new, and we're thinking about that right now. We advertise in the *Times Literary Supplement* and in the *New Statesman*. The only daily paper in which we advertise regularly is the *Guardian*; it's got the best literary page of any British paper. We also advertise the more obviously commercial books in the *Observer*, the *Sunday Times*, occasionally the *Times* and other places. We also advertise in *London Magazine*, in *Encounter* sometimes, and in quite small, specialized papers if we feel they've got the right kind of readership.

Q: Is there a circle, or are there circles in England connected perhaps with publications like *Encounter*, which, if favorably disposed to a book, can really make it go?

Calder: Oh, I think so. Ultimately every writer gets to know other writers; they have their friends and they have their enemies. The thing to do is to get your books reviewed by your friends and not by your enemies. You can influence that to a certain extent. You can at least have the friends make an effort to review the book, rather than just wait for the literary editors to send it out. Aside from that, we also promote lecture tours and public readings and all that kind of thing.

Q: Is there anything now like, say, the old *Athenaeum* under Murry that can really make an impact on intellectuals as a group?

Calder: Well, we're about to buy up a major London bookshop. When we do that, we're going to in fact use it not only for selling books, but to create a literary circle around it that will meet regularly and have public meetings. That I think will help us in various ways. It is essential, if you have writers of a similar type, that they form themselves into some sort of group to create an image that's recognizable to journalists as a news item from time to time. The public then builds up some sort of cliché that you can use to launch new authors.

Q: Is Calder and Boyars interested in the way Grove Press seems to be becoming interested in buying up films and selling them?

Calder: Well, I rather doubt it. You see, Grove has become more and more interested in sensational publishing as such. We'll publish anything we like, whatever the legal risk. But we are not particularly interested in publishing any sort of rot-gut, good, bad, or indifferent. Grove is. We're completely uninterested in pornography as such. No prejudice against it, but that's for somebody else, not for us. We're doing quite a lot in the theatre; we have our own theatrical agency and we publish a lot of plays. Our theatrical agency helps to pay the rent, brings in quite a lot of money, and helps to sell, of course, books of plays. Aside from that, I'm quite involved in theatrical activities. We have our own theatrical review. We're interested in what goes on in the theatre, because a lot of the best English writing today is theatrical. In fact, I think the novel is going into a certain decline. Also the rewards of the theatre are greater than those of the novel. A writer who can do both is pretty often putting more energy into the theatre, and, of course, into films. We *are* interested in films as literary properties; we publish scripts. We might eventually become interested in films in a more direct way, other than just publishing film scripts and selling film rights of our novels. But we haven't really started to think about that yet. That's a possible future development. I don't think we're going to be interested in simply being a commercial film distributor as Grove has become.

Q: Do you give authors advances on novels that you like?

Calder: You have to. We give them advances, but over and above the advance, if an author is getting on with a book and has a great financial problem, well, we do just tend to keep on advancing to keep him alive for the time being. You have to help your authors. That's perhaps not commercially wise, but you've just got to do it if you want to keep a certain kind of author, if you want to have the right kind of relationship with your authors. In this country we have the Arts Council which now gives quite a lot of money each year in grants to authors. Normally it's a grant that will give them six months to a year to finish a new book. It might be renewed for a second year, but there are a great many claimants. We are quite good at getting money out of the Arts Council for our authors, partly because they are the kind of authors who need grants. But they do take us seriously, and they know that if we put up an application it's not a frivolous one. I suppose this year we'll raise something like ten thousand pounds from the Arts Council for our authors, which is something like 15 percent of the total advance money available.

Q: Thank you, Mr. Calder.

Maurice Callard

MAURICE CALLARD was born in 1912 in Gosport, Hants, and educated at the Gosport County Grammar School. He has worked as a hairdresser in the family business at Gosport, except for an interval of several years' service in the Palestine Police Force. He is married to Margaret Joan Gouldie and has two children. His novels include *The City Called Holy* (1954), *The World and the Flesh* (1960), and *Across the Frontier* (1964).

The interview took place in Callard's home in Gosport.

Q: Would you say that it's impossible for a writer, unless he's already very solidly established or unless he happened somehow to stumble onto a good thing that sells in enormous numbers, to live from his writing?

Callard: Yes. If you mean sales of his novels, it's impossible. Graham Greene, I think, is an exception. Somebody once said that only Graham Greene in England could live from the royalties of his books. That is, the hardback copies. That's probably an exaggeration, because there are some popular novelists who can; not of the quality of Graham Greene, to be sure, but people like Georgette Heyer, who writes historical novels. I believe they print editions of forty thousand copies of her books, and she turns out a book every year. But the serious novelist who's trying to write well I think does find it extremely difficult. This is partly because there isn't much of a market, because not only has the library lowered the value of the book itself, but I think that the people who use the

76

libraries become the lowest common denominator. I mean, they are *readers*, thank God. We don't want them to give up reading, but they look for something fairly easy to read.

It's just very difficult. What one hopes to do is gradually, slowly, to break through, but I'm getting a bit old for it now and a bit indolent. I don't write as much as I ought to. It's very hard to get established, I'm sure of that. I don't think there's any easy way; I don't think having been to a university would help. In fact, it could possibly be a hindrance, because practically everyone has been to a university nowadays. And if you haven't, you necessarily must have some sort of fresh outlook. For example, Alan Sillitoe.

Q: Would you say that one of the ways of getting established would be to leave the provinces and go to London? To get into the literary mainstream? To associate with the right people who would then drop one's name in the right places?

Callard: It may be that sooner or later you can break in through journalism and have people say, "Oh, that well-known journalist." But I don't think at the outset it would sell any more of one's books, because I've had examples given to me of people whose names are quite well known as literary figures, and publishers have told me what their novels sell. It's not too good. So I think that it would be a long process, but then there's always a disadvantage in doing that, and I personally have always avoided it. I've never joined any clique, club, or anything, because I think, well, if you get in, you'll become like them to a great extent; and that's really what an author doesn't want to do. Because, frankly, a lot of the novels turned out by young chaps from a university could be written by any of them. They all have the same outlook.

Q: Was it, then, a conscious choice on your part to stay in Gosport?

Callard: No, it's just really personal finance. I think if I'd had money, I'd have gone and lived in North Africa.

Q: But not to London.

The Writer's Place

Callard: No, I don't think so.

Q: Why not?

Callard: Why not? If you mean London literary life, no, I wouldn't care for it. I'd like to be away from it.

Q: Do you ever discuss your writing with other writers?

Callard: When you discuss your writing with other writers, all they talk about is their own writing. I haven't done it very much, no. I have friends—a fellow who was at school with me, who has made a bit of a name as a novelist. He lives in Germany, and has lived in Germany since the war. Occasionally I see him, perhaps once every five years, and we talk all the time about books. But I haven't got anybody else that I can talk to about books. It doesn't worry me. I think about it, but I don't really talk about it.

Q: In other words, it's not necessary for your writing, or even helpful?

Callard: I don't quite know. I'm invited occasionally to go and talk to writers' circles in the district, particularly the local one. The invitation crops up every two years. I'm sure they must be getting fed up with me, but I always find it rather interesting and refreshing to have a chat to them about writing. But I'd rather, on the whole, think it out myself. I've been working now for five or six years on an entirely new technique, which I haven't quite got off yet.

Q: A novel?

Callard: Yes. Why the novel is written, actually. I want to do something where the impact of the words on the page is greater than in an ordinary narrative. To do this, I'm choosing a very simple subject and looking at it through the eyes of two protagonists. It's written in the first person, in the present tense, and in alternate outlooks—first from A and then from B. There's plenty of action, but the action is going on not only in the person, but his reactions to the other person and what they're doing.

78

Maurice Callard

There are several other technical devices which I've used, but the main idea of it is to let the reader look at the person quite nakedly, without any of *my* narrative or description. *There's* the person, you see.

Q: So you're dissatisfied with the more conventional type of novel? Or with its function?

Callard: To some extent. I think we've had far too many novels. We're simply snowed under with novels every week. The way people live too has some effect on their reading habits. There now are so many other diversions. Whereas even fifty years ago, there was comparatively nothing. When I was a boy, on Sundays there were no cinemas, everyone got dressed up in their Sunday best and of an evening we stood round the piano singing songs, or, I suppose, when that was over we read . . . Though I didn't read much as a young boy. We had three books in my house: Ethel M. Dell's *The Rocks of Valpré*, H. G. Wells's *Mr. Britling Sees It Through*, and Jane Austen's *Emma*, of which the first couple of pages were missing. It was all small print, and I don't think I ever read any of them anyway.

Q: To come back to the matter of the library and payments to the author. If a public lending right system were introduced, do you believe it would solve any of the major problems of authors?

Callard: No, I don't think it would. You see, the number of people writing is so big, and the number that go into the library must necessarily be a small proportion of those, that I don't think it would affect a great many people anyway. And also it would hardly affect making the successful author wealthier, whereas the chap who was trying to get established might not get his book into the library at all. Or he'll probably get his books into this library and that library by the sheer idiosyncrasy of the librarian; or because it had been reviewed and people came and asked for it. But there's no guarantee that all the libraries over the country would take the book. I don't know how many libraries there are, but I suppose about a thousand of my books would go into libraries. And of course a book in the library hasn't got a very long life; it might last ten years. Sometimes the libraries will have a book rebound, which costs them far more money than they will ever pay the author to keep the book going in the library.

Q: What is your view of the British Arts Council grants and bursaries?

Callard: I read about various people having them. I don't know anything more than that.

Q: Do you think it's a good idea?

Callard: I don't know very much about it, but I imagine it is to people who get them. I have read of one or two of my contemporaries who've got grants.

Q: Would you be tempted by having a chance to teach creative writing? Is this something that would interest you as a writer?

Callard: I love talking to people about things which interest me, and I've done a lot of lecturing. I would be interested, but in this country if you haven't got the academic qualifications, I don't think you'd stand much chance. I don't know, there may be a chance now, but I left school before I got anything like that.

Q: What caused you to begin writing novels?

Callard: Mainly because I had no success with short stories. I wanted to be a writer when I was in school. I left school at a most unfortunate time, in 1931 when the Depression was at its worst. In England here we had some three million unemployed out of a labor force of eighteen million. I wanted to go into journalism really, but the papers were amalgamating, two making do with one staff. I tried several local places. They said, well, come back in two or three years' time, things may be better. I never had the money to be able to do that, so I had to find something else. As a matter of fact I went into the family business, which was ladies' hairdressing. And that's what I still do; I've never been able to get

Maurice Callard

quite out of it. But for six years I was in Palestine, in the Palestine Police Force.

Q: Is the story in *Across the Frontier* at all real? Did you base it on a real story while you were in Palestine?

Callard: Well, I did once take a girl in a pickup a short distance. I didn't have any conversation with her at all. She was a Turkish Jewess, and she was being extradited, and I took her from Nazareth to Accra, or somewhere like that. And I sat at the back of the pickup and she sat at the other side, and neither of us said a word the whole time. But that is the genesis of the book.

Q: Your style reminds me a little bit of Hemingway's. Would you say that he in any way interested you as a writer?

Callard: Yes. Hemingway has; but, more than Hemingway, Scott Fitzgerald is my hero. Not all of Scott Fitzgerald, but *The Great Gatsby. The Great Gatsby*—well, I don't know if I do now, but I used to know it by heart. I thought it was lovely. There's a sort of—I know it's criticized on all sorts of grounds—but there's a sort of music in it that is beautiful English.

Q: You said earlier that you moved from the short story to the novel. Could you elaborate on that?

Callard: Well, I was writing short stories and they weren't getting accepted. And I thought, well, in the time taken up writing a few short stories I could easily write a novel. Besides, when I came home from Palestine, I had a good subject to write about. At least I knew the background would be interesting. *Across the Frontier,* for instance, would make a wonderful film, because if it was filmed in the natural setting, in color, you couldn't go wrong. As a matter of fact, just before it was published, when it was in proof, all the film companies were looking at it. I shouldn't be surprised if it wouldn't be filmed one day.

Q: It might be hard to produce, however.

Callard: Well, that is the point, of course. There was a producer

81

who made an offer for *The End of the Visit*, which was published by Doubleday in America and in this country by Hutchinson. Hutchinson's New York office wrote to London and said, this chap's made a firm offer for the film rights. It wasn't very much, $4,000 or something like that. It was a lot to me, but it wasn't a vast amount. They wrote down from London and said, did I accept it and would I reply quickly because this producer chap was off somewhere. I did reply and I didn't hear for six months, so I wrote and said, what about this $4,000? And they said, we haven't heard anything from New York, we'll check up. Which I thought was a bit slack. At any rate, they checked up with New York, and they said, well, unfortunately there was a snag, namely that the producer belonged to a—you might not believe this—to an American-Egyptian film company, where the directors were Americans and Egyptians. One of the conditions of the company was that the film had to be made in Egypt. Egypt, incidentally, is—well, you probably know—is a very, very big film-making country. They make most of the films for the Arabic-speaking world, which after all is a good part of the earth, really. All of Pakistan, the Middle East, North Africa, and a good bit of East Africa. They make a hell of a lot of films. Anyway, this was at the time of a bit of trouble between Nasser and the Americans, and the film just didn't get made.

Q: Do you write at all with things like film rights in mind?

Callard: No, I don't really, although I've always been alive to the fact that novels written about exotic places like the Middle East could be made into films, and quite on the cards. If I did, I think I would have more characters; I tend to keep my characters to two always, and the others are not really very important. I think two is really enough for a novel.

Q: How did you, by the way, flesh out this incident that led to *Across the Frontier* where you drove the girl to some small frontier town? How did you come to associate this with a longer story?

Callard: Well, the situation of the girl affected me at the time. If

82

you live in Palestine, you are much more alive to the flotsam and jetsam of human beings than you would be in Minnesota or in Hampshire. Particularly in England, because we're an island, and we have a little problem nowadays with the recent immigrants, but in a country like Palestine, which is nearly surrounded by other countries from which people come in from all directions, it's a constant problem. In the days when Britain held the mandate of the country, of course it was a pretty small country. The coastal belt comes back about twenty, thirty miles. Then there are some hills and then you're down in the desert. There isn't a lot of room for people to live in. No doubt the Jews have made a much better job of it than anyone's done before, because they've got all the technique of turning the desert into a garden. I used often in the course of my duty to find people who'd been wandering around. I came across a chap who had escaped from Russia in 1920. From 1920 until somewhere around 1943, he'd been shuttled from country to country. He got into Persia, and they found him in Persia and said, where are your papers? And he said, no papers. They kicked him out, you see. They pushed him somewhere else. He'd go to Syria, Lebanon, Palestine, Egypt, like this. A terrible situation. He couldn't get back to Russia for some reason. He was stateless, by that time. He had people in Russia, he said. And of course we had no alternative in a small country like that than to go on doing what the other people were doing. Off he had to go. If he had been living in the country he had to be brought up in court. But if you just caught him as he came in, you could push him out again in forty-eight hours. What one used to do was take him to the frontier in a car, and say, right, there's the frontier; off you go. You'd watch him go over the frontier and then of course you drove away, knowing damn well he'd probably come back again. A terrible situation for these people. This girl, you see, she'd—come to think of it she did say one or two things; she said something about the Turks treating the Jews worse than the Germans had ever done. She'd been persecuted and apparently separated from her family. We were sending her back to Turkey, at least sending her back to Lebanon.

The Writer's Place

Q: The idea came to you much later?

Callard: Well, the idea of writing about it came much later, but I thought about it a lot, you know. One would naturally think about those things. What sort of life is it for anybody? Never settle there; you'll never get any roots because at any moment there might be a knock at the door saying, where are your papers, and off you go again.

Q: Have you ever received letters from people who've read your novels, this novel in particular?

Callard: I've had a few letters from people who've said that my evocation of Jerusalem and the country reminded them of the old days, that sort of thing. But not of anyone being affected by the story of that girl, for instance.

Q: This novel seems to be focusing on a moral problem.

Callard: Yes.

Q: A man is forced to choose between the woman he loves and the whole weight of his tradition and training. Do you see the story as a kind of allegory that a reader can see and apply to his own life?

Callard: Yes, well, I particularly wanted the people who read the book to be a little concerned about the condition of people like that girl. I don't suppose any of them ever do anything, but there must be some small awakening of the collective consciousness of the people who've read that book. They must think, well there are people like that, and what a terrible thing. If it could grow enough, somebody might do something about it. The problem is treated in another book, *Flotsam* by Erich Remarque, which deals with Jews in Germany getting into Switzerland in 1938. It's not anything like my story, but it's the same problem.

Q: In other words, would you say that a writer has some sort of obligation to society to try, through his work, to change it?

Callard: No, I wouldn't say so. No, I think his obligation is to be as ruthful as he can, and if the society that he's living in doesn't please him, I think he ought to write about the unpleasing aspects of it. And then everyone says, what a terrible book that is. But the point is that it's the people in the society that are terrible—if the author is truthful. And they might do something about it themselves. People talk nowadays about the sex, the violence in books, but the point is there's a lot of sex and a lot of violence in life and you can't expect authors not to write about it. I think when they write about it they're not necessarily approving of it. They're probably neither approving or disapproving, they're simply writing about it. That's the attitude I would take.

Q: Would you agree there's a kind of ricochet effect in that the novel picks up what society is doing and mirrors it? But society looks into the mirror and sees itself for what it is for the first time?

Callard: I think there is. Unfortunately this does happen. An author may be quite honest and may write about something which is not at all pleasing. And I think there are people who will say, well there you are, that's the way we ought to act. I'm not at all sure that Somerset Maugham's not right at the end of *Theatre* when he says that it is not art which imitates life, it's life which imitates art. There is this ricochet, as you call it.

Q: What kind of novels, besides the ones that you've mentioned by F. Scott Fitzgerald and Hemingway and Greene, interest you? Or does the reading of novels interest you at all?

Callard: Till I was about thirty, I very seldom read a novel at all. I used to read a lot of history and things like that. But in the last fifteen years or so, I've read novels. But I very often read the same novel again. I've read *Fiesta* quite a lot of times, and *Madame Bovary* I've read several times. Stendhal—I like reading Stendhal. I read rather like a carpenter looking at a table. I don't read novels in a way that anyone else can read a novel, because I simply start dissecting it from the word go: watching the style and the tricks and that sort of thing. And if I see through it too easily I don't go on reading. Does that sound pretentious?

The Writer's Place

Q: Do you pick up material for your own writing from your reading?

Callard: Material which I use in the novels? I suppose so, but not consciously. I've just read Guy Endore's book about De Sade: *Saint and Sinner*, I think it's called. This is interesting because it's not like a novel, really; it's a sort of discussion of the character of De Sade. It's got bits of a lecture that he gave; it's got all sorts of things in it. Some letters are real, some are fictitious. The whole thing hangs together quite well. I read that because it was a new sort of format. And this is really what I look for, a book that's different.

Q: Does the kind of thing that's going on in the United States now, for example Truman Capote's *In Cold Blood* or Norman Mailer's journalistic, documentary work, interest you?

Callard: I think they're getting at something. I sympathize with what they're trying to do.

Q: What do you think of organizations like the Author's Society and PEN? Was it disillusionment that caused you to resign from PEN?

Callard: No, it wasn't that. I joined it, and I found that it, well, meant nothing to me because I was never in London. I could never go along to any of their meetings, and I just let it drop. The way they operate internationally I admire, but there wasn't very much in it for me and not much that I could give to it either. So I let it go for a year and then I let it drop.

Q: You don't see any useful function that these organizations are performing, outside of giving lectures? Do you see them as possible means for improving the lot of the writer financially?

Callard: PEN has been in existence for forty-odd years, I suppose. 1926, was it? I don't know that it's improved the lot of the writer in that time. Then again, there are all sorts of writers, aren't there? I daresay if you spoke to someone like William Cowper, whom I met at a PEN meeting, he'd probably say that it had improved his ot. But for a writer like me, I don't think anything could improve my lot. I just have to go on writing.

Q: Earlier you said that your novels had been published by various publishers. Why various publishers?

Callard: Well, my first book was published by Jonathan Cape. I sent it to them on the general principle that they were one of the best, from a literary point of view, of all the publishers in London. Therefore, if it got refused by them, I shouldn't be so terribly disappointed; I could always offer it to somebody else. But if I started at the bottom of my list, and I got refused, I should be disappointed because I'd think there was less chance of it being taken higher up the list. But Cape took it, and they were very pleased with it. They did quite well with it, really. They also took my second book about a year later with hardly any reflection. I think they kept it a week or so, then wrote back and said it was very good. They published that and it fell a bit flat. It sold about the same as the first novel, but it didn't improve much on the first novel. So when I sent them the third one, of course, they made all sorts of excuses; they didn't want it. This, I think you'll find, is the general run of things. They give you a couple of tries, and if you don't get over the four or five thousand mark in sales, they let somebody else take a chance. My third book I sent to Hutchinson. I don't quite know why I sent it to Hutchinson, but I had to find somebody else. I didn't have an agent at the time. At any rate, I sent it to Hutchinson and they took it. But they refused my next book; they refused *Across the Frontier*. They refused it because they said—they liked it, actually; in fact, one of the editors said it was literature—it would sell very well from an established writer and if it was a fifth or sixth book. But for a new writer, it's not the sort of book that the bookseller will be falling over himself to get into the shop. So they said, write something else. And I wrote something else, which they didn't like. And so I had to find someone other than Hutchinson. I picked on Peter Davis because they were a small publisher, and I sent it there. I sent them a light novel, and they wrote back and said they'd like something a bit

more serious. They weren't so interested in light novels. So I sen
them *Across the Frontier*, and they liked it.

Q: Would you say that your writing is at all influenced by the taste:
of publishers?

Callard: Yes, I think it has to be. I think a writer is under all sorts o.
pressure. I have an agent named Curtis Brown now, but I placec
all my books myself. One's under all sorts of pressure. You go anc
see a publisher and he says, well, of course, it's all right, but can'
you write something about England? Something like that. You g
and worry about this for weeks and weeks and think, I really mus
give up this Middle East business and start on something abou
England. That's one of the things that does affect you. The thing
that people say to you. Or you read reviews and, of course, you
don't *really* take any notice of them, but you can't hel
remembering that someone said this is too much like Hemingway
or something. Some remark, and you brood on it. It does make
you change a bit, I think.

Q: Do you ever change a story to suit the taste of a particula
publisher or magazine?

Callard: I wouldn't twist my story to put in something which .
didn't want in there. But I think that this again is a sort of pressure
or influence that's always there. When you come, for instance, to
describe a love scene, it wouldn't be much good describing it in
the way that Stendhal describes that love scene with Mme de
Renal. He takes about a chapter and they get to holding hands.
You know very well that that's not going to wash, you see. So you
do tend to write in the accepted idiom, because you know that thi:
is what people are looking for in that particular circumstance fo
those two characters.

Q: Do you find that the literary establishment, the reviewers, the
publisher's readers, perhaps even the publishers belong to the
same social group, by and large?

Callard: I think all publishers do, yes.

Q: They share the prejudices of their class?

Callard: I don't know whether they have the prejudices of their class, but I imagine they have because you never get a publisher that's worked himself up through the ranks, as it were. They go from the university straight into publishing at a fairly high level—editor or junior director, something like that. In this country they do. They all seem about the same. I thought they were all men of the world, very much men of the world. Probably they all travel quite a lot. The ones I've met have served in the Forces and they've been here, there, and everywhere, and have a pretty broad outlook. But I don't really know anything about the prejudices of their class.

Q: In other words, you don't feel the effects of an old boy network?

Callard: I believe this has more of an effect on criticism and reviewing than it has on publishing. Because I think publishers, if they've led an academic life and have gone straight into publishing, would be most excited to find a book which was coming from a class which was not their own. I think they'd be very pleased to find that. To find another Lawrence, or someone like that. I think they're really looking, I'm sure they're looking in England and have been for the last fifteen years or so, for the writer who is *not* from the educated classes. Of course, unfortunately the normal fellow who doesn't have a good education just can't write, can he? He just doesn't have the ability to put it down at all. But given the sort of grammar school chap who's never risen above a certain level, like myself, I can write about people the publishers never meet. I think this is an advantage.

Q: Do you think that the reviewers, for example, refuse to take someone seriously who doesn't meet the literary requirements which they've been conditioned to expect?

Callard: What happens when a book is published is that it's sent round to eighty reviewers or so, a hundred reviewers. Each reviewer has got a pile to get through that week. The chances of even getting a review are very, very small, unless you're an established writer. Very small. And if you get mentioned in the *Times* or the *Telegraph*, then you've done extremely well. Because out of the hundred books published every week, how many get any reviews? I think reviewers obviously have to review the work of established writers to begin with. Well, this accounts for about one or two reviews a week. Then they tend to look for the extraordinary sort of book. But I don't suppose any writer's got much time for reviewers, really.

Q: You said that the sales of your books have not been affected substantially by reviews.

Callard: I don't think it matters at all. Some of them write very clever little things about your book, and you feel they've quite misunderstood what you've been getting at. You feel a bit annoyed, not because they say nasty things, because I don't think it makes any difference to sales. I don't think it makes any difference to the book either. But you feel it's a rather cheap way of scoring a debating point. I had a book reviewed by John Wain, the novelist, in the *Observer* once. In the course of a short paragraph he'd made references to six writers, from Congreve to Hemingway, including Greene and several others. This seemed to me simply a little bit of showing off. Rather pointless. I really forget anyway what the point was now. George Orwell was mentioned too. Yes, I remember. The point was that he was endorsing Orwell's view that in all books about the East, the East is the greatest character. Which in the particular book, my second book (about a man who lost his heart to the desert), the point of the book was that nothing else mattered to him but the desert. In this rather facetious remark, he really missed the point, because that's what it was, the East *was* the greatest character. Then in the following week, after having been criticized for evoking the atmosphere of the desert, you get a different reviewer who starts off, "The evocation of the atmosphere of Malaya in his book is something . . ." He praises it to high heaven! Makes you wonder what to do next.

Q: Do you think it's possible to change this: the way books are published now, the way they're circulated, the way the whole thing works?

Callard: Well, it's very difficult to change it because I don't think the reviews do anything one way or the other—they're marginal anyway. But the fact is that the book is mentioned. No matter what's said about it, someone who reads the review will be interested for some personal reason, and will go to the library and order it, or go and buy it. Getting the book mentioned is the main thing. Publishers don't seem to be able to advertise. In any case, their next week's issues are going to swamp last week's. But if I published a book and it was mentioned in the *Daily Telegraph*, say, for three or four consecutive weeks, I'd be quite pleased no matter what was said about it, because someone would notice it. For that reason I think reviews are quite important and one's only too glad to have any review. Because the title of the book is there in heavy print and someone's going to notice it.

Q: After this novel that you're working on now, do you plan to go on writing novels or more plays?

Callard: I like writing plays, actually, but plays are difficult to place. As I said, I'm really very indolent. I have written a comedy which I sent to the Richmond Theatre. They kept it for about six months and sent it back with a short note saying they didn't want it. I left it lying around for the last six months; I must really get down to sending it to somebody. It's difficult to get a play placed in the West End, of course, largely because of the vast expense of putting a play on. I don't know what the present cost of putting a novel out is, but when I last inquired—about ten years ago—they reckoned it cost about a thousand pounds to publish a novel. It costs, I believe, about ten thousand pounds to put on a play. And of course, people don't like risking their money. So the West End tends to be full of musicals, many of which have had long runs in

91

the States and have come over with a fairly good chance of being successful. Or, alternatively, very light comedy things with a personable, well-known young actor.

Q: How about television—BBC or independent television—does this tempt you as a possible market for your work?

Callard: Yes, I have tried plays for television. *Across the Frontier* is going to be done on television. I didn't do the dramatizing of it but it's going to be done sometime this summer on the BBC. I don't know how they're going to make a play of it, but . . .

Q: Have they consulted you in making the script itself?

Callard: No, they just bought the rights of it.

Q: But you are interested in writing for television?

Callard: Yes. Here again one always feels that there's a bit of a closed shop, when you see the same names of writers appearing so often, time and time again. Of course a lot of them are under contract. Once they've written a few successful plays, they tend to go under contract for a series. It is a bit difficult to break into that I imagine. But there again they're probably looking for something a bit different. Well, this is always a dilemma, because if it's too different they're afraid to run it. If it's not different enough from anything that's gone before, they say, well, we have plenty of this. I knew a film writer, a chap called Kenneth Hales. He's written quite a few British films, and he was telling me that producers used to go to him and say to him, now look here, give us something a bit new. And he said he'd write for six months and think up something which hadn't been done before, and he'd take it along to them and they'd have a look at it and say, marvelous, just what we want, just what we want. Absolutely new, you see. And then he'd walk out of the office and he reckoned that immediately after he'd gone, they'd get on the phone to another couple of writers saying, come over here and knock this into shape. It's a jolly good story, but we can't have this and we can't have that. By the time it was finished, it was more or less the usual run of the mill. The explanation is that these people who are risking a lot of money say, well, for goodness sake, let's do something which we know worked all right last time. Of course, the days of this may soon be over, because there's a move now for smaller cinemas. There's one going up in Edinburgh where they're going to have three cinemas in the same building, seating I think seven hundred, five hundred, and three hundred. So that they can show films that are made for a minority audience, you see. The big super cinema which came along just after the war had two thousand seats. Of course, these won't take the minority films, for obvious reasons.

Q: To ask you a hypothetical question, if you were to do it over again, starting now as a young writer, which direction would you move in? Do you think you'd move in more or less the same direction you did?

Callard: It is hypothetical, isn't it? I should like to have written about the Middle East; after having been there for six years I felt there was something to write about. So I think I would have written novels. But I really, all my life, have wanted to write plays. You see, I have such a limited amount of time that I had to say to myself, now what can I do in the next year? Shall I spend it writing a play, which may never get finished or may never be put on? Or shall I do something which I know I can do a bit better or at least I know I can get done, a novel? Well, I mean it's quite possible that any novel I write might come shooting back from the publishers.

Q: What is the position, would you say, of the novelist, for yourself as a novelist, in this relatively small community of Gosport?

Callard: The morning after I had my first novel published I walked back from High Street and I thought everybody would be cheering. But no one's taken any notice, really. A very large number of people know I am a novelist, and I think they sort of like it. This isn't a very flourishing cultural center, Gosport. We have no theatre, no commercial theatre. I suppose anyone who writes anything is regarded as a bit remarkable. I get a bit of notoriety sometimes when writing to the weekly news about libraries and things like that. There was a proposition to spend a quarter of a million pounds on a library building at a time when the books in the public library were pretty poor really. The debate which was reported in the local newspaper mentioned all the wonders that we were gong to have—a roof garden, for instance—but not a single reference to any books in the library. This struck me as typical. The amount spent on books is a small proportion really of what the rate payer pays in rates. Well, I worked it out, and I suppose probably a fifth or maybe a quarter goes to books, to buying books. The rest is administration, upkeep of the buildings, and cost of the staff and that sort of thing. Not very much goes on books really. In this town they spend 6000 pounds a year. They've got six libraries. That's a thousand pounds, or twenty pounds a week. And you can't buy many books for that.

Q: You mentioned earlier that you would rather live in North Africa. Why is that? Would it help your writing to be away from Gosport?

Callard: Yes, I think it probably would. I think it would. A writer's a human being after all. Once you get to a nice warm climate you might be tempted not to write. There's something to be said for being austere. I went to Palestine with the intention of writing when I was there. But I wrote practically nothing in the six years I was there. I complained about it to a friend of mine once, and he said, the inspiration of this country will come when you're about two thousand miles away from it. Which is probably true. Most of my books are about Englishmen who turn their backs on England, in some way or another. And I think will probably continue to be so.

Q: What would you say is it in England that makes so many English writers want to turn their backs on it?

Callard: Well, the successful ones leave for tax reasons. But if it were possible for the unsuccessful ones to leave, I think they'd leave because of the rather depressing climate.

Q: Physical climate?

Callard: No, no. The social climate and the political climate. This is a country with a great empire which has gone down. I think people as old as I am know and feel the difference there is in the air. It was nice to be the center of a big empire, whatever they say. You know, you felt good about it. But to be on the periphery now of the world is not so nice. Mind you, going to Malta is not going to solve that problem. It will sort itself out in time and Britain will find some other place in the world. I think we're all a bit conscious of the slightness of things. Not a very invigorating atmosphere to be in. Quite frankly, the artist is better off if you don't have things like the welfare state. Once you get down to everybody being treated the same, the subject matter to a great extent is gone.

Q: Thank you, Mr. Callard.

Roald Dahl

ROALD DAHL was born in Llandaff, South Wales, in 1916 and educated at Repton. He is married to the actress Patricia Neal, and has three children. During the last war he served as a pilot in the RAF and subsequently did free-lance writing. He is probably best known for his short stories (some of which have appeared in the *New Yorker*), collected in *Someone Like You* (1953) and *Kiss Kiss* (1960). In recent years he has concentrated on writing children's books.

The interview took place in Dahl's home at Great Missenden, Bucks.

Q: Does the old boy network extend to literature? And if so, what is the size of the mesh?

Dahl: Of course, it exists and of course it extends to literature. It's always consisted of people of wealth, but in the last hundred years it's consisted of men who've gone to the British public schools. One may get an equally fine education at the grammar schools, but there's no question that you don't get the same character education, however ghastly they used to be and they were pretty bad when I went to one, Repton. My headmaster became the archbishop of Canterbury, Geoffrey Fisher. He used to whack boys on the bottom and bring them a basin and a sponge to wash the blood off afterwards. This is just about finished in the public schools; they've become humanized. And also extremely expensive. What makes parents pay these high fees? It's not just to get their sons into the old boy network. It's to build their character. That's the real reason they do it. They build the best parts of your character: courage, the refusal to give up. It is from their number, certainly in the last World War, that virtually all the officers in all the branches of the armed forces were drawn.

Q: Is it then, in your view, the character-building capacity of these schools that is responsible for producing such a high percentage of British writers?

Dahl: There's another reason for that. On the average, the people who have enough money to send their children to these schools are people with better brains than the people who don't, and these brains are transmitted to their children. It's a question of genetics and breeding.

Q: Then why don't they come so much from the grammar schools?

Dahl: Well, they're going to catch up. This is a very new thing. It's only in the last thirty years or so that fine grammar schools have been matching the education given by the public schools. Now when the sons of these graduates continue to go to grammar schools, I think they'll catch up.

Q: How do you think your own writing was affected by the public school experience?

Dahl: If I'd gone to a grammar school instead, I'm certain I would not have had the education in English that I got. I'll never forget my English master at Repton offering the whole form half-a-crown, which was six times then what it is now, for every split infinitive we could find in the *Times*. We never found one, but we've never forgotten what a split infinitive is, and I certainly have never split an infinitive since then.

Q: Could he still make that offer now?

Dahl: I think he could, but only for the *Times*. And I'll give anyone half-a-crown who finds a split infinitive in my work. These are the sort of things that add up to make a writer — not, of course, that not splitting infinitives will do that. But it's knowing how to use the language properly.

Q: Was it also perhaps the fact that public schools, by being primarily residential, forced the potential writer into groups of similarly minded boys, who then caught fire from each other?

Dahl: I'm not a believer in writers' living together. I don't know if you meant that. When you find groups of writers and group teach-ins and all that sort of thing, they are usually writers who are so uncertain of themselves that they're all gathering together to give themselves confidence and strength. Actors always move in groups and gather in groups in the evening. I know, my wife is one. This is because they are so filled with uncertainty and lack of confidence. On the whole, a successful writer doesn't do that.

Q: Yet all the established writers in England seem to know each other.

Dahl: But they don't see each other very often. Yes, I know Victor Pritchett and H. E. Bates and, from the old times, Hemingway. I know or knew them quite well. How? By running across them in places, but not by making dates to meet them again or having them to dinner much or anything like that. When you do run across each other, you talk a lot for a short while, and there's an immediate sympathy.

Q: But aren't there bars, cafés, clubs in London which are known to be patronized by writers? A latter-day Bloomsbury perhaps?

Dahl: I wouldn't say so, no. Absolutely not. You'd have a job to find anything like that. The Author's League has, I think, club facilities, but I don't think you'll find anyone there to speak of. The Bloomsbury lot gathered together from a great feeling of insecurity. They were not really successful at the time, were they? And how much of a circle were they, after all? Four or five people perhaps; the Woolfs, Strachey, and so on. It's bad for writers to get together like this. I can remember Hemingway talking for quite a long time on this point, saying that writers should *never* cluster together in groups. Painters, of course, do gather together. The impressionists did, because they were poverty-stricken and unsuccessful and miserable.

Q: Yet Hemingway seemed unable to move about without a Boswell of some kind.

Dahl: Yes, but they weren't really much, and then only at the end of his life.

Q: How about writers gathering together in universities? Or, for that matter, the tremendous importance of universities in shaping literary taste and even influencing sales directly by requiring books in courses?

Dahl: You've come to the wrong man if you want any praise of universities in general. I'm very much against them, except where they train people for the professions, doctors, lawyers, architects, and the rest of it. In the arts, I think they are an enormous waste of time. I refused to go to a university when I was eighteen. My mother offered me Oxford or Cambridge and I said, no, and took a job and went to East Africa. That, I thought, was a much better education.

I think it's splendid that American universities are more and more preoccupied with literature and even more splendid that they give jobs to professors and writers. What I don't hold with is what they teach. I don't think you can teach the novel or the short story. You get a class of people who want to be writers and there's probably an absolute minimum of talent among them. You get a celebrated writer in to teach them and he goes through with it all and there's nothing in it.

Writing comes from two things: an inherent talent, and, secondly, having something to write about — and you're not going to get that in college. About three weeks ago I was asked to judge the short story competition of the University of Kent in Canterbury. I said all right, thinking it would be rather exciting and fun. So I got sent these eight or ten entries, which had obviously been carefully weeded out as the best. They were appalling, absolutely appalling: pretentious, foolish, without any form or style. Useless. I don't think you can teach this stuff.

If I were eighteen and assuming I had some talent and wanted to be a writer, I'd say, "My goodness, I've just got to get all the experience I can of people and the world, and hope that I will finally get something to write about." I'd steer clear of every university in the world.

Q: What do you mean by "something to write about"? An attitude or merely a collection of experiences?

Dahl: Not just plot, no. You can't develop a character in a story, however briefly, unless you know something about people. Unless he's an unusual genius, an eighteen-year-old can't do that. The best way of learning about people is first of all to learn about their foibles and filthy habits; then you can blackmail them on paper. People have far less nice characteristics than nasty ones, all people, and they all pretend to have far less nasty than nice ones.

Q: The duty of the writer is to expose the folly of mankind?

Dahl: He only exposes it insofar as it adds to the entertaining qualities of his work. My job, if I write a story, is purely to entertain. If there's an undercurrent of social commentary running through it, this is not done purposefully. That's just how you feel, about people and things, and that's bound to creep into your writing occasionally. You'll find that in any writer, good or bad. Shaw is a good example of this. Most writers tend to be compassionate, liberal-minded kinds of people. I should think virtually all of them are by now pretty fiercely antiwar and have said so.

Q: Should they say so in their writing?

Dahl: No. If they say so in their writing, then they'll probably screw up their writing. If you're writing what you hope will be a fine novel and you can't make room in it for a sermon, naturally, don't do it. No; they should say so in lectures, in pamphlets, in brief articles in magazines, in public — not that I think it carries much weight.

Q: What do you think of the notion of critics like Ortega or Forster, in *Aspects of the Novel*, that what matters in literary art is not the story but the ideas? That the story is a kind of barbarous residue which civilized humanity has, alas, not yet grown out of?

Dahl: No, I don't agree at all. I've got the concentration to read philosophy if I wanted to, but I loathe it. I like reading adventures. I love good stories and good plots and exciting adventures. The last thing in the world I want to read is Nietzsche. It's not my line and it's none of my business really. No philosopher has ever changed the world, except Marx.

Q: What kinds of novels do you read? Do you prefer reading nonfiction to fiction? What do you think of novelists like Simenon or Joyce Cary who loathe reading novels?

Dahl: I know a lot of novelists who read nothing but novels. Hemingway was one of them. I've never understood Simenon's reputation. Everyone I meet raves about him and says how beautifully he writes. Well, I don't think he writes beautifully at all. Rather dull detective stories, with some bloody old inspector chasing somebody else.

Q: Thank you, Mr. Dahl.

Margaret Drabble

MARGARET DRABBLE was born in 1939 in Sheffield and educated at the Mount School and at Newnham College, Cambridge (where she got a First in English). She is married to the actor Clive Swift and has three children. Her novels include *A Summer Birdcage* (1963), *The Millstone* (1965), *Jerusalem the Golden* (1967), and *The Needle's Eye* (1972). She has also published a critical study of Wordsworth (1966).

The interview took place in Miss Drabble's home in Hampstead.

Q: Do you consider yourself to be part of a literary group? Or do you think that your association with any literary grouping has had an influence on your career?

Drabble: This is something I'm very interested in because I've always been looking for some kind of literary circle to belong to . . . Well, not really, because I don't suppose I would like it if I did. But I've never found anything going at all. I don't think there is a literary scene in this country, or if there is, I don't know anything about it. I suppose by now I've met quite a lot of writers, and I've met most of the people I would want to meet.

Q: How did you meet them?

Drabble: I suppose a lot of them at publishers' parties, that kind of event, in fairly formal surroundings. One or two of the older writers have very kindly made overtures toward me, like C. P.

Snow and J. B. Priestley; they have invited me personally round and that kind of thing.

Q: From reading your books?

Drabble: From reading the books. But most of the writers I've just met about — the people I have met. The only person I have made any overtures toward myself is Angus Wilson whom I admire tremendously and whom I kept writing to and telling I admired him, and finally we did get together after corresponding on various things and we went on this Arts Council tour. I don't know if you've heard about these Arts Council tours for writers? They've got a new idea of sending writers out on tour to fairly remote parts of England and we were the pioneer tour. Angus and I, and Nell Donne and Christopher Logue went off to Anglesea in North Wales together, and talked in schools and technical colleges and evening meetings and little theatres and that kind of thing.

Q: What kind of schools?

Drabble: Oh, any. I mean secondary, modern Welsh-speaking schools — a tremendous wide range of people, in fact.

Q: Did you read from your work?

Drabble: No. We talked really. I mean, our aim was to get them talking, which some of them wouldn't; and when they wouldn't one had to talk to oneself. But in the evenings we all four sat on a platform or whatever was there and one of us led off with some subject like, say, revolution, or women in the novel and that kind of thing, and then we all joined in and talked amongst ourselves, and then threw it open to the audience. Some audiences were very lively and some were not so lively. What I got out of it was that I very much liked being with other writers. I enjoyed their company very much and found out a lot about them. Angus Wilson — well, I have always known one would like him. He's a tremendously communicative and likable person. And that was very valuable. But I did notice that Christopher and Nell knew each other quite well, and they also knew Angus, I think. So I probably was the only person who did not know anybody when we set off.

Q: At Cambridge you didn't move in any — what might be called — circle of writers?

Drabble: Not at all. No. I moved totally in a theatrical circle at Cambridge. I did a lot of acting. In fact, I did know one or two people who have subsequently written. I was an assistant editor at some point but really I was not very conscientious. One keeps in touch, that's all. There's a fellow named Jim Hunter who's a novelist whom I've seen once or twice since Cambridge. He lives in Bristol. That's it, you know. And there's a poet called William Dunlop whom I knew well at Cambridge who disappeared to Seattle and has never been heard of since. Theodore Roethke was there, who promptly died as soon as William got there, and just silence followed, you know. But he was on the poets' scene, and in fact he took me to one or two parties where I met Sylvia Plath and Ted Hughes and people like that. But the poets are very much a different scene from the novelists anywhere, I think. But I'd say I'd met them all, you know, but no more. I couldn't call any of them personal friends.

Q: Would you say that in Cambridge you had a chance to talk about your own work?

Drabble: Not at all. No. I mean not with *me*. There could have been if one had been a poet or if that would have been what one was really interested in. But I found the atmosphere there very forbidding and very destructive. In fact, anything I wrote I kept very, very much to myself. I didn't show anything to anybody till the year after I came down from Cambridge.

Q: So you didn't regret not having the chance to show people your work? In fact, you didn't want to?

Drabble: I didn't want to, really. I might have wanted to if they had

104

been nicer about it, or if I had felt they would be nicer about it. No, I was too interested in just getting on with life there. And after that, I've worked very much in a vacuum as far as work goes. I mean, totally in isolation, I think. I just finish my books and send them off to the publisher and the publisher — and *only* the publisher — has made a comment.

Q: In one of your books you mention F. R. Leavis. Do you think that Leavis had any influence on your writing at all? Or did any academic at Cambridge have, would you say, an influence on the way you write? Consciously or unconsciously?

Drabble: It's terribly hard to say. I think that, in fact, the atmosphere that Leavis created — and I don't blame Leavis for this — was very, very difficult for anyone with any creative ambitions to live in. It was so destructive: the standards were so high. And this thing about minor writers — in fact, I've just written my first letter to the press about this, to the *TLS*, because Leavis made some awful crack about me last week in the *TLS*. So I was stirred up by the editor ringing me and saying, you can't take that lying down; and I wrote back. But, in fact, it's absolutely true. The point I made was that if you're a would-be writer at the age of eighteen, you're not to know whether you're a minor writer or major writer, you just know that's what you want to do. And there you are with Leavis and everyone telling you that Arnold Bennett is beneath contempt, you know; and if people like that are beneath contempt, why should one ever dare to begin. That kind of atmosphere, I think, is most depressing. On the other hand as a critic, I admire Leavis enormously. I'm sure he's right about the people whom he admires, and the Great Tradition is what I believe in as a novelist. I mean, his preoccupations are my preoccupations. I'm very much a moralist or would think myself so. So I think he has affected me deeply, and it was just good luck that he did not stop me completely.

Q: Would you say that your writing has been in the tradition? I'm thinking of the comments of one of your personae on Jane

105

Austen. Would you repudiate those comments in your own person?

Drabble: I don't wholly repudiate them. No, I go along with them. I do think she's narrow. Still they were comments of a character in a situation; as a critic I wouldn't say it at all, but as a human being I say it. You know, from my situation or from the situation of the character in the book, I feel it very strongly. I think she's a pernicious and terrible influence, Jane Austen, sort of malicious and exclusive and socially unjust, really. The social injustice of which her books reek: people might say this isn't historically accurate, but I don't care about the accuracy. It's the feeling or response, the human response. I couldn't write a literary essay in these terms on Jane Austen, because one has to be fair when one writes something critical, but as a writer, as a person responding to them I feel this very strongly.

Q: John Wain in his autobiography talks about seeing Kingsley Amis write a novel and enjoying it so much that he sat down himself and wrote *Hurry on Down*. Was there anything remotely like this in your experience? What suddenly made you want to write your first novel?

Drabble: I'd always wanted to write, I think, simply because I enjoyed other people's books so much. Some books were inaccessibly marvelous like the books one admires most, *Middlemarch*, for example. I used to sit down and think, God I can't face ever starting to write a book. Then I would read something that was more near to me, like *Anglo-Saxon Attitudes*. In fact, *Henderson the Rain King* I remember reading just before I started my book, and I thought, this is not impossible. You know, it's a book that's human and of our time, and it's not a classic. It's written now. And reading those two books I thought I really must have a go. The reason why I actually got down to do it was that I had nothing else to do. I got married and I was expecting a baby and that's practically why I wrote the book, but in terms of literary inspiration it was simply the fact that one stopped reading that classical, that nineteenth-century Tripos stuff. I also read something which affected me profoundly just after I finished my part two at Cambridge. I read Simone de Beauvoir's *Second Sex*. This seemed to me to be wonderful material and so important to me as a person. It was material that nobody had used and I could use and nobody had ever used as far as I could see as I would use it. I think that again meant something to me.

Q: When you sat down to write your first novel, did you have some social purpose in mind, some sense of presenting a particular predicament, a particular kind of person?

Drabble: Not really, no. Though in fact, when I look at it, I can see now what the predicament was. I was in Cambridge last week and some girls in their last year came up to me and said, is it really so awful when one leaves? I hadn't realized I was writing about that at all. It simply hadn't crossed my mind. I was just writing about life, you know. I thought that was all there was to it. I didn't realize it was a problem. I was writing about things as they impinged on me then. I don't think I do that quite so much now. I wouldn't like to write a book that was socially neutral. I mean I'd always come down on any issue, but in fact, no, I think I write very privately.

Q: What do you think, for example, about the school of, for lack of a better name, Vietnam poets in the United States? Do you feel this should be considered criticism rather than fiction or poetry?

Drabble: It's not something I would want to do or could do, but I admire them for doing it. I think that political theory can produce very great works of art, but *I* can't do it. I don't want to do it. I think I am a private writer, really. And also I don't believe in, I really don't have enough faith in influencing anybody to try. Christopher Logue, for instance, says things like: "I hope that, if you are not changed when you have read these poems, throw them in the rubbish bin." Well, this seems to me fantastic to think that one could change someone's attitude on life, you know. I just want to make a fairly modest statement about something very

The Writer's Place

specific. I admire their courage, I really do, but I don't think I could ever do it.

Q: You mentioned earlier that you met a number of writers at publishers' parties and so forth. Do you find that having met them and talked to them has in any way changed your writing, or is this part of your life quite removed from your own writing?

Drabble: Completely removed. One never talks about writing anyway. I mean, they talk about whom you know and whom you don't know. In fact, I don't really go to an awful lot of parties, because I never have time and they are usually at terribly inconvenient times of day. I can't remember any literary discussion of any sort, except in this Arts Council tour, which was interesting because there we were all fairly relaxed and got to know each other quite well over the whole week and one was able to talk, but at parties one can't talk, I don't think. And I can't think of anybody that I talk to about writing, except possibly my sister,* who is a novelist, and we talk about acting, we talk about problems.

Q: Do you miss the lack of opportunity to talk about your own work, about literature in general?

Drabble: No, not really. I would miss it if there was no outlet for it at all, but one can do it on formal occasions, I mean one can do it for instance in radio programs, interviews, when everybody is all geared up to talk about it. I find this really quite interesting. One gets some quite interesting stuff out of the BBC from that point of view. And also I do a bit of lecturing, which is a chance for me to discuss my work and other people's work and to see what kind of response you get from the audience. And sometimes one gets quite a good response from students. I had a marvelous evening in Cambridge not so long ago with the English Society or whatever it's called, and they were frightfully good and very, very interesting on creative writing. Obviously all suffering from Leavis paralysis, poor things. On that kind of occasion, one can

*Drabble's sister publishes under the name of A. S. Byatt. (Ed.)

talk about it. I only feel I'm going to bore people stiff unless it's actually set up for me. I don't think I've ever sat down in this house and talked about writing. I have a friend who reads enormously and we talk about the books we've read, but that's a different thing.

Q: You spoke about your work with the Arts Council. Are you in agreement with their policy of giving grants to writers? What do you think of their work in general?

Drabble: I think it's terribly difficult for them to know what to do with their subsidies. They did have the scheme of giving subsidies to individual writers, but it creates such ill feeling and I can understand why. I would say possibly sending people on tours and paying them to do it is a more useful way of spending the money because it gives the writer something to do, rather than just handing them out something on a plate. I think they should subsidize little magazines and things like that, which they do. But I think the idea, the principle of subsidizing individual writers is very difficult indeed. I'd much rather that the government passed its public lending right bill for the libraries and we could all make a bit more money that way, which would be very beneficial to writers who don't sell an enormous number of copies. They would make so much more a year. They'd have earned it rather than having been given it.

Q: In the United States, so-called creative writers are very often and increasingly connected with the universities, as professors or occasional lecturers, judges of literary competitions, or whatever. They seem to earn a significant fraction of their income from the universities. Do you think this is happening in England? Do you think it's a good thing?

Drabble: I think it happens very little here actually. And I think it's a dangerous thing myself. I know people who do it successfully, who have anyway an academic turn of mind and are good at it. Someone like Angus Wilson has never been to a university even and is now lecturing. I should imagine he's a marvelous person to work with because he does communicate so well, but he is fifty something and he has been through it all. He's written his books, or some of his books, and he's all right. I think it's very dangerous for a writer of my age to start doing it. I personally think I might enjoy it, but I'm not sure it wouldn't be a terrible drain of energy and I'd hate to feel that I was relying on it for income. I think there's a very frivolous attitude among a lot of writers in this country which I rather go along with: that one would rather be on bread and butter from doing bits of TV and screenplays and things like that and leave oneself totally free so that one's so-called creative writing is completely uncommitted and unaffected. I also think that then there's a chance that it's more related to some kind of real activity. I mean earning one's living in a free-lance way. I'm very attracted — not that I've any other option because of domestic life — but free-lance living appeals to me very much and I know a lot of writers who feel the same way about it.

Q: At least one of your books has been made into a film. Are you at all attracted to writing directly for films? Do you think that the film is taking away the audience that used to read novels? Does the consciousness of this in any way affect your writing?

Drabble: Not at all, no. All I want to do is to write novels. That's all I'm interested in. That's all I take seriously. The other things I'm interested in and do for pleasure or for money or for society. I mean, it's a sociable job doing a film; you meet the people and you talk about it, but it would never cross my mind to try and write a marvelous film because people weren't buying my novels or weren't reading my novels. The novel, well, it's a different, it's a serious thing that I've got to do, whereas I don't think I'd ever write an original screenplay. I'd quite like to, just to see if one could, but I've never done it. And somehow my mind doesn't work that way. Sometimes I get asked to do things and I just know, well I've said yes to one or two things I know I shouldn't have done, just to see if I could. But of course one can't tell if one hasn't tried it.

Q: In the U.S., especially after McLuhan, there seems to be a feeling among a great many younger people that writing is by and large passé, that what matters now is films. Do you think this is at all happening in England? That the people who "matter" are no longer writing novels, or are beginning to move away from the novel?

Drabble: I don't know if people that "matter" are moving into film. A lot of people are, but none of them matter in my view. There are very few good films, really very few good films that have anything like the intellectual quality or the creative quality of a good novel. I personally feel this. Some films I'm very deeply impressed by, but there are so few of them and so much trivial rubbish. As for television as a medium, I cannot see anyone taking it seriously. One can create something quite interesting and quite entertaining, but nothing more. Because it's a cooperative effort which in itself can't produce an individual voice. An elaborate structure can't be reproduced, I don't think. I've watched one or two of the most celebrated TV programs which were supposed to — I don't know what they were supposed to do, but everyone said how wonderful they were — I watched some terrible rubbish about pop music and Buddhist monks burning themselves in Vietnam and corpses in Belsen. A novelist wouldn't dare to do it. Its intellectual content was so slight and the claims it made were so enormous. I have very little sympathy with that kind of thing. It seems to me that they're kidding themselves and they're kidding themselves for money, which is the worst way of doing it.

Q: Would you say this is inherent in the medium or simply because of the people who go into it?

Drabble: The people who go into it. I can see that one could use the medium. I'm not saying, I don't wish to say, that I haven't seen films which are of the quality of novels. I have. But very, very few and I don't think I could do it, because I don't work that way. I think a lot of people are just kidding themselves that that's where they ought to be because they get a minimum of two thousand pounds for it, instead of a maximum of a hundred pounds as my advance. I suppose some people have a genuine feeling for it, but it's such a seductive medium and I've known some very good people who've ended up writing absolute rubbish. I suppose someone comes along with a lot of backing and a nice idea and they think, yes, that would be nice.

Q: What kind of books do you read? Do you, for instance, find that you still like reading novels?

Drabble: I do enjoy reading novels very much — good novels. But reading bad novels is a frightfully destructive thing to do, because one gets one's mind all messed up with them. I don't read an awful lot of contemporary novels, although I do a certain amount of obligatory reading, like books by friends, or books that you're reviewing or whose author you're going to meet next evening. So I read, I suppose, a certain amount, but I feel that possibly one ought to read other things more. I do read quite a lot about other kinds of things. I try to. There's so much one hasn't read. One hasn't read all of the classics yet. I read classic novels, and I would defend reading nineteenth-century novels absolutely. This seems to me a very valuable thing for a novelist to do, and it means a lot to me.

Q: What would you say you get out of them? In terms of your own work?

Drabble: In terms of my own work: continuity, a sense of what can be done, and what could be done with the medium, which I get far more from reading old novels than I do from reading new ones. Possibly because I've got an old-fashioned mind naturally. Over the last year or two I've got a bit more indulgent toward the avant-garde in the novel, but the experimental novel — well, a lot of it seems to be like people making films about Buddhist monks. It seems to me very irrelevant.

Q: Whom would you name among the younger people whom you like reading?

Drabble: Oh, dear, I do have this awful leaning toward the conventional novel. Whom do I enjoy reading? They're all older people. Well, I did read a novel by Piers Paul Read the other day, called *The Junkers*, which seemed to me very fine. I'm sure he's going to do something very good. It's not entirely a conventional novel, it's faintly experimental. My favorite experimental novelist is Doris Lessing — *The Golden Notebook*, actually. It's an absolutely marvelous book and has profoundly affected me, I think. But I only read it a couple of years ago, so it couldn't have affected me for very long. (*laughter*) She seems to me to be writing on the highest level with the highest commitment to the form. And she seems to really know and to care about what she's doing, which is very rare.

Q: Would you say that your writing a book on Arnold Bennett in any way reflects on your own novels? Is your right-hand critical sense, as it were, completely divorced from your left-hand creative sense?

Drabble: I don't think it's completely divorced because obviously I admire that type of solid novel more than some people do. I've always admired Bennett as a writer. But really there are personal reasons which have nothing to do with writing about why I wanted to write about him. That's really because he comes from the same background — I think he's my great, great uncle. His background is so similar to mine in so many ways: the potteries, for instance; my grandparents were brought up in the potteries, my great-grandfather was a potter. And he has this kind of feeling for provincial life, which is so similar to what I was brought up in that I identify with it a great deal and am very sympathetic. Or at least I was. The more I read about him the less sympathetic I get. I feel very personally about his background, which is why I wanted to do a book on him.

Q: You mentioned before that you enjoyed living in London. I notice a great many English writers seem to disappear from London. Angus Wilson, for example. Or even more, they go abroad. Why do you think this is? Does it at all tempt you?

Drabble: I guess it is the income tax. It's a terrible thing. I think it's

113

shocking. No, I wouldn't. It seems to me that if you are making that much money, you can afford to live in England anyway. It's not a very expensive country to live in. I don't want to leave London. Possibly as people get elderly they can't stand the row. But I like it very much. I don't think all of them want to leave London, do they? Some of them do. Some people just like country life; I hate it. I certainly wouldn't want to go abroad. That seems to me a fatal step for a writer to take; it's a step toward disintegration. I wouldn't mind going abroad for six months, you know. Well, I wouldn't even like to do that actually. Anyway I couldn't, so I'm saying that possibly out of sour grapes, but I obviously couldn't with the children and so on. But I don't really want to, anyway. I like traveling, but I always like to come back again.

Q: Do you think of yourself as an *English* novelist? Do you see, say, important differences between your situation as an *English* novelist and that of an American novelist? Take, for example, Dickens writing about characteristically English places and social situations. Would you consider yourself an English novelist in any analogous sense?

Drabble: I think I would; yes I would. Because I don't know about anywhere else, therefore I write about what I know about, and that's England. I don't think I'll ever get to know anywhere else well enough, except to use it as an occasional backdrop, as a symbol of disorientation. I do feel, as I've said, very closely connected with a literary tradition of some sort or another. Of women writers possibly. I read Virginia Woolf's *A Room of One's Own* for the first time two or three months ago and I felt *so* in sympathy with everything she said about the tradition of women writing and where it's going. And I know that's what I'm part of, and I don't think it can be the same in the States for a writer. I don't think one could feel that way about the English tradition. One couldn't feel a part of it in quite the same way. And I don't feel part of your tradition at all. I mean, I read American books with great admiration, but I just don't know what the scenery looks like, and it's like reading about China, you know, to me.

Q: You mention Virginia Woolf. It strikes me that your style sometimes approaches that of Virginia Woolf. Is this conscious?

Drabble: I now must make an awful confession. *A Room of One's Own* is the only book I've ever read of hers. I'm in the middle of *Mrs. Dalloway*, which I'm enjoying very much, but I can't possibly have felt anything about it because I haven't read it.

Q: I'm thinking of *To The Lighthouse*.

Drabble: Yes, I haven't read it. I must. I know I must. I tried to read them when I was about seventeen and found them frightfully heavy going, and I recognize I must now come to terms with them. Because *A Room of One's Own* seems to me such a lucid and intelligent and moving book, that I thought I must get round to them.

Q: What do you think of the financial situation of the novelist in England? Do you think there is still enough of an audience to support novel writing in England? Do you envision your audience at all? Do you meet them occasionally?

Drabble: I really don't know. I suppose I do meet them occasionally. I get letters from time to time, but they don't really add up to a picture. One gets letters from all kinds of people. There's a certain type of woman that I get letters from; she's an intelligent housebound housewife and I know what they're all about, I really do. But that's just part of it, and I don't think they're great book buyers, because on the whole they don't have any money. I don't know who buys books. I know this is heresy and I wouldn't like the Society of Authors to hear me, but I don't think that a novelist should expect necessarily to earn a good living out of writing novels, because one can't pretend it's either a full-time activity or exactly a service to the community if one does it. One does it for oneself. If you're paid, so much the better. I make more money than I ever expected out of writing novels. I'm absolutely staggered by the fact that one can earn a decent living out of it. It's amazing to me. I wouldn't have expected it. Any more than had I been a poet, I would have expected to drive a Rolls Royce; it's just not the kind of thing that one sets out to do. I'd have thought that a lot of people were earning quite a good living from novels. Perhaps it is in a way surprising.

Q: Some writers claim that they consciously popularize what they write, because they know that so-called serious fiction just won't sell. They have to make it more palatable to their readers. Is this something you've ever been tempted to do?

Drabble: I'm surprised that people say that. I've never thought of it. My only aim is to get my novels as serious as I possibly can. I mean they started off lightweight but simply because I couldn't make them anything else, but I certainly wouldn't aim to sell. I really don't want to. I'm not interested in selling. I get terribly embarrassed when publishers start talking about sales, because this isn't what I'm after. What I'm after is writing something that I can take seriously myself. Well, I know what I can take seriously and I'm not prepared to put anything in that I don't want to be in there. I have heard of that kind of thing, but I wouldn't know how to do it. I don't know how a writer can look at it that way. One wants people to reread the book, but that's an artistic preoccupation.

Q: Has your publisher had any influence on your writing at all? Or your publisher's reader?

Drabble: Not really, no. With my first book they made me cut out a bit of subplot, and they were probably quite right. I was so diffident in those days, I'd have cut the whole book if they told me to. But no, they really say very very little about it. I hand over the manuscript and they make one or two suggestions about where I've been inconsistent about what they were wearing on a certain day and that kind of thing. With the last one, I did get one or two suggestions. They said there wasn't enough of the background for one of the families. I can't remember which now, and in fact I hadn't really finished the book when I handed it over, because I couldn't resolve the ending. So I was quite glad to go back on that. But you know, I would only do it if I thought they were right. They also made one or two suggestions which I thought were ridiculous and couldn't have done anyway. So really: very, very little influence.

Q: In *The Waterfall*, you shift from third to first person, which seems vaguely experimental. Would you say this is the direction in which you are moving now? Toward more experimental kinds of writing? Are you working on a novel now that you would say is like this?

Drabble: Well, I am. But I don't really want it to be experimental. It only gets experimental when I can't cope with it. When I can't get into a third or first person narrative, what I want to put into it, then I have to do something else about it. But this is a failure of technique, I think, on my part rather than a positive ambition. In *The Waterfall*, I think I was finally quite pleased with it because it wasn't experimental in the sense that one didn't know what was going on. I *hate* books which are deliberately confusing. I aim to be lucid. If one doesn't know what one's writing, I don't see why one should write it. But I did find it impossible. I wrote the first chunk in the third person and found it impossible to continue with, because it did not seem to me to tell anything like the whole story. And so I evolved. I didn't intend when I started the book to have this shifting, but it did seem quite a useful device, having got it set up. But it wasn't my aim at all to write it experimentally. It just happened that way. And in fact, I think I can see that one might possibly use extracts from diaries and things like that, but I don't really approve of it. I read a very interesting book by a man called Richard Wolheim, *A Family Romance*. It's his first novel. He's a professor of philosophy and it's all done in diary technique and it's based very closely on Michel Butor's *L'emploi du temps*. It's very interesting and a very good book, but it's cheating in a way because it means you never have to sustain any passage or any sequence, that your structure is in little chunks, and this is really a rather lazy way of writing, I think. That sounds offensive, but I know that I'd rather have a structure that is bigger and with more sustained passages in it than just page lengths of contrasting ideas, like B. S. Johnson. It seems to me that anybody can write a book in twenty-six chapters and shuffle them around; the difficulty is to get the chapters in the right order. The problem is to make your book the right shape, not to make it shapeless.

Q: When you write a novel, have you plotted out the entire course of the novel?

Drabble: Not at all.

Q: How do you begin? What gives you the idea?

Drabble: Well, I *think.* I worry about it for about six months or so, and then when I get enough worry in my mind, enough anxieties, I then . . . Well, I also need a first chapter, I have to have a beginning and then I can go and resolve it; and it's got to be a concrete beginning. I've just begun with a new novel. I've only just started, actually, with an event that actually happened to me, which was buying a bottle of wine in an off-license, and the woman in front was buying everything in the shop. This somehow connected very much with the theme of the book, the theme that was worrying me, that I wanted to write about. And so having got this very definite idea, a scene in my mind, I then start. As I write, the act of writing to me clarifies what happens next. I know the subject matter, I know the characters, but I don't know the events, and the events occur to me as I go on.

Q: William Trevor in his review in the *New Statesman* of *The Waterfall* comments on similar situations in your novels. One thing that I noticed is that somehow the heroines begin to grow older. I wonder if there is a conscious autobiographical element in your novels? Are you working out your own problems?

Drabble: It's almost inevitable, I think, that one should write about one's own age group and the preoccupations of it. In fact, it's not strictly true, chronologically, because *Jerusalem the Golden*, which is my last book but one, has my youngest heroine of all. She's a schoolgirl going up to twenty, younger than any of the others, though I wrote the book when I was twenty-seven or so. But on the whole I do tend to date myself up with them and this is because the problem of what's around me is what I am interested in on the whole.

Q: Would you say that you put people into your books that you know?

Drabble: Yes, certainly yes.

Q: What reactions do you get?

Drabble: They don't know. They can't recognize themselves, I don't think. If I make it recognizable it's because I wanted them to know and then they are pleased, I hope. If it's a really nasty, unsympathetic portrait, I hope they don't know, or I hope they're dead.

Q: How does your family life relate to your working life?

Drabble: I think if I could go abroad for six months, I might just fall to pieces because my working habits are so closely tied up with my domestic ones. It used to gall me very much that I had to start work at half past eight in the evening when everyone else was finished and I was completely exhausted by children. But having done this for so many years, I don't think I could stop. I can't write for more than two hours at a time unless I'm really finishing a book or in some very crucial moment. The thought of sitting in a room writing—I don't know how I could adapt to it. Perhaps in middle age when one might have the money to go away or the money to send one's children off, I might get used to it, but certainly at the moment it's the last thing I'd want. And money doesn't seem to me to be relevant really, so long as one's got enough to live on. If one wants to make money, if one wants to be a multimillionaire like the production writers, why not do something else? It doesn't seem to me to connect up. I mean, if one's aim is to be rich, there are a lot of ways of getting rich, and I think one would have the wit to find them out.

Q: How about Johnson's remark that no one but a fool wrote for anything but money?

Drabble: Well, I don't know. I do write a lot of things for money. I write scripts or reviews or articles for money. It's got to be something I'm interested in. I wouldn't *just* write something frightfully boring for it. But a novel: I would *hate* to think I was writing it in order to get royalties, because that would compromise me. This is the problem I have in writing for films and television, which I don't really like doing because I know I've got to justify the amount I've been paid, which is out of proportion to the amount of effort I'm prepared or capable of putting into it. With a novel I can put endless effort into it, because I care and I know what I'm doing, but with anything else I simply can't. I feel guilty and upset by the fact I've been commissioned. I think commissioning is fatal.

Q: How do you manage — as someone who writes for television and journals — how do you manage to find time to write your novels?

Drabble: Well, I'm quite a hard worker when I get down to it, but as I said I only write a couple of hours at a time. It's quite easy to find a couple of hours. I have a room in town now where I go out to work, and I go out four days a week. I'm not saying I work four days a week because there's so much else to do. I'm always slightly pushed for time, but I quite like that. I don't mind it at all. I quite like the idea of being under pressure and I quite like the idea of having to get back for the children's tea. It limits one's activities in a good way, I think.

Q: Do you work on more than one novel at a time?

Drabble: No, no.

Q: But you are working on the Bennett book and on your next novel at the same time.

120

Drabble: Yes, I am. But the Bennett is a very different kind of activity. And frankly, I haven't written much of it yet. I'm really only reading at the moment, doing the research; which is good because I hate reading aimlessly. I try to read with a purpose.

Q: What about William Trevor's remark about the recurring situations? Is this a conscious feature of your work? Did you read the review?

Drabble: I did read the review, yes. Perhaps they're just archetypal situations. (*laughter*) No, I suppose it's true. I do find situations recur in life, and naturally one's preoccupied with the same kind of things. I'm not going to do it again next time, though. I'm going to try to write about a man next time. It will probably all work out the same, but, even so. . . .

Q: From his point of view?

Drabble: No. At the moment I'm doing it in the third person, but I may give it up. I may have to introduce a woman character in the first person later on. (*laughter*) In fact, I can see her coming up already. That's a weakness of some sort.

Q: Thank you, Miss Drabble.

Roy Fuller

Roy Fuller was born in 1912 in Oldham and educated at Blackpool High School. He is married to Kathleen Smith and has one son. He is a trained solicitor and until his retirement in the late 1960s worked for various building societies. In 1968 he was elected professor of poetry at Oxford. His publications include *Poems* (1939), *Savage Gold* (1946), *Image of a Society* (1956), *Collected Poems* (1962), and *Owls and Artificers* (1971).

The interview took place in a small London hotel.

Q: Are you teaching here in London as well as in Oxford now that you're professor of poetry?

Fuller: Well, the peculiarity of the job is that I don't teach at all.

Q: You mentioned you were lecturing in London.

Fuller: Ah, well that's really the notoriety of the Oxford election catching up on me. That's one of several engagements I've taken to appear in summer schools. If I hadn't got the Oxford election I don't suppose I should have been asked.

Q: This is the first time you've done this sort of thing?

Fuller: It's the first time I've done it in any kind of organized or regular way. Over the years one's had to appear just simply through being about, but I haven't done it regularly. In my life as a lawyer, of course, I've done quite a deal of lecturing, not on literature but on law. So the idea of standing up and spouting isn't foreign to me.

122

Q: What are your feelings about lecturing on poetry, talking about literature in an academic way?

Fuller: Well, I'm not an academic, of course; I never went to a university. So my discoveries about literature were simple and I usually find that I make contact with the audience because they're probably in as great a state of ignorance and doubt as I am. But I'm not an academic at all. In fact, nowadays, I just really try to confine myself to reading and talking about my own verse. I only venture into more general fields if I'm forced to.

Q: Does lecturing appeal to you?

Fuller: No, quite honestly it doesn't. It's the tightness of English literary life. One very often gets asked by people and they're so friendly that you can hardly refuse. I don't particularly like it and I don't need to do it for the money, so I don't know why I do it. It's the obligation of friendship mainly, I think.

Q: You've lived your creative life always in double, working first in law and now as a professor.

Fuller: Yes. I left school when I was sixteen and was articled to a solicitor. I qualified as a solicitor at twenty-one and worked as a solicitor until the end of March this year, when I retired from regular practice. For thirty years I was a tame corporation lawyer and I've now gone on the board of the corporation, which means that I don't do a regular lawyer's job; I simply appear at board meetings and that, of course, is very much less arduous.

Q: Do you regret this career?

Fuller: Yes, by and large. Because I've never had enough time for writing. Also I think I could have made my mark in a different field. I've always been rather too good a lawyer to let the law languish and allow me to concentrate on my other side. I've really worked hard as a lawyer all my life and, looking back, I see that I haven't had enough time. I think it was not too bad when I just wrote verse, but I had always wanted to write prose fiction, and after the war I embarked on it in a serious way. I wrote seven or eight novels. That was when the difficulties really started. To write poetry and prose and be a full-time lawyer all at once is too difficult.

Q: Yet your experiences as a lawyer seem to have provided some of the material for your fiction, in *Image of a Society*, for example.

Fuller: Yes. The curious thing is that I don't think I've used it enough. Particularly in the recent novels I've dealt with the literary life rather than exploiting the life I know quite well. I wanted to do more about the world of affairs in fiction, but it's never quite worked out that way. I don't know what other life would have been satisfactory, mind you, and this is the crux of the problem you're dealing with, isn't it? Is there such a thing as a satisfactory literary life?

Q: Do you find your present life of appearing at board meetings, of lecturing at Oxford, of having more time for writing is more satisfactory to you?

Fuller: I think it will be. At the moment it's like trying to establish new brain channels after forty years of going to an office every day. I'm still not used to having this time and this freedom. It's a most curious sensation. And I've now got to the position where it's as though I were the possessor of a modest fortune, which comes in the form of a pension. I'm free from literary chores, or theoretically free, whereas if I'd done this twenty or thirty years ago, I wouldn't have been. I should have been subject to the same pressures in the literary field, it seems to me, as I have been in the legal field. So although one regrets being a lawyer, it would have been very difficult to choose some other occupation which would have enabled me to live.

Q: Are you writing more now that you've got the extra time?

Fuller: Yes. The position is a little complicated by the fact that a new burden was added, by having to do three lectures a year and so on. But quite plainly, thinking about it in an Arnold Bennett way, at the end of a year one is able to say one's written far many more words than one did before.

Roy Fuller

Q: Are you still concentrating on poetry?

Fuller: Well, I've been doing these lectures. I've got a few poems in hand and I've started a novel. My guess is that the amount of poetry I write won't be significantly increased by having most of my time free for literature. That's just a guess, but until one starts a productive poetic period one simply can't tell how it's going to turn out.

Q: Is the contact with students worthwhile in your writing?

Fuller: I think it is, yes, I think so. In my case it's probably less of a novelty or stimulus, because I have a son who is a poet. So I've had a contact for the last ten or fifteen years with the younger generation. In fact a lot of my friends were first friends of my son. Luckily therefore, I've never been out of touch with what's going on among the younger generation. But yes, I do like feeling I'm not a complete has-been.

Q: Did you find it difficult to keep in touch with literary trends, while you were devoting more of your time to the law?

Fuller: I don't think so, really. I've never lived a literary life, and, well, obviously time has been against me. I suppose my friends have been divided half and half between the law and literature. I've never felt myself falling behind in the sense of being embedded in one particular literary period. I've always contributed to little magazines. I've never become a grand old man, or a grand middle-aged man of literature, partly because I was part of a curious generation. Although I was born at a time so that I came to maturity in the 1930s, I wasn't at all known as a poet until the forties. And then I was writing during the forties the kind of poetry which became popular in the fifties, so that I've never felt superannuated in that way.

Q: In one of your poems you mention Alan Ross. Are there other literary friends, people professionally concerned with literature with whom you might have formed a group?

Fuller: In retrospect, yes, I think it might have been a group.

The Writer's Place

Although at the time one didn't regard it as a group. Very early in my writing career I sent poems to John Lehmann who was editing *New Writing*. He made the supreme effort of getting to know me personally on the evidence of these poems, which were very bad indeed. So I've known John Lehmann since about 1937 personally, quite apart from his reputation. I've kept up that friendship all the time. I met Alan Ross quite by accident during the war. We happened to be in the same bedroom in an officer's club in London, so that he's been a personal friend ever since then. Any literary activities he's been engaged in, I've been associated with, I suppose, through friendship. But I think in the case of both John Lehmann and Alan Ross, it's less personal friendship than similarity of outlook and feelings about what literature should be. In recent years, I've contributed to a little magazine called *The Review*, which was founded in 1961 and is edited by a young man who was a contemporary of my son's at Oxford. Personal friendship enters into that. But, on the other hand, I wouldn't have been allowed to contribute to this thing, which is very severely edited, had it not been for some desire of the editor to have my work in it. Inevitably, in the small metropolitan literary society of London one does fall into these associations. I think they're nourished, certainly in my case, less by personal friendship than by continuing sympathies.

Q: Has your conception of what literature is and ought to do changed much since the thirties?

Fuller: Not much, no. I think I'm one of the people who has changed least since the thirties.

Q: Do you still feel that literature should have political content?

Fuller: I would take a less severe view there than I did in the thirties. I feel that a literature which ignores the things which press most men at the time that the literature comes into being is running a great risk of being negligible. But I wouldn't want now, as I probably did in the thirties, to lay down a blueprint for writers, to say you must deal with this or that subject. I take a much more general view. On the other hand, I still feel that a poetry which can't deal with the topics which engross and obsess us is likely in the end not to turn out to be much good.

Q: Is this true of a poet like Stevens whose social situation at least parallels yours very closely?

Fuller: Well, Stevens is a very interesting case, and I'm a great admirer of Stevens. My admiration for him has grown a good deal in the last ten years. Stevens is, in a sense, full of the particular period in which he was writing. I find Stevens's thirties poems, for example, much more comprehensible if one thinks of the social content behind them. "The Man with the Blue Guitar," for instance. A lot of critics go wrong about Stevens by ignoring the social context of Stevens. He's very much alive to workers' movements and communism. I think this comes out tremendously in his letters. In fact, Stevens's position is similar to the one I have reached myself. That's to say, the idea that Stevens is a kind of dandy, immersed in literature, or that all his poetry is about writing poems seems to me an entire misconception. I see him as absolutely concerned with mankind in quite ordinary connotations. I know this doesn't come out on the printed page, but it's there behind all the poetry.

Q: Did you consciously, in the thirties, try to distinguish yourself from the groups that were then in existence, the Auden-Isherwood group or the pacifist group around Huxley and Heard?

Fuller: I think there was nothing conscious about this; it just happened. It's something people find very difficult to grasp about the so-called public school communists of the thirties, the Audens and Spenders and Day Lewises: one looked down one's nose very much at them. They were not thought to be proper communists at all. It wasn't simply a matter of dissociating oneself but just a feeling that one was entirely different. I never went to public school, never went to a university, and in the thirties, when I was politically engaged, I was in the provinces; I wasn't in London at

127

all. My active political experience was a provincial experience, very different from what went on in London. It was entirely without any literary context, just simple day-to-day political activity — disseminating leaflets and selling the *Daily Worker*.

Q: Did you write any of these leaflets yourself?

Fuller: No. Being a lawyer and being politically active was a very difficult business. My political involvement, in the sense of being involved in day-to-day politics, occupied a comparatively short period at the beginning of the thirties. My sympathy with working class movements was largely theoretical after about 1935, but I never lost, as other people did, the fundamental belief in socialism and the materialist conception of history. Although I would have reservations about a number of things now, I had no reservations about them at all in the thirties. Even so, fundamentally I still have the same opinions.

I admired Auden and Spender as poets, but I didn't particularly admire them as politicians. In fact, I remember writing an article about Spender in very scathing terms. I was absolutely excited about his early poems — those before his first book, the ones that appeared in the *Oxford Poetry* of the time. Later people, like Alun Lewis and so on, I never made contact with. For one thing, they never appeared in metropolitan literary society at all, and of course one's life was disorganized by the war.

Q: Were you at all influenced, as you were beginning your career, by Marxist critics?

Fuller: Yes, I was, very much. Both by the official critics of the day, whose names are now probably forgotten, and by critics of the previous period, like Plekhanov and Lunacharski. In fact, Lunacharski may very well have still been about when I first started writing. Yes, I was influenced. It's very easy, I think, to sneer at the people in the thirties, and in the forties and fifties in the case of Upward, to sneer at their worrying whether one was on the party line, because it seems to those who didn't go through that period just a matter of dogma and words. But behind all this

128

was an enormous concern for the fate of humanity. The question of what literature should reflect was merely the end result of a very strong emotional feeling that one could, through one's writings, perhaps influence the course of events for the good. This is what I find so tremendously touching in Edward Upward, particularly the second volume of his novel. This concern for humanity in his case has led to the most ludicrous and appalling consequences in his literary life. Luckily, I suppose, I escaped the terrible pressures of the party line and what literature should contain. Apart from a very brief period in the thirties when my poems were very arid and didactic, I bypassed, I think, the more stringent requirements of Marxist literary theory. I was probably critical of official Marxist pronouncements much earlier than the end of the thirties, but, broadly speaking, the original Marxist conception of literature remained with me.

Q: What about the poetry of the fifties, which by and large lacks the social content of earlier poetry? Is this lack one of the problems modern poets have inherited?

Fuller: Absolutely. After the war, for about ten years there was a period of English poetry which seemed to be abysmal to me, with very low technical standards. There were eclectic magazines and critical views, and a poetry full of feeling, ill-expressed and ill-digested. Then when the poets of the fifties came along, the young Larkins and the young Amises and the young Wains, one couldn't help welcoming the return to technical competence and to common sense and also to a poetry which was depicting the ordinary life of the poet. What their poetry lacked was any kind of system of belief to incorporate into it: the complicated, general issues of human life. They themselves, or some of them, looked back to the thirties as a golden age when one could be easily committed, when there were ready-made issues for poetry to embody. But of course this wasn't so at all in the thirties. One had the same agonies about whether one's life and whether one's work was correctly and properly and adequately reflecting the time. Just as the fifties people did. It was never easy. It may seem in

The Writer's Place

retrospect that all you've got to do is write a poem about the Spanish Civil War or unemployment or the rise of fascism, but when one was in it, it was by no means easy. Nobody, it seems to me, ever did the thing successfully. Take a poem like Spender's "Vienna," which attempts to do this. It was always thought to be a bad poem, and I still think it's a bad poem. But it was a very brave and indeed noble attempt to write a large-scale poem which wouldn't be a mechanical, political slogan, but a felt poetry about the political issues and events taking place.

Q: Is there now again a possibility for good political poetry?

Fuller: Very much so. As was apparent all the time, the so-called affluent society merely masked issues which were still there. Now the young, having got to the point of despising the affluent societies, see the real issues underneath, like the race question and the colonial wars. They want to express these themes in their poetry. One isn't satisfied — one never is. For a variety of reasons it would perhaps be tedious to go into, the technical basis for writing an adequate poetry about these issues has somehow been lost. Whereas when the fifties poets emerged, I wanted a better system of belief, now that the sixties poets have emerged — or perhaps one should talk about the seventies poets — I would want a better technical system in poetry to express the things which undoubtedly they feel and see in a way which one can't help sympathizing with, very deeply.

Q: How do you reconcile the problem of writing poetry which is politically committed or at least politically interested, but which is read only by the same people who produce poetry or by intellectuals who already have more or less identical sympathies?

Fuller: I can't reconcile it, and never have. I never am likely to. There is a great gulf between society and art which always exists or has existed since the time of Pope perhaps. So far as the poet is concerned, I've always felt he should write as though his audience were a big one. He knows perfectly well, or at least he did in the thirties, that in England his audience was going to be about 2000.

Until the middle of the war, I don't suppose I ever published in any periodical which had a circulation of more than about 2500. But it didn't ever strike me then that I was writing esoteric poetry. I wasn't writing for posterity; I was writing for a theoretical largish audience. I've never had any trouble about this, in the actual process of writing. I've never thought: this'll tickle the palates of 2000 people. I've always tried to be as clear as I could. My poetry isn't easy, I don't think, but it's always worked toward being clear. In a way it's a ludicrous kind of activity, writing poetry with social content for people who are never going to read it; yes, one's compelled to agree. But then this seems to be the way that art works in a society like ours. As one gets older, one does acquire a larger and larger audience. Think of T. S. Eliot. When I first read Eliot at school, he was utterly ignored by the universities. Sounds comic, doesn't it?—that a don at Oxford would no more think of recommending his students to read T. S. Eliot than he would have told them to jump off the end of a pier. The mere process of time certainly brings readers. I know this isn't an answer, but that's the way I think literature works, how all art works in our society.

Q: Was the larger audience the reason you shifted to prose, to fiction?

Fuller: Not really, no. I always wanted to write prose fiction. This was a very early ambition. It so happens I've written the kind of prose fiction which has found not much more readership than my poetry. My novels have not been successful in any kind of popular way. So I would say that even now I'm probably better known as a poet than I am as a prose fiction writer. All the same, there are things that one can say in prose fiction that one can't say in poetry. So there is a motive there, but it's not the prime motive.

Q: Are you concerned that the society should keep the poet or the writer in general alive, when he cannot sell enough to keep himself?

Fuller: This is a very ticklish problem and I don't pretend to have found the answer to it. There are obvious fields where the state — in England usually through the agency of the Arts Council — ought to provide financial assistance. For one thing, these days, because of printing costs, it's extremely difficult to run a little magazine out of the editor's own pocket, or the editor's friends' pockets. This could easily be done in the thirties and was fairly easy still in the forties. I certainly think literary magazines ought to be subsidized, though with certain safeguards. Possibly publishers ought to be subsidized for quite obviously noncommercial but viable books. And prizes and rewards for work actually done are also useful and acceptable. But I'm very much against keeping writers in a state of perpetual studenthood. For one thing, it's awfully difficult to judge who are worth supporting and who aren't. And once one starts doling out largess very indiscriminately, one's got a mass of writers pressing forward to become the beneficiaries of this largess, writers whom, under any rational standard, one wouldn't want to encourage. Although the capitalist system, as applied to works of art, is very often harsh and difficult, I'm not sure that it has any worse results than a public dole system. It's very difficult to apply standards in the realm of public grants. In this country, to my way of thinking, far too many indifferent writers have been sustained and expect to go on being sustained, when really the time has come for them to drop to the bottom of the heap.

Q: What do you think of the poetry-reading circuit as a way of financing poetry? Or of becoming poet in residence?

Fuller: The dangers are obvious. Poets tend to become performers who not only select poems but write poems which are going to make an effect by the emotional or comic response from the audience. You get routine acts, rather like in an old-fashioned vaudeville tour. A chap takes an act around the country as he used to do in vaudeville, playing first the big town and then the secondary town. I can't think that's good for poets. The temptation is to do more and more of it, of course, since you can make a good living at it. The poet in residence thing, I would have welcomed at an earlier stage in my career. If I could have escaped the law or received a more or less equivalent income attached to some university campus, I would have probably done it. But whether it is right for a poet to go to a university to do some postgraduate work and establish himself as a poet and then go on to some other campus — whether this is right or not, I don't know. It may be too narrow a life.

Q: Are there fewer possibilities for a writer to become known in England now than when you began writing?

Fuller: It's very much easier for a young writer to get, either with book reviews or poems, into periodicals which have quite substantial circulations. In fact, they often get into some of the newspapers. This was unknown in my day, partly because book reviewers in a society which had a large mass of unemployed clung onto their jobs. The idea of a young man just down from the university reviewing books for the *Sunday Times* or the *Observer* would have been unheard of in my day. It's possible someone like Spender or Auden might have done a book review or two, but then they were very special because there was quite an apparatus of publicity attached to their names. But my son when he came down from Oxford, was almost immediately writing for—in fact probably while he was still at Oxford—was writing for the *Observer*.

I think one's first book, now, if one shows any talent at all, will be snapped up by a reputable publisher. This wasn't so in my day. I had the greatest difficulty, and so did some of my friends, in getting my first book published. Writers get better known now, simply because of the growth of the media for gossip and publicity, things like color supplements and magazine programs on television and, to a lesser and more serious extent, the BBC Third Programme. They eat up material about certain writers. And as in all gossip columns, characters are invented, aren't they? This doesn't depend on any kind of merit. A figure is established in the public mind of a poet or a novelist, and because that figure becomes known, the gossip writer or journalist keeps on writing

The Writer's Place

about him. So you have this *dramatis personae* of all sorts of writers who keep getting publicity. This has grown enormously in my time, and nowadays bears no relationship to what it was in the thirties.

Q: How would you describe the beginnings of your own career, your attempt to get published, to make a name for yourself?

Fuller: It started simply by sending out poems. I was in the provinces and had no contacts at all with the literary world through any kind of friendship or knowledge. I began by sending poems and short stories to periodicals. Later, round about 1937, I came to London and got to know one or two people concerned with little magazines, but nobody in the "high literary racket." I became very friendly with the man who edited *Twentieth Century Verse*, which was a parallel publication to Geoffrey Grigson's *New Verse*. I published several poems in *New Verse*, but I never met Grigson until after the war. I did know Julian Symons, who edited *Twentieth Century Verse*, and became friendly with him. It was entirely a matter of sending poems out, and apart from one or two people like John Lehmann and Julian Symons, I didn't really know any well-known literary figures until late in the war and after the war.

Q: Did it make a crucial difference to you to leave the provinces for London?

Fuller: Yes, I think so.

Q: How?

Fuller: It's hard to say. For one thing I was always madly keen to come to London. I wanted to escape from the particular lower middle class milieu into which I was born and which had really nothing to offer me.

I was born in the industrial part of Lancashire, which I have a great affinity for and roots in. But unfortunately I left that part of Lancashire when I was ten or eleven. I went to live in another part of Lancashire which was by the seaside and which had no

134

integrated social background. I never liked the town I lived in from the age of eleven to my early twenties. I was eager to escape from there. Whether I would have wanted to escape from a provincial city or not I don't know. Probably not. But a small seaside town in the provinces was not for me. I don't think my career was helped by coming to London. This was entirely a matter of spiritual satisfaction. When I came to write prose fiction, London played a great part in that. I've got a sort of provincial attitude toward London. I'm amazed by it still, and I like describing the central part of London in my fiction. But I don't think, as far as meeting people and that kind of thing, that London made very much difference.

Q: Doesn't London offer you greater opportunities to speak seriously about literary subjects, to discuss your own work rather than lecture on it? Does this help your own work or provide material for it?

Fuller: No, not with me personally. I've been very lucky in having my son during the last fifteen years or so to read most of my stuff; I've always relied enormously on his judgment. If I hadn't had him, I think probably I would have wanted much more to find some congenial, preferably younger writer in London to consult. This is enormously helpful to a writer, and I think far too many English writers just go on relying on their own judgment, not taking stock of the generations coming up below them. I know it's difficult to establish contact in that way, and I've been particularly fortunate, I think.

Q: Have you at all been tempted by the possibility of reaching larger audiences through radio or television?

Fuller: No, it's never crossed my mind. I've usually accepted invitations to read on the radio, but with the BBC Third Programme, it's only like appearing in a magazine with a fairly large circulation. It's quite a large audience but it's not a dramatically large audience. I've never been tempted to write anything specific for either radio or television. As for appearing as a personality on television, I've always tried to avoid that as being irrelevant.

Q: What about the trend in poetry to put things across aurally or visually rather than in print?

Fuller: Young people have a greater power than my generation has to enjoy simply the sound of things. But whether they actually understand more through the ear than one does oneself may be doubted. I can't help thinking there's an inbuilt limit of capacity in the human ear to take in consecutive thoughts and complicated ideas. But they seem much more prepared than my generation was, to sit back and let words wash over them. Whether there is going to be any supplanting of more traditional ways of presenting literature one simply can't guess. I wouldn't have thought, really, that there was any fundamental difference. I think it's true that nowadays you get a larger theoretical audience, or indeed a larger audience in practice for art. But the cultural tradition, it seems to me, goes on being handed down with a comparatively restricted audience. Thinking of my grand-children they're still just as hooked on the printed page as ever I was. They're absolutely avid readers. It's true their father is a university don, but the power of the printed page—that can't be taken away. Whether there is a sort of secondary audience around this cultured nucleus in art, whether there's a barrier between the two, I wouldn't like to say. I'd much prefer to think that it was possible for educationalists to lead the new mass of literates, the new mass of people who are undergoing further education, to regard the printed page with less suspicion. That would be my desire.

Q: Does concrete poetry interest you at all?

Fuller: No. I saw it done before in the twenties and I pretty well recognized its limitations then. Some of the things look quite nice, agreeable to hang on the wall and so on, but I don't honestly see any significance in them. For one thing, the content of concrete poetry is so limited, such a little *frisson* of aesthetic communication, that one quickly tires of it. It's true I've written quite a number of short poems just containing one idea, and that sort of poem does appeal to me very much, perhaps a concrete poem of another kind. I don't despise the form, but for a man to devote his life to writing concrete poems seems to me a very restricted mode of activity.

Q: Young writers, nowadays, are almost universally university-trained, if not university-oriented. What do you make of this, especially as someone who did not go to a university?

Fuller: This is a rather disturbing phenomenon. It's very significant, for example, that one of the most interesting little magazines which has appeared since the thirties, namely *The Review*, which I think was founded in 1961, attracted a number of poets and critics around it and almost without exception they were young university dons. It's very difficult for a man with any literary ability at all to avoid being siphoned off into university channels, postgraduate work, and then some teaching post which he accepts because he sees it as providing sufficient leisure to write. Whether *The Review* is typical of the state of affairs that results from all this, I don't know. But although it gathered together a number of extremely interesting critics, *The Review* never really found poets in large numbers. The critical part of *The Review* grew and grew and the original poetry part shrunk and shrunk. They never found an Auden, not even anyone approaching an Auden. That's what distinguishes it from *New Verse*, which was also very sharply critical, but of course had a large poetry section in it, where not only Auden and Spender and MacNeice published, but many other excellent poets whose names are probably forgotten now. I regard with some dismay poetry being exclusively the province of the university don, but certainly it seems as if it's likely to remain the province of the university-educated: not only the graduate but the postgraduate man too. A writer now wants to postpone for as long as he can—if he's any talent at all—entering into any gainful employment which won't give him enough time to write. Who can blame him? When I've confessed that my life as a lawyer has never really given me enough time, one can't blame a man for taking a job that provides him with fairly long vacations. But it's a disturbing phenomenon and it's not going to be solved by public doles. My suggestion, a rather frivolous one, is that these large corporations, like Imperial Chemicals and so on, should put a few poets on their boards of directors at an early age, which would just let them come in once a fortnight, see something of the world of affairs, and draw about 5000 pounds a year director's fees. But that's not likely to happen.

Q: How did the company that you were working for react to your double life?

Fuller: At first, of course, I was able to keep it dark, when I was an obscure poet—and indeed that obscurity lasted for a very considerable time. Then it was impossible to keep it dark. There probably was a certain amount of suspicion at first, although they were always very kind and, latterly, they seemed to take pleasure, in a way, in reflected kudos. The Stevens parallel is interesting, because from his letters—I mean the archives of the Hartford Insurance Company have never been revealed—but reading through the lines of the personal letters one sees that he established himself by being an efficient lawyer; and he established himself by that means as a poet as well. I always had a fairly responsible job, and in my latter years with my building society I had a very responsible job, so they never were able to accuse me of being a better poet than lawyer—which I suppose is the main thing when one is working for a corporation.

Q: Thank you, Mr. Fuller.

Giles Gordon

GILES GORDON was born in 1940 in Edinburgh and educated at the Edinburgh Academy. He has extensive experience in publishing, having worked for Oliver & Boyd, Secker & Warburg, Hutchinson, Penguin, and (as editorial director) for Victor Gollancz. He now combines as writer and agent with Anthony Sheil Associates. He is married to Margaret Estoe, a well-known (under the name of Gordon) children's book illustrator. His publications include *Pictures from an Exhibition* (1970), *The Umbrella Man* (1971), *About a Marriage* (1972), and three volumes of poetry, *Look out Any Date* (1963), *Two and Two Make One* (1966), and *Two Elegies* (1968).

The interview took place in a small pub in London.

Q: Does Gollancz tend to keep up with what's new, to publish new poetry in the way Cape does? I've noticed that your own poetry is published by relatively small presses. Is Cape the only large publisher willing to take the risks of publishing poetry?

Gordon: Cape is the only big publisher at present who's doing a lot of poetry with imagination. Chatto & Windus, Macmillan, and one or two other publishers will churn out the slim vol of, you know, forty-eight pages at twenty-five shillings. But this is increasingly not the way to publish poetry successfully. We've just published a volume of poems by a Scottish poet called Iain Crichton-Smith. We've published his poems, frankly, because we publish his novels, and he wanted his poems published, which is a very cynical way to publish poetry. But in fact he thinks of himself

The Writer's Place

primarily as a poet; and indeed is primarily thought of as a poet. I know British publishers tend not to give sales figures, but we've sold six hundred copies of that in a couple of months and that actually is terribly good—which is appalling, because it's obviously terribly bad. I suspect that of that six hundred about five hundred and fifty copies went to libraries. To be fair, we don't publish much poetry. We're going to publish more in the future, but this is the first volume we've done for four years.

Q: Your own poems, however, have been published by presses which are much smaller.

Gordon: Yes. Turret Books is affiliated to a bookshop called The Turret Bookshop in South Kensington. That was set up by a man called Bernard Stone, who is a bookseller specializing in poetry. He went into association with Edward Lucie-Smith, the poet. Lucie-Smith set up this series of Turret Books and published about thirty volumes in a limited edition of only a hundred and fifty copies each. Mine's been out of print for quite some time, and I think they're nearly all out of print now. They're all in identical format, by people ranging from Ted Hughes, Christopher Logue, Peter Redgrove, Sylvia Plath, right down to completely unknown people. He published entirely what he liked without any particular aesthetic. The complete set is fetching enormous prices now in good second-hand bookshops here, which is very depressing. Because people are buying them as collectors' items rather than because of the poetry.

Q: Is he continuing to publish?

Gordon: He's not. He's stopped for the moment, for all kinds of personal reasons. I think partly because he's doing too many other things, partly because he felt they made a certain impact and a certain splash. But none of them were reviewed here either.

Q: Why not?

Gordon: Because he didn't send copies out to reviewers, because they were all limited editions. Many of the poems in them are being published by the various poets in their own collections, in larger collections. Because they were mostly only twenty-four or thirty pages.

Q: Has anything taken the place of this series?

Gordon: Not to my knowledge, except for Cape and, possibly, a small press that publishes nothing but poetry and is making more and more of an impact called Fulcrum. They started by publishing Basil Bunting. He was their first scoop, when nobody had heard of Basil Bunting yet. They've gone on publishing a lot of American poetry.

Q: How did you get involved with the group around Turret Bookshop or the Turret Press, if it can be called a group?

Gordon: I wasn't involved with it, actually. I've never belonged to any group of that kind, though most poets of this country do actually and very consciously belong to some group.

Q: Did you submit your poems to Lucie-Smith?

Gordon: I didn't submit them, no. I know Lucie-Smith quite well and indeed he's doing a book for us. Some of my poems were broadcast, a sequence of poems, two sequences actually; they were broadcast on the radio and he heard them and said he'd like to consider them.

Q: You say almost every poet in England belongs to some group or other. Can you identify some of these groups?

Gordon: It's difficult to put this into words, in the sense that most people would say any given poet belongs to group X. In a loose sense, there's the group which is probably the most influential, around George MacBeth, who produces nearly all the poetry that goes out on the radio. He's the most influential person in Britain with regard to getting poetry across to the most people. Almost every poem that goes out on the radio is chosen by him or is rejected by him if it doesn't go out. And obviously more people hear poetry than read it in any magazine. He has the great

The Writer's Place

advantage of being totally antifactional and quite incorruptible in the sense that he would not broadcast somebody's poem because he happened to like them, or know them, or drink in the same pub with them. He will turn down poems if he doesn't like them by the greatest in the land. But needless to say, he does have his preferences, and a lot of people, nearly always the people who fail to get their poems on programs, naturally say he's very prejudiced and partisan. But most reasonably objective people would say that George MacBeth doesn't use his power badly. There is a group around him.

Q: Is it a political group in any sense?

Gordon: It's more a generation group, which prefers a particular kind of post-movement poetry, post-Alvarez poetry. People like George MacBeth himself, Edward Lucie-Smith, Peter Porter; they're the best-known ones. Philip Hobsbaum I suppose. Lots of others. Another group is the group around Fulcrum, who are post-McLuhan poets, less interested in literate poetry, more interested in noises and effects, concrete poetry, spoken poetry.

Q: Are there groups at all around publishers or magazines? A *London Magazine* group?

Gordon: There's certainly a *London Magazine* group, yes.

Q: Do these groups overlap at all?

Gordon: They overlap occasionally, but they're fairly distinct. Nobody in the Fulcrum group would get poems into the *London Magazine*, I don't think. I personally detest the *London Magazine* poetry. The *London Magazine* has become terribly nostalgic, a sort of memorial to the thirties, a lot of us think. It resurrects people like Edward Upward, who's the rage in England at this very moment and has been for about the last ten days. I'd never heard of Edward Upward, I'm ashamed to say. I've asked this question of about ten people of my own generation recently, and none of us had heard of Edward Upward.

Q: Does your generation have a magazine of its own?

Gordon: No, definitely not. There are a few magazines—*Ambit*, *Stand*—fewer in England than in Scotland and Ireland and Wales. I personally think, being Scottish, that the best poetry in Britain at the moment is being written by Scottish poets, notably, Norman MacCaig, George Mackay Brown, and Iain Crichton-Smith. The Penguin Modern Poet series is doing a volume on MacCaig, Mackay Brown, and Crichton-Smith, which is nice. There's a great deal of resentment, I think, by English editors toward Scottish poets. So a book like that coming out in the Penguin series, which has a vast circulation, will do nothing but good for Scottish poetry. Scottish poets today, all stemming from MacDiarmid—who's virtually stopped writing anything interesting, though he's still writing—has much more to do with life and what's going on. It's much less cerebral than English poetry, less ostrich-like. It's much more open.

Q: Why is that, do you think?

Gordon: Most English poets live in London, I think, with very few exceptions. Even Ted Hughes, who claims not to live in London, is in London a great deal of the time. The only one I can think of who isn't is Philip Larkin, of the younger poets. I think there's nothing worse for a writer than to live in London, if he's serious about writing. It's far worse here than in America, I think, where only a very small percentage of writers live in New York.

Q: Why then do you live in London?

Gordon: Well, I live in London because I need a job. Publishing doesn't exist in Britain outside London, alas. I come from Edinburgh and started working for a publishing house there. Now it's been bought out by the *Financial Times*—Oliver & Boyd. Nelson's no longer exists as a publishing house in Edinburgh. Collins in Glasgow is now hardly publishing anything in Scotland; it's merely a printing works. Chambers and Blackwood are minute. No Scottish publishing house now seems to feel any responsibility at all toward Scottish writers, which is sad. It's ridiculous, for instance, that we should be publishing people like

143

Iain Crichton-Smith and George Mackay Brown, and doing very, very well with them. Because obviously they ought to be published in Scotland.

Q: What is your estimate of the work of the Scottish Arts Council?

Gordon: I don't know enough about it. That's a cagey reply, I know.

Q: Well, if the publishers aren't doing enough, perhaps the Arts Council should step in?

Gordon: Yes, well, they're beginning to do more, but they don't have much money to spend on writers. They have quite a lot to spend on artists, on painters and sculptors. And quite a bit on music, but they don't do much for writers.

Q: Do the Scottish poets, if you include yourself in that group, keep pretty much to themselves in London?

Gordon: No, not at all. No, not in London. Because there aren't many in London. The only one I can think of—and I don't think of myself in that way, actually—is Barry Cole, who works for the Central Office of Information. But he doesn't keep himself to himself.

Q: They're not nationalistic?

Gordon: No. If they were, they wouldn't be in London. The only nationalistic ones are the ones living in Scotland, who are very nationalistic and often quite humorless about it, and actually would refuse to live in England.

Q: Do you find that most of the poets of your generation are involved in the same professions, in publishing, in teaching?

Gordon: I'm afraid so, yes. Almost entirely. More and more writers, novelists and poets mainly, seem to be working in publishing, which I'm sure is not a good thing. It must all be part and parcel of the fact that fewer and fewer people are

144

reading interesting new writers. I mean interesting in the sense of experimental. It's a word I hate, but it conveys what I mean: people who are trying to do something new and different. They do seem to work in publishing, or in something like the BBC or the Central Office of Information, or in advertising, or as teachers.

Q: Why do you think this is not a good thing?

Gordon: Almost as a reflex action. One is slightly embarrassed at spending the whole of one's life involved with the written word. In my case, I can't help thinking that if I were a shepherd or fisherman or farmer it would be much healthier for my writing.

Q: Does your job in any way influence the kind of poetry you write?

Gordon: Not in the least, no. I don't think so. I keep the two absolutely separate.

Q: To what extent do you discuss your work with the poets whom you meet?

Gordon: It used to be common, I think, about eight years ago, to discuss poetry when there was an official group called "The Group" meeting once a week. That was run by Edward Lucie-Smith and Philip Hobsbaum, where twenty or thirty poets were meeting every Friday evening and one poet was reading his or her poems. Poems, that is, that had before then been circulated among the other members of the group, so that people would go not just having heard them and then commenting on them, but would have read them and thought about them a bit and then could talk about them. A lot of people seemed to find this very constructive. There is a lesser version of this going on now by a man called George Wightman, who also works for the BBC. It doesn't seem to be as influential in that people don't seem to be benefiting by it, as far as their own writing goes.

Q: How large is this group?

The Writer's Place

Gordon: I don't know, I've never been there. I think it's about twelve people, but I'm guessing. It may be more.

Q: Did "The Group" stop almost at once?

Gordon: No. It ran for a long time. It stopped about five or six years ago.

Q: Was it modeled on the Group 47?

Gordon: Yes, that I think was how it began.

Q: To what extent, if you don't discuss your own work, do you discuss the work of other poets? What kind of literary conversations go on, at meetings, at gatherings, at parties?

Gordon: It all tends to be terribly superficial, but I suppose it always does, doesn't it? More than one thinks. People tend to say, I like X, or I don't like X, and the subject changes slightly. I think it depends on how well you know people. With poets I know well as personal friends I will find myself talking seriously. To take a specific example, a week ago my wife and I had dinner at the house of the editor of a magazine called *Ambit*. Peter Porter and his wife were there along with two other people and we spent most of the evening, about four hours, talking about poetry and poets, and being very specific about likes and dislikes: the way people were writing and what influenced them. That was good and interesting. But one doesn't do that kind of thing, I think, at a party.

Q: What do you think of the way or ways reputations are made now? Do those reputations correspond, in your view, to ability?

Gordon: By no means, no.

Q: What's wrong? What can be done about it?

Gordon: I think it's being proved rapidly that nothing can be done. And it's being proved largely through the work of the Arts Council. The literature panel of the Arts Council, I think, is rapidly, completely, and utterly failing in every single respect. On

146

the whole, money has been given to the wrong people for the wrong reasons. The wrong people are applying. And this obviously is tied up with reputations to a certain extent. It's tied up with who sponsors people. Only poets get money who have been put up by some other writer, or by a publisher or editor. The real answer I think is that there are so few poets of any great merit writing in this country at the moment. I would say Ted Hughes stands head and shoulders above everyone else.

Q: Do you think belonging to a group can aid a writer's reputation?

Gordon: Very much so, yes.

Q: Has it helped you?

Gordon: No. Nor Hughes or Larkin. Neither has been involved in the literary world in London. Hughes is now but he wasn't, and both manage to be more substantial writers than most of us. They do manage to keep above it. I imagine it would be very difficult if you wanted to be uncompromising and wouldn't kowtow to anybody.

But the whole thing is so inbred. Basically, the people who are writing the stuff are the people who are buying other people's stuff. Everyone's taking in their own washing. There was a case recently—this is being rather bitchy—where the literary editor of a well-known weekly sent a novel out to be reviewed by his regular novel reviewer. When the review came in with four or five novels reviewed, and one particular one omitted, the literary editor got on to him and said, "Look, why haven't you reviewed this?" The reviewer said, "I thought it was terrible." The literary editor said, "Well, I'm sorry you must review it, because X is the editor of another magazine." This is surely very unhealthy and corrupt, to put it at its highest level.

Q: Do you think that poetry is really not reaching a public other than poets themselves?

Gordon: I think it's not, as the sales would indicate.

The Writer's Place

Q: What about the universities? Is it reaching the people in the university?

Gordon: It's reaching a few people in the universities, in English departments, but on the whole most universities in this country are not interested in contemporary writing. One of the few exceptions, I think, is East Anglia, where Angus Wilson and Malcolm Bradbury teach, and where they do have real live writers. And rather good writers, who are actually there on the campus. That's much more like the American thing, and we are now beginning to have a few writers in residence at universities.

Q: Do you find that attractive?

Gordon: I personally think it's terribly important from everybody's point of view. I think it would be nice from the writer's point of view because he's got a certain financial security. He doesn't have to have a nine to five job. He can actually take time off and write, which is very rare in this country. I think it's good for the students because they're coming up against a living writer, and that makes them at least think of new novels and new poetry, instead of Chaucer and Shakespeare all the time.

Q: Doesn't the subject matter of poetry become restricted by the fact of poets teaching in universities? More so perhaps than by being employed by a publishing company?

Gordon: Because they'll be subjective about it?

Q: I'm thinking of America now, where so many poets are in residence and continually reading poems by their students, continually thinking poetry, continually writing poems about criticism, about their students, and so on.

Gordon: Well, it obviously could be a problem, but I don't think a serious one here, because most of the poets—as opposed to novelists—associated with universities here are not teaching anything specifically. They just happen to be there. Take, for instance, a friend of mine, who until now has been an editor at Macmillan, Kevin Crossley-Holland, who is a poet himself. He's just been made the Gregory Fellow at Leeds University. What in effect this means is that for the next two years he has got to be at Leeds University. He doesn't have to give a single lecture, he doesn't have to do anything. He's just got to be available to any student who may or may not want to talk to him, about anything under the sun. Meanwhile, he's supposed to get on with his own writing, though he doesn't have to show anything at the end. That's ideal, even if he's not paid much. What he's paid, in fact, wouldn't be anything like enough to live on, if he wasn't publishing criticism and his own work.

Q: Is there anything in England like the American "tour" of various universities, where a poet will go from university to university reading his poems?

Gordon: Not really. This is something that the Arts Council have tried to set up recently. This spring, at the suggestion of Julian Mitchell, the novelist, they set up two tours of writers. There were four writers in each group—one was a novelist, one was a poet, one was a playwright, and one was something else. They went on tours of various towns and various parts of Britain. One group went to Wales; the other went to the Midlands. These were quite successful, but they received a *terrific* amount of publicity in the press here, which is some indication that such a thing is new. They went to bookshops, they went to universities, they went to schools, they went to all kinds of places. The most humiliating thing about both tours happened I think during the Welsh one. Margaret Drabble, the novelist, was in a bookshop to sign copies of her book and she wasn't recognized by anybody. Lots of people came up to her and asked her how much this book was or could they have that book. They mistook her for an assistant in the bookshop. Which sums up what the British think of their writers.

Q: There's nothing less formal than this kind of arrangement through the British Arts Council? No individual possibility of going from university to university to read one's poems?

Gordon: No. Not officially, anyway. There are odd things.

Lancaster University or some people at Lancaster University are organizing a series of poetry readings at the Edinburgh Festival this year. There are four of them and they've got three poets and I got a letter the other day from the chap organizing to say, would you like to be the fourth? He then ended up by saying, of course we won't be able to pay any fee for getting there, or any fee for doing it. If I were to do it, which I can't because I shall be out of the country then, I should have to pay for it out of my own pocket.

Q: Is poetry doomed to remain unpopular? Can anything be done to change this situation?

Gordon: No, nothing significant. I'm very pessimistic about that, and I think it's unrealistic not to be. Recently I attended a reading in London by Kenneth Koch. There weren't more than about forty or fifty people there. I've read to groups together with good poets or well-known poets, and there've only been ten or twelve people.

Q: Where does the fault lie?

Gordon: I think the fault probably lies in our educational system, where contemporary poetry is not given any kind of treatment at all. It's just thought of as something moderately eccentric and quaint, rather than as an integral part of life and literature. I think it is wrong to think of poetry in isolation. This applies to all writing in this country. Even a book like *Portnoy's Complaint*, which has done reasonably well here, has achieved nothing like the effect it did in America. It's just a wonder for a day or two.

Q: And yet there are novelists certainly who can earn their living, serious novelists, by writing; and there don't seem to be any serious poets who can do so.

Gordon: No.

Q: Perhaps T. S. Eliot was the last who could.

Gordon: I think Ted Hughes can. But admittedly not through writing poetry, but by editing other poets, by organizing

150

international conferences, by writing introductions to children's books, by having some of his poems anthologized. But not through writing new poetry.

Q: What influence do you exericse at Gollancz's in publishing poetry?

Gordon: Well, I have all the influence here, in poetry. If I want to do a book of poems sufficiently eagerly, if I behave myself, I'm allowed to do it. As long as I don't do too many.

Q: Does Gollancz have an annual allotment?

Gordon: Of poetry? No, not really. Perhaps two or three. But actually, there is no poet who is not being published now that I personally would like to publish in this country.

Q: Do you solicit manuscripts of poetry?

Gordon: Yes. I solicited Iain Crichton-Smith's, I suppose, in the sense that I wrote to him and said, can we consider your next collection? Some publishers are having difficulty in publishing enough poetry. They want to publish poetry, but they're having difficulty in getting enough that they like. It just isn't around. I personally think it's nonsense—all the people who say nobody'll publish poetry here. Any poet who's half good can get his poetry published quite easily. I hope that doesn't sound too authoritative.

Q: Has poetry reached a dead end?

Gordon: No, not necessarily. I just think that one has surely got to face the fact that possibly the time in which one lives and works oneself is a time when there aren't many good writers writing in one's own country. Isn't it reasonable that this must happen?

Q: What poets in other countries would you say are interesting?

Gordon: I'd say [Miroslav] Holub, the Czech for a start and [Vasco] Popa, the Hungarian. I like a lot of East European poetry very much.

The Writer's Place

Q: Ginsberg, Ferlinghetti, Corso?

Gordon: Oh, I think so, yes. But we now think of Ginsberg as almost historical. They're of the past rather than the present. People like Snodgrass, who I think is a very fine poet, is hardly known here at all. His last book was very badly reviewed indeed. There is definitely a clique in favor of Berryman. Berryman's star is on the rise here, I think.

Q: What clique?

Gordon: People who have some influence in the world of poetry—reviewers, literary editors—who are doing all they can to get Berryman's poetry published in magazines and reviewed and favorably criticized at some length and with some seriousness.

Q: Not a literary conspiracy?

Gordon: No, no. It's literary enthusiasm, if you like.

Q: What is the cause of this?

Gordon: People are surprised. Yesterday I saw a Cypriot poet called Taner Baybars who lives in England and who writes in English. He was terribly surprised. He said, have you read Berryman? Isn't he marvelous? It's fantastic the way one gets this kind of reaction. People don't expect other people here to have read most American poets. I don't know what caused it. Isn't Berryman's poetry very European? Perhaps this is it, in content and in approach. We're very cautious about our poets; we prefer them to be traditional and classical.

Q: Yet Ginsberg and Ferlinghetti, who are not, seem to have been popular in England.

Gordon: Yes, but more as figures than as poets.

Q: What about concrete poetry? Is that already past?

Gordon: I think it's been at about the same level of interest for quite a few years now.

152

Q: Is English poetry moving in a Berryman-like direction?

Gordon: Yes. I suspect he would be the biggest influence in the next few years, just as without any doubt Sylvia Plath has been since she died, much more so than Ted Hughes or Larkin, who I think have had relatively little influence on their contemporaries.

Q: Thank you, Mr. Gordon.

Ian Hamilton

IAN HAMILTON was born in 1938 in King's Lynn and educated at Darlington Grammar School and Keble College, Oxford. He is married to Gisela Dietzel and has one son. Besides being poetry and fiction editor for the *TLS* from 1965 to 1972, he founded and helped edit the well-known literary magazine *The Review*. His publications include various editions of modern verse, two volumes of poems, *Pretending Not to Sleep* (1964) and *The Visit* (1970), as well as a book of criticism, *A Poetry Chronicle* (1973).

The interview took place in the London offices of the *TLS*.

Q: What policies, aside from preserving the anonymity of the reviewer, does the *TLS* have toward reviewing? How, for example, do you select the books you plan to review? Do you have any conscious emphases on kinds of literary work you select?

Hamilton: Not really. I don't think in a paper like the *TLS*, which is a large, wide-ranging setup, one can afford to omit much of anything.

Q: What happens to the books when they come in?

Hamilton: The books go on the main shelves in the main office, and the books that fall in my area come to me. That is, all the books that are literary books: poetry and fiction and so on. Each week, to take fiction as an example, one has, say, twenty-five novels come in, and on a particular day, one browses through these. Clearly with novels, you can with some confidence eliminate perhaps a half dozen of those. All the crime novels

154

Ian Hamilton

would go off to one particular reviewer who is a regular crime reviewer. All the science fiction novels would go off to a science fiction reviewer.

Q: Before they reach your desk at all?

Hamilton: No, no, no. I would send them off, after having sifted them out. Then we simply have a panel of regular fiction contributors who probably do anything up to three books a week, in the case of the very short 250 word reviews. Here's the real difficulty of making the editorial decision. On a book that seems moderately competent, which is all right but nothing very special, you allocate 250 words on the basis of just having looked through it. But this isn't a rigid instruction that we give out to reviewers. If a reviewer then reads it and feels that this book is worth more, or worth less, or worth nothing at all, he will say so, and we'll take his word for it. You have to have reviewers, therefore, whom you can trust to do a lot of the kind of editorial work of the most refined sort. But one is always worried about missing some masterpiece, about having thrown it perhaps in the wastepaper basket or something. Obviously, there have been cases where this has happened. Every paper that has been going for any length of time has its nightmares, its skeletons in the cupboard. We have quite a few of those. For example, *Catch 22* was sent out to a quite inappropriate reviewer, and was dismissed very, very briefly, as I remember. It obviously had gone to somebody who had not really examined the book closely. I was not here at that time, I must say in my defense. It's not one of my own skeletons I am exhibiting. But had that been looked at with sufficient care, it would have been clear that this reviewer would take against it.

Q: Did you inherit a stable of reviewers when you came here?

Hamilton: One or two of them, yes.

Q: You had the option of dismissing them if you so desired?

Hamilton: Well, yes. One kind of forgets to send certain people books after a point if they don't seem to be up to standard and so on. This is always very difficult, because there are some free-lance book reviewers who depend on regular work. Their whole lives can be altered just because of a change in the literary editorship of some paper. One has to prevent that sort of feeling from influencing one too much. You know there are people whom one simply has to get rid of.

Q: How do you go about selecting, or how *did* you go about selecting reviewers?

Hamilton: Well, first of all there are obviously people whose performance one knows about from having seen them review elsewhere. Also, we get a lot of people who write in asking to review books and we always treat such requests seriously, at least to the extent that we ask the applicant to submit specimens of his work. It's unlikely that we would employ someone with no experience at all, in other words, somebody who had not done a certain amount of writing in either literary magazines or university publications of one sort or another. On the other hand, there are cases of people who haven't done any journalism who have sent in essays that they have written, or have taken a book, tried it out, and have turned out to be okay. One is always having to keep an ear and an eye open in this way.

Q: Do you find that most of your reviewers are authors themselves?

Hamilton: A lot of them are, yes. Many poetry reviewers write poetry, but fewer fiction reviewers, it seems to me, tend to write fiction or publish novels. But one or two, of course, do. In fact, oddly enough, I have found that novelists tend not to make the best fiction reviewers. There have been people whose novels one admires and to whom one has offered books to review—this is a generalization, naturally—and they haven't been anything like as good as one would expect from their performance in fiction.

Q: Do you favor sending poetry for review to poets of a particular school? Especially in view of the kind of poetry you write yourself?

Ian Hamilton

Hamilton: No, not really, I think. Because there are "schools," one tends to gravitate toward one school or another oneself to some degree. One has partisan views, of course, but these one has to try and keep under control. You can't edit poetry in the *TLS* in the same way as you might edit it in a little magazine. In other words, you can't adopt a single set of criteria and set about promoting them in a polemical way. Nevertheless, it is the case that one would probably not—at least regularly—send books to somebody whose views seem to you appallingly wrong. There can be disagreements over certain books, to be sure. You would still maintain somebody in employment even though he disagreed with you over particular books. Where somebody did seem, let's say, to be absolutely sold on the Black Mountain school of poetry or something, so that this seemed to him the only kind of poetry that ought to get written, one would probably not send collections of Black Mountain poetry to that person, because you know what you are going to get for a start. On the other hand, of course, there are other reviewers who take the view that Black Mountain poetry is precisely the kind of poetry that ought *not* to get written. You must be rather careful of that as well.

Q: Do you get accused of being prejudiced against certain kinds of poetry?

Hamilton: Oh, yes, yes. You have to be cautious. My whole habit as an editor—and because I also edit a small magazine—is to edit in a fairly polemical way, I suppose. I do have very firm ideas about what I like and don't like. But I think it would be wrong to carry these over wholesale into the *TLS*. On the other hand, one does have one's views and so on, and there are critics whom one admires. Part of one's admiration, naturally, has to do with the fact that they like the kind of poets that one likes oneself. One can't altogether pretend that one is adopting a totally neutral, open stance, because I think such a stance is impossible. Still, you have to try to temper this, moderate it, something that is not always easy.

157

Q: Do you find yourself being supervised by the chief editor, being asked, say, to be less polemical?

Hamilton: This has never happened, actually. But certainly he reserves the right to do so. He is the editor of the paper and he reads everything that goes into it. His decision is final on what goes in. But there have been no instances of there being a dispute over such an issue, no.

I don't think actually—looking over the period that I have been editing poetry—that it would be easy for somebody, who didn't know who was doing the editing, to work out a map of what this particular editor believed or didn't believe. Whether that's a sort of backhanded apology is another matter. It's more difficult even in poetry, I think, than in fiction. Poets divide themselves up into warring camps, and poets get more steamed up about things. There is more of what one calls gang warfare on the poetry scene than in the novel business.

Q: Do you feel yourself under any kind of pressure to influence you to take sides in these skirmishes?

Hamilton: No, people will send in poems, and they will quarrel with reviews that have been written. They might feel, if they belong to a particular school, that their school was not being treated as generously as it might be. But there is no real pressure, no.

Q: What about the literary gatherings you go to? Do these exercise an influence on you? Sorry, if I'm asking too bluntly.

Hamilton: I don't go to many affairs. You mean the difficulty of knowing people as personal friends or acquaintances? And then having to make decisions about their work? This is a problem, yes. This could be said to be one argument for anonymity, of course.

Q: Is it real anonymity? I mean, is it only the general reading public which is kept in the dark, whereas to "those in the know" it's perfectly clear who the author of a particular review is?

Hamilton: It oughtn't to be clear, because we don't let it out. We don't, of course, have any means of preventing somebody who has reviewed a book for the *TLS* going around saying that he has reviewed it. He might well do this. It does, in fact, happen. So, consequently, word can get around about a particular book, particularly in the universities where you have a fairly tight community. The news that X or Y is reviewing the latest book by A or B is, you know, likely to get around.

Q: Is this rarely the case, or often the case?

Hamilton: I don't know. I think probably rarely. Yes, rarely.

Q: What do you make of the usual charge that anonymity is merely a mask for malice, that only a signature can keep the reviewer honest?

Hamilton: Yes, this is a danger. There is a danger in anonymity. Personally, if I were the editor, it would not be an anonymous paper, let's put it like that. On the other hand, I can see some kind of case for it. I certainly do know reviewers who write more astringently, when they write anonymously, than they do when they are writing under their own names. Some might say more "acrimoniously" and also more cowardly and maliciously and so on. But that would be mere opinion. Still, it does seem to me that one could give instances where anonymity is a good thing. There are cases of people who are in, say, positions in government or the civil service, etc., and are obviously well informed on particular subjects, but who would not be able to write about them under their own names. So one can, therefore, by the anonymous convention, get at some otherwise inaccessible areas. I mean, I would not say this is the key, but you can get at more expert opinion on some topics by maintaining anonymity.

One of the dangers is, as you say, the narrowness and backbiting and even backstabbing that anonymity encourages. But I have not seen a lot of that, actually. I think the real danger is that it encourages a certain kind of bland, pontifical assumption of absolute authority, particularly in matters of literary criticism where it does not seem to me that there are many absolute standards lying around. This seems to me philosophically unacceptable, that one shouldn't own up to one's view and agree to the proposition that one's view is relative and personal and conditioned by this, that, and the next thing. In other words, the assumption of anonymity in matters of literary criticism seems to me to be wrong, though less so in matter of fact, I suppose, and in academic research.

Q: Do you ever find that you need to modify what your reviewers write?

Hamilton: Well, I think every person who edits does to some extent, yes; but not unless somebody seems to me to be going off his head, getting a bit intemperate or overstating the case. Or if someone is writing inelegantly and clumsily, and I want to straighten it out. We try to consult with the reviewer about it, but this is not always possible. Small changes are made at the last minute and so on. But on the whole, I insist that the reviewers are consulted.

Q: How about cutting out sections? Is this more common?

Hamilton: Yes, you have to do a bit of that.

Q: Do you ever get any reactions about cutting from the reviewers?

Hamilton: Not often. I think most professional reviewers accept that this is part of the business. They might feel, why cut me and not him? Or why cut that excellently turned sentence and not that monster? But it's not a great problem.

Q: The *TLS* seems to have changed in the last few years, changed, if one may say so, in the direction of greater "popularity": long articles in the style of the *New York Review of Books* or signed essays. Do you envision further moves in this direction?

Hamilton: Well, we did introduce signed articles about two years ago. But I would not have thought that either of those two things that you cite was a move in the direction of popularity. I don't

160

think there has been any general move of that kind, certainly not as a matter of deliberate policy. But the introduction of the signed article obviously made a difference to the appearance of the paper. And there seemed, perhaps, to be more going on in it, that not every piece was a book review and so on. We also introduced the "commentary" column, which is a weekly news review, a little thing which again might be said to be a concession to modishness.

Q: What about your special issues?

Hamilton: Well, we've had those for some years. It has always been the case that we've had a number of special issues: one usually tied to the Frankfurt Book Fair, and one which we call the "Export," a number of special copies designed for export. It's usually been the practice to invent a theme which in the first issue would be covered in terms of England or the United Kingdom, and in the second in terms of abroad, Europe, and so forth. We have had up to four of those kinds of issues. In 1965, there were, I think, four issues on "Sound in the Sixties"; one on England, one on America, one on the Commonwealth, and one on Europe. But we always have the two. This year we're having two on money in writing.

Q: Is there a weekly, fixed allotment for fiction, which you don't customarily exceed?

Hamilton: There's always one page, sometimes there are two. This would depend on the overall size of the paper, which would depend on the amount of advertising, whether it's a twenty-four–page paper or a twenty-eight–page paper. So we get a plan of the advertising allocation for that particular issue. For a large paper, we tend to have two fiction pages, but, of course, we always have the one. Sometimes we have had three fiction pages, especially in large issues.

Q: Do you see yourself developing in the direction of the *NYRB*, with longer review essays?

Hamilton: Well, the quarrel really is between coverage, on the one

161

hand, which a lot of people value in the *TLS*—it does cover most books for the public—and the clear value of the long review. We try to get the best of both worlds by having a long middle page article and a long front page article, which amount to about 3,000 words each, but which can be longer. And at the same time, we try to maintain a very broad coverage of the whole field of what is published.

Q: How is the distribution of the lead article decided on? Proportionally? So many to fiction, so many to history, so many to science?

Hamilton: Well, it's fairly random actually, again depending on what books appear. We have had front page articles on poets and novelists.

Q: Who makes the decision?

Hamilton: That would be decided here in editorial discussion. If it seemed to me that there was a case for a lead review being allocated to a particular poet or a novelist, then I would put this up to the editor and get his view on it.

Q: Thank you, Mr. Hamilton.

L. P. Hartley

L. P. HARTLEY was born in 1895 and died in 1972. He was educated at Harrow and Balliol College, Oxford. His publications include *Night Fears* (1924), *The Shrimp and the Anemone* (1944)—which established his reputation as a novelist—*Eustace and Hilda* (1947), *The Go-Between* (1953), *The Hireling* (1957), *The Betrayal* (1966), and *My Sister's Keeper* (1970).

The interview took place in Hartley's Kensington apartment.

Q: Is it a good thing for a writer to maintain a connection with a university? Your own close friendship with David Cecil indicates that you do care about what the academic intelligence has to say about your work.

Hartley: We were at Oxford together. That's how I met David Cecil. I had come out of the army after the First World War and he'd never been in the army. He's much too young; there are about eight years between us.

I do think it's a good thing that writers should have links with universities, because I don't see otherwise how they could live unless they had private means. Of course, it's true that a good many cease to write when they go to a university; they find their teaching activities enough. David Cecil was an exception.

Q: Did your own years at the university help or impede your creativity?

Hartley: I think they helped me, because I wrote some short stories when I was there, which I was able to publish because I was

163

editor of a little university magazine. I could put in what I wanted to and that was a great thing, because I don't think anybody else would have published them. They *were* published eventually by Putnam's. I was very lucky over that.

Q: Did you belong to any circle or movement at Oxford?

Hartley: Well, I belonged to a good many circles which were sort of contiguous, but I don't know which one I belonged to most. I think I had more friends outside college than I had inside. I frequently went out to Garsington, something I very much enjoyed.

Q: Did Garsington inspire you in any way?

Hartley: Well, I think it was inspiring. Lady Ottoline [Morrell] was a great inspirer. I should always say that. When I knew her the great days of Garsington were over, because she didn't see the Bloomsbury group as much as she used to. Lytton Strachey and Virginia Woolf and all those people had rather faded out of the picture.

Q: In what way would you say you were inspired by her?

Hartley: She had the most inspiring personality. You only had to be in the same room with her; she gave out something.

Q: Lady Nelly and Eustace?

Hartley: (*laughing*) No, that was somebody else I was thinking of; no, not her.

Q: Some of the writers associated with Garsington, Huxley and Lawrence for example, used her in their fiction. Were you tempted?

Hartley: Well, I mixed her up a little bit with one character in *The Boat*, but it wasn't principally meant for her. But I did draw on her a little bit for that.

Q: Do you think the character of your writing would have changed if you had not been part of this circle?

Hartley: Yes, I think it very likely would; or I might not even have gone on writing. I suppose I should have, but she was very encouraging, you know. It's encouragement one wants when one's starting out.

Q: Was it possible to speak to her about literary subjects?

Hartley: Oh, yes, almost about nothing else. I mean, that's what she wanted. And painting even more. I think painting is what she really was chiefly interested in.

Q: Did she inquire after your own writing?

Hartley: I can't remember whether she did. Hers was a kind of salon. She brought up a subject, not in the deliberate way of French salons, but she threw a ball into the air and hoped that people would catch it.

Q: Did you discuss your writing with other members of your college?

Hartley: Oh, I think so, certainly with David Cecil. I did get encouragement and a feeling that people were interested, so it was never like talking in an empty room.

   I think Aldous Huxley and Lawrence used Lady Ottoline rather badly. Aldous Huxley always said he did not put her into *Crome Yellow*, though he did put her husband into it, which she rather resented. Mr. Wimbush, I think he was called.

Q: Was Hermione Roddice in Lawrence's *Women in Love* an accurate portrait?

Hartley: Well, it's a very suggestive portrait of one side of her. Her voice and passionate temperament and everything come in, don't they? Yes, I think it is really rather like her; more than she liked to think.

Q: Has the world of English letters suffered because there is no Lady Ottoline anymore?

Hartley: Yes, I think it has. There's no literary hostess anymore.

The Writer's Place

In fact, in all of London there's no hostess as there used to be. Lady Colfax and Nancy Cunard had parties for lions of various sorts.

Q: Do you still meet authors yourself now? To discuss literature?

Hartley: Well, I do at parties, cocktail parties and dinner parties and so on. Literature is never left out at such affairs, but it's more often what contemporaries are doing than deciding what Jane Austen's greatest novel was. No, I don't think at any of the parties I go to literature would ever not be discussed in some form or other, because it's what people have in common. I don't go to parties where people talk about horses or something of that sort.

Q: Do you keep up with contemporary literature?

Hartley: Well, I do to some extent, because I'm on the committee that awards a little prize: the Heinemann Committee of the Royal Society of Literature, and for that I have to read a certain number of books. We gradually winnow them, you know, the committee does, until we find something we can agree about for the prize. So I do read a good many books which are ultimately cast aside.

Q: What is your feeling about the state of contemporary British literature as opposed to twenty or thirty years ago?

Hartley: The reviewers on the whole are much more savage. I've had one or two disagreeable reviews. They like to take a very strong line for or against a book, especially novels, so as to give a rave notice or a really damning one. I suppose that's easier to read for the public. It was not my practice when I was a reviewer, which I was for a great many years. Now reviewers don't always read the books very carefully. They get an overall impression and go to town on that. There's a great deal of, not exactly showing off, on the part of the reviewer, but they don't really study the book or try to get inside it.

Q: Have you ever been helped by a review?

Hartley: No, I don't think I have, or not very much, except for encouragement and notice. I wouldn't say that many reviewers had actually helped me. One did a little while ago and I was trying to think who it was. I think it's very difficult to help a writer unless he's got some glaring defect that you could point out.

Q: What was your own procedure when you were reviewing books? Your own sense of your function?

Hartley: I read the book as fairly as I could, you know, and said as far as I could what my opinion was—good or bad, so to speak. But I don't think I ever got my knife really into a writer; and I was never an *engaged* reviewer as so many are now. You can tell almost from what paper the review is coming out in, and the leaning of the reviewer, whether you'll get a good review or not, though one sometimes has a surprise over that.

Q: Do you think the presuppositions of your readers have changed appreciably since the war? That you now have a different reader than you did twenty or thirty years ago?

Hartley: I've just written a novel, which I've given to one or two of my friends to read. There's a certain amount of homosexuality in it, something I haven't done before. The last friend I lent it to liked the book very much, but she said, "You must make it quite clear that this story happened several years ago, because the young now have no sense of responsibility whatsoever." Do you think that's true? I don't know. I know so very few young people. Of course, it makes a difference because nearly all my novels were about some form of responsibility. And this one certainly is.

Q: What, in your view, is the health of the novel as a form? Moribund? About to become extinct?

Hartley: Well, I think as individualism tends to become extinct and is swallowed up in some form of collectivism, that certainly does weaken the novel. Because to me a novel is about characters, their problems, and their differences from each other. You can't really write a novel about people who are all alike.

Q: Do you still read novels yourself? I mean, for pleasure?

Hartley: Well, in my case it's something that's grown on me. For eighteen years, I used to read about six novels a week, among other books, and write about them, comment on them. I did at one time three articles a week, when I was in Venice. I think it's given me a sort of distaste for reading novels, a satiety, you know. At one time when I went into a room and saw the books, I went to look at them. Now I turn away from them. But I still get great pleasure in writing.

Q: Does the material for your fiction come out of your life, or more out of your reading and imagination?

Hartley: I think I dig it out of my own entrails, so to speak. And I probably write the same story in different forms every time. I can see the kind of form they take: usually the hero is someone who for one reason or another has some kind of secret that he can't divulge, and who becomes more and more lonely as a consequence of this. Some of my novels are one-man or one-woman novels, and the other characters are gradually thrown aside. The hero is left isolated with himself. That's what seems to me to happen.

Q: Are your novels autobiographical?

Hartley: Oh, yes they are. At least *Shrimp and Anemone* was. I mean, they have autobiographical features, but they end up by being much less autobiographical than they began.

Q: Why do you write novels?

Hartley: I suppose it's partly because I have to do something to justify my existence. And I do enjoy writing. There's never been a long time when I haven't been without some idea. It comes into my mind, I never know quite how. When one novel has been finished, I don't take much interest in it after that; and then something is waiting in a queue, so to speak. At least that's what I hope will happen.

Q: How do you react to the criticisms David Cecil levels against the Victorian novel? That it is not intellectual, that it does not come

168

honestly to grips with sexual problems. Is it necessary for a novel to have ideas? To be socially involved?

Hartley: Does he say that? Oh dear, he must have changed his mind since then. Well, I think it's quite a good thing for a novel to have an idea. Stendhal had ideas, or if not ideas, he had a kind of ideal character. And I suppose Hardy's novels, which perhaps is what David Cecil was thinking about, are all founded on an idea, on a fatalistic idea.

Q: How do your ideas appear? Ideas for plot, for example?

Hartley: I think of the situation before I think of the character.

Q: How much of a mulling-over period precedes the actual writing?

Hartley: Not very much that I'm aware of, because I can't really think about a novel when I'm not actually in front of the paper I'm writing on. But I suppose a certain amount goes on subconsciously; I'm sure it does. And sometimes if it's been going well, as I think, little things keep occurring to me and then I rush to write them down before I forget, little fragments of dialogue or something.

Q: Do you plot out the novel in advance?

Hartley: I think I do know what the end is going to be. But otherwise I just go on hoping for the best, though I know what the last page is going to say, more or less.

Q: What about names of characters?

Hartley: No, I'm very bad at names. Indeed, it's been a great worry to me, that particular thing. I think the name should suit the character, but I very often would like to call them Smith and Jones.

Q: Do you find that relations with your publishers on titles of novels or changes in novels are amicable or useful?

Hartley: Some have condemned them violently, but without

suggesting much change; just saying this is one of the worst books they've ever read. My publisher's reader said that about *Facial Justice* and *The Hireling*. He couldn't bear either of them. However, they did quite well; he was wrong, I think.

Q: In other words, you do all your revisions yourself. There's never any question of a publisher's reader suggesting revisions?

Hartley: Well, a publisher has. My old editor at Putnam's used the blue pencil quite a lot. It used to annoy me to see the typescript come back with marks on it. He was the only one who really took a lot of personal interest in my books or made drastic suggestions.

Q: What would you say were the major literary influences on your work?

Hartley: Nathaniel Hawthorne and Henry James; and they resemble each other, don't they?

Q: I suppose James would have denied that, particularly in respect to the isolated condition of the writer in America, the lack of tradition.

Hartley: Actually, I did some lectures on Hawthorne, at Cambridge. And nobody had ever heard of him; it was very disappointing. Somebody at England's seat of learning said to me, "He wrote a book called *The Scarlet Woman*, didn't he?" Now what am I to say to someone as ignorant as that? And then of course there were no doubt two or three Americans in the audience who knew much more about Hawthorne than I did, because I rather got it all up. I've read a great deal about Hawthorne. And as you know a great deal is known, but a great deal is not known.

Q: In what way would you say that James and Hawthorne have influenced your writing?

Hartley: James influenced me very much stylistically at one time. I used to copy his manner, and I couldn't help it. I thought it was really enough if one had produced a Jamesian sentence, like "Ah, she beautifully waited"—that sort of thing. I loved all that.

Hawthorne I felt a sort of affinity of mind with. Apart from his being a very beautiful writer, perhaps one of the best writers who have ever written fiction. Nobody could ever turn out a better sentence than Hawthorne could. And also his particular problems—those moral problems—are the kind that interest me.

Q: What do you make of James's great catalogue of social and traditional advantages the English writer could draw on, but the American could not? Do you think there's much truth in that?

Hartley: No, I really don't. And the fact that the American novelist of the day had no Epsom and no Ascot, no castles, no abbeys, no stately homes . . .

Q: No interesting crimes . . .

Hartley: It was Hawthorne who said that: "no gloomy wrongs." But he proved very much that there were plenty of sad and gloomy wrongs in America. He couldn't have been more mistaken over that.

Q: Is it becoming more difficult for an English writer to be an English writer, in the sense that there is no interest any more, at least on a serious level, for writing that is intimately tied to a particular place?

Hartley: Well, we give a prize at the Royal Literature Society for a regional novel. We were left some money, about three thousand pounds, to found a prize for a regional novel. So we dutifully have to go round and find a novel which is properly regional. This one, say, has to be dismissed because it's not regional enough. We do generally find one, not a very good one, that is about the Tyneside, or some district in Yorkshire or Gloucestershire.

Q: Is this something you consciously avoid when you write?

Hartley: I do. I generally write about London. I did write a novel about the Fens once, because I was brought up there. But it wasn't so much about the Fens as about my boyhood in the Fens.

171

Q: Why London? Aren't there grave disadvantages to a writer staying in London? Various distractions?

Hartley: Well, I suppose you do get interrupted by the telephone. It depends on what sort of ambience one can write best in. I have tried to go away and stay in a hotel where nobody knows where one is, or can get at one, but it hasn't worked very well. I think I perhaps want companionship every now and then. Angus Wilson, I'm sure, could write in any circumstances whatsoever. He's got such fluency of mind and pen. But I wouldn't like to shut myself up altogether like Hawthorne did under the eaves, for thirteen years.

Q: Thank you, Mr. Hartley.

Bill Hopkins

BILL HOPKINS was born in 1918 in Cardiff, South Wales, and was educated privately. He worked in journalism and publishing from 1946 to 1957. His first and only novel, *The Divine and the Decay* (1958), came under strong critical attack in the British press as an expression of neo-fascist sentiments. Associated with the Angries—especially with Colin Wilson—Hopkins faded from the literary scene in the early sixties and now deals in antiques.

The interview took place in Hopkins's London apartment.

Q: What is your impression of the literary machine, so to speak, in Great Britain: the methods of reviewing—or of getting reviewed—advertising, publishers' parties, publicity, all that kind of thing?

Hopkins: I do think it's a system. I think it's an almost inextricable part of how literary reputations have been made for the last two hundred years. That's probably the reason why literature, on the whole, has been so boring and stupid and futile: why it's been so repetitive. Because the people who are in literary society tend to encourage those who are very close to their own way of thinking. But, on the other hand, familiarity breeds contempt, so that most of the writers who have considerable reputations are fairly self-contemptuous. They turn on those who were their friends. I see them gathering in groups at cocktail parties. By "I see" I mean in the past tense: I saw. I was sickened by the whole society. I was, as you probably know, attacked by virtually every major reviewer in England, largely because I wasn't dependent on them in the

173

least. Of course, I was in a way dependent financially. I ran into a very bad time because of that, but I was tough and could make my living outside literature. As such, I just haven't mixed in literary society in recent years. They do phone me occasionally and ask me to go to a party. But I never go. Writers bore me and they bore themselves, I think.

Do I think most reputations are justified from this sort of circuit? No, I don't. But they know it themselves. The only time literary society becomes exciting and literature becomes front-page news is when some completely unknown person, with a sense of his own uniqueness, bursts through and isn't stopped. Eventually, they're all brought down, of course; they're tamed. Whether it's a good thing or not, I don't know. That depends on what humanity wishes for itself. If literature is going to be an entertaining medium, then it's a good thing if people can hear the same insane, humorous anecdotes again and again. But I think that literature is educational and revelational; therefore, people must come from the outside. It does seem, however, to be something of a problem that people aren't attracted to each other with the recognition of talent, not in literature.

Q: What should be the alternative?

Hopkins: Men with decent brains and curiosity about the unknown becoming publishers, turning their capital to publishing, and publishing only those people who interest them. I've got a very high estimate of public intelligence, and I think the public would always make a very interesting new book—one that was thinking along new lines—a best seller. This, I know, is very much a minority view.

Q: Would you abolish reviewing?

Hopkins: Yes, I would. Entirely. All the books that I publish in the future will not *ever* go out to reviewers. I don't want reviewers. I don't want money from my writing at all. I don't even want fame. I'm considering publishing under another name, and changing periodically.

I'm going to launch a new magazine with my own capital, which I've earned myself in the last four years. I'm going to form my own publishing company. I hope to buy my own theatre eventually. I think most creative people should do this, or else resign themselves to being in the hands of others. That's generally quite foolish.

I come from an extremely interesting family, and I've had an extremely interesting life myself. Virtually every generation in the last hundred years or so has produced men and women in public life. My father was a famous actor and he died penniless at forty-four. He was head of the bill at the Alhambra and at the Colosseum. I've been myself at the point where I've been quite famous, in the sense that I've been on the front pages of newspapers, not on the literary page. And I've seen just how worthless it all is, how all these awful publishers and editors approach me and try to get contributions because one's name is fashionable. As soon as one drops out, as I dropped out, then immediately one is deserted.

This is really, I think, what is maddening about America, where the talented men are brought down early. They're persuaded that they're terribly important when they know damned well they're not. I've had people in raptures about my work, but I've known it's absolute rubbish comparatively—you know, with what I'm going to do, I hope. People mislead one so. Literary society is really cancerous for that. My solution is solitude: to cultivate people who don't know that one happens to write, and to try, for God's sake, to sidestep any fame or any publicity at all.

It's very difficult. Incidentally, if you go back into old records about me, you'll find that ten years ago I held a completely opposite view. That was because I was very optimistic about people. I'm no longer optimistic about people at all. But I'm invincibly optimistic about a minority of people. Anything I write or create will have to be appreciated by a few people, and if they like it sufficiently, they'll talk to others, and gradually one will sell a few thousand copies. That will *mean* something. But this

175

business of a great crash of publicity, and an organized boom for a book, is pernicious, I think. When Colin Wilson wrote *The Outsider*, it was the equivalent, I suppose, of Byron writing *Childe Harold*: waking up one morning and finding himself famous. Well, I remember Colin in exactly the same situation, and remember saying to him then exactly the same thing, "There must be a complete reversal of this. Watch." He said, "Nonsense, nonsense. It must go on if I go on working like this." About six or eight months later, I was in Fleet Street in one of the pubs there, talking to John Raymond and a few of the others, and they told me that a hatchet job was being prepared for *Religion and the Rebel* before it even appeared.

Q: Since we're on Wilson, could you say something about your connection with the Angries?

Hopkins: Yes, I was instrumental in forming that group. I met virtually every major writer of that time in or around the environs of Soho. We fostered such an excitement, talking in all-night cafés—not restaurants, we never had any money. We used to exchange ideas with genuine excitement and passion. Someone would outline an idea for a story or a play or a poem, and we were all immensely critical, but constructively so. We gave each other significance, and it was no surprise to me that within two or three years we were all famous.

Let me strike a parallel in the arts. When William Blake went around, for a long time he was alone. Then one day he met a little, mediocre artist called Samuel Palmer. Well, Samuel Palmer was a virtual nonentity, but Blake struck him with a revelationary impact and from that moment on Samuel Palmer's work was completely transformed. Today he's rated one of the most exciting painters of his time, directly because of William Blake's influence.

I would say that when you have a company of people who are like-minded, and they're predominantly writers, then a stranger—a doctor, say—could enter their circle and become a writer. If anyone has participated in a circle like that, as I have, then everything is inevitable from it. My feeling would be, though, to try to cut this ghastly cancerous misunderstanding of the great majority of people that they're unimportant. They all think that someone is great, therefore they're small; instead of thinking they too could be great. If they had a sense of significance and self-belief, they could inject it into others. And soon, between them, they could all become creative. In fact, the arts as such only exist by default of the majority, I'm afraid. I don't know how long the majority are going to endure this form of robbery. As the capitalists were once said to have robbed the poor, so I think the so-called artists of today have robbed most people of the understanding that they too have the same talent, though not the same opportunity.

Q: Did the Angries have something in common, something besides, say, meeting at the same cafés? Did you have similar ideas, and, if you did, what were the sources of those ideas?

Hopkins: There was no similarity of ideas as such. Writers automatically come together and like each other, because they're the rare ones with the feeling of significance. I never had anything in common with John Osborne, never had anything in common with someone like Stuart Holroyd, never had something in common with Peter Hastings, but we all, when we met, understood one another, and shrugged at the differences. It was nice that there were others working, even if the ideas were completely contradictory and, in fact, destructive to one's own.

That's what draws people together. If you were writing a book which you thought terribly exciting and original, but fraught with difficulties, you'd be likely to say to me, "Well, what should I do with this? This is the problem, and what would you do in this circumstance, with this character and this character and this character?" Now, you wouldn't be interested in my ideas as such; you'd be interested in talking aloud and bouncing your ideas back off me. As another writer, I would understand this perfectly. So I would try to provoke you, in conversation, to try to spring the ideas in you. I know that I couldn't suggest the ideas to you, because you'd reject them. We all reject ideas. The more convinced we are of something, the blinder we become. You know, the path of intelligence is contrary to the path of creation. So I would throw ideas around, deliberately trying to provoke you into saying, "No. That isn't the way it is at all. No. This is the way it should be. How can you say that, if this person is in this position. As I see it, this is the only thing that can happen to him." Already, as soon as you've said that, you've seen the way ahead for your own book. I was necessary, but in fact the work was entirely your own. That's the way circles *do* work, and I can't see them working in any other way. Wives are useless, and girl friends, because all they do is say, "Yes, dear. Delightful! How original, dear. Oh, that will startle people!" Absolutely hopeless! As a claque is hopeless. But the Angries as a group had basically nothing in common, except that we all knew the frightful loneliness of creating.

Q: Didn't you have in common the fact that you were angry, or was that simply part of the publicity?

Hopkins: We were never angry. I mean, if we were to reverse positions, and I were to start questioning you, your ideas would emerge as positive and someone might well coin the description "angry" about you. But you wouldn't be angry at all! It's simply that you were talking passionately. I always thought this angry business was rubbish, because I was never angry about anything or anyone.

I was brought up quite differently from most people, by a family which believed each of us was unique. I was expected to be famous. I was brought up with that idea. I remember as a child, crossing Westminster bridge and seeing on the newspaper placards that my father had died, and I thought everyone's father's death was announced in this fashion. I was brought up to believe I was highly significant and I've always carried this around with me. I think that's probably the rapport that's generally made me the center of the circles in which I moved.

It's worth analyzing this, because it's important, not for me or for this generation, but for future generations—how these things can be possibly artificially created in a society.

Q: Do any of these circles exist now?

Hopkins: It's much more difficult now. Because a cup of tea or a cup of coffee is much more expensive. Nowadays they don't like people sitting in a café for hours; they want to take away your empty cup and replace it with another. Rent is much more.

Q: But then there's the British Arts Council, ready to step in with bursaries and grants-in-aid.

Hopkins: They don't mean a thing. You see, they only offer bursaries and grants to people without any pride. Any man who's original in his thinking wouldn't accept help from anyone. I've never at any time had any help, nor wanted help. In fact, any offers of that sort, I rejected.

Q: Of course, there is the tradition of patronage by the aristocracy. Couldn't the Arts Council be viewed as a substitute for that?

Hopkins: No, that's all gone. The Arts Council gives money to the completely wrong people. I won't name names, but all the grants and bursaries I've seen handed out were a waste of public money. In fact, I don't see why writers should have ratepayers' money. We're enemies of the state, basically; we intend to change the state—I mean, those of us who are significant. If we're entertainers, for Christ's sake entertain so well that you get your money. If I needed money so desperately, I should take a guitar—and I can't play one—and make a spectacle of myself outside cinema queues to earn money. But I certainly wouldn't ask another man for it, and certainly not from the state. It's illogical. How can I, wanting to change everything, ask for a grant from the state?

Q: On the other hand, shouldn't the state want to keep its creative people in touch with itself, channel their energies so as to help rather than harm the state?

The Writer's Place

Hopkins: No, I don't think so. Established people, bodies, institutions are quite comfortable without change, thank you very much. Merchants of change are definitely not acceptable and shouldn't be acceptable. After all, if you're one of the "haves" what the hell is the point of listening to the "have-nots"?

Q: Well, if you don't listen to them, they may gather sufficient force to overwhelm you.

Hopkins: You mean, a state that allows bursaries and grants in the way of Hyde Park Corner? A place where if you let off steam, there'll be no revolution? Ah, yes. In that case, it's up to every artist not to accept a grant in order to build the dam up higher till it bursts with a bang.

I don't think the arts should be helped. Writers should be so exciting that people clamor to give them money. And they should refuse. If you've got something new to say, you need no help.

Q: Then the writer's born, not made?

Hopkins: No, I think the writer's made. Most people so neglect themselves, it's astonishing when a few cultivate themselves a little more and become artists. And once they succeed and they're on a silver platter, they find they're all alone, terribly alone.

My mother used to say to me, "You shouldn't think so much. It's dangerous." I used to smile at that and think that this, in a phrase, is the epitaph of the adult world. They never dared go too far. They were cowards. But now I see what she meant. I think that the weak, when they are very weak, must be safeguarded. I don't like them, don't misunderstand me. I'm not a humanist, but I think the weak should be left with Catholicism or with any other orthodoxy to give them happiness and security. My interest is only in the minority, who will be alone and will go alone.

My ideas are polysemous. That's how I would describe them anyway. The *Twentieth Century* magazine described me as "the dark angel of English literature," and *The Observer* called me "a future dictator."

Am I a right-winger? I love the past, I love England, I'm a

patriot, I'm a royalist, I'm all sorts of ridiculous, insolent, arrogant, anachronistic things. But right wing? I think not, somehow. Nothing to do with a group.

Q: To move on to something different—or is it?—what did you mean to suggest by the ending of *The Divine and the Decay*?

Hopkins: That if you believe strongly enough, you can change the objective world. I know that's insanity.

Q: You said originally that you planned a continuation of the novel, that it would be part of a cycle. What were you thinking of following it up with? A Utopia? Some kind of revised *Also Sprach Zarathustra*?

Hopkins: It would certainly lead to very ecstatic understanding, which I don't think would be acceptable at this moment. But times are changing. When I wrote that book, I was attacked, as you know, as a fascist and everything else by the left wing. It was so exasperating for this to be seen in a political sense. Maddening. Particularly maddening that the mystical understanding was so overlooked. Now I hope to write another book which will go even further.

But first I had to attend to the financial realities. The fact of the matter is that, after that book, I should have brought out another immediately, *Time of Totality*. I don't know if it was reported in America, but my house caught fire and I lost *Time of Totality* and a play, *The Titans*, which was just about to go to a theatre. I lost everything. That put me in trouble. I just wasn't up to writing them again. I had no money, my name was mud, I was tied to a contract with a left-wing publisher, a millionaire who supported *Tribune* magazine which was attacking me with every issue. He hated my ideas. God knows why he took me on. He never released me from my contract, and I wouldn't write another word for him. I was really in a terrible situation.

Q: To come back to what you were saying earlier about the absence of successors to the Angries. Is this really attributable only to economics?

The Writer's Place

Hopkins: Yes, economics does come heavily into it. It's impossible to live now as we used to live, on three or four pounds a week. Secondly, any really creative person needs a long period of incubation, of solitude. Before you can go to people, you've got to have gone into the wilderness. In times when a reputation can be achieved by a pop-singer singing one song and immediately becoming world-famous, then I don't think there's much of a temptation for a writer to endure the long grinding years of formation, if it's money or fame they're after.

Q: What about the writer who lets himself be supported by a university, as poet or playwright or novelist in residence?

Hopkins: I think universities ought to keep away from literature—unless universities are *producing* writers. Literature should not be a form of snobbery, and I am afraid it is at the moment. You know, who knows whom?

I've turned down money offers from universities to lecture. But to my shame, when I was very broke, I sold some of my old manuscripts to a university in America, Texas I think. I certainly wouldn't do it again.

As far as I'm concerned, a writer is basically a vagabond. The only commerce he has is ideas. It's wrong to give him any kind of authority; it persuades him he's important. I've been more reviled than most writers, and it's done me a power of good. It's increased my willpower, it's made me redefine my understanding of being an alien in society, it's increased my powers for survival.

Q: Thank you, Mr. Hopkins.

Richard Hughes

RICHARD HUGHES was born in 1900 and educated at Charterhouse and Oriel College, Oxford. He is married to Frances Bazley and has five children. The London production of his first play, *The Sisters' Tragedy* (1922), brought him early to the notice of critics, but his reputation was only established with *A High Wind in Jamaica* (1929). He has also written short stories, poems, children's stories, history, and radio and screen plays. He is now at work on the third volume of his massive serial novel, *The Human Predicament*, the first two volumes of which are *The Fox in the Attic* (1961) and *The Wooden Shepherdess* (1973).

The interview took place in Hughes's home in Talsarnau, Wales.

Q: Looking at English literature of the teens and twenties, I am struck by how many major writers knew each other intimately. Part of the reason for this seems to have been that they met through literary hostesses, especially Ottoline Morrell.

Hughes: Yes. But I myself didn't know Ottoline Morrell well, I only went to Garsington a couple of times when I was an undergraduate. The place I knew best while I was at Oxford was Masefield's house on Boars Hill. I used to go out there pretty well once a week and met a lot of other people there—other writers.

Q: Did this experience help you?

Hughes: Tremendously, as a young writer myself. Masefield and

183

The Writer's Place

Robert Graves particularly—who was more nearly my contemporary of course—helped me. Masefield was incredibly patient with reading and commenting on young writers' work. And Graves was always discussing technique, but when I say technique I mean psychological technique more than anything else: what happens inside a poet, what makes the poem.

Q: Did he also read your work? Or only Masefield?

Hughes: Oh yes, both. At that time I was mostly writing verse.

Q: Did you read his work as well, and comment on it?

Hughes: Yes: but I took a lot of notice of what *he* said, whereas I don't think he took any of what I said. After all, although we had overlapped at school by a year he was an established poet by the time I became an undergraduate. He had a wife and two children by that time, and had been away at the war.

Q: If you had gone to, say, Bristol instead of Oxford, would it have changed your career appreciably?

Hughes: I'm sure it would. I didn't get much academic education at all; I wasn't really looking for it. I got mine mostly from Masefield, and Graves. Then Yeats came and lived at Oxford for about a year while I was up. And there were others: Blunden was then an undergraduate, and Alan Porter and David Cecil.

Q: Do you think that the fact that other writers were at the same place where you were, at the time when you were beginning to write, was important?

Hughes: Oh, very. You see, that was while one was still trying to find one's feet and get one's ideas. Then I wrote a one-act play, which Masefield had performed in his drawing room: he sent it to Sybil Thorndike, and it got put on in London while I still was an undergraduate. I was also writing regularly then for two London weeklies and for the *Manchester Guardian*—book reviews, mostly, but also poems and short stories.

Q: Do you think that Oxford and perhaps to a lesser extent Cambridge still perform a similar function?

Hughes: I'm told they don't. Everybody's much more tied to the academic treadmill now then they used to be.

Q: How do you mean that?

Hughes: Well, I mean that it matters much more today what exams you pass and what Honours you get. I went up with a scholarship at Oriel and a school exhibition, with which record normally you would be expected to get a First. I got a Fourth! As I said, I was working entirely for myself as a budding writer and not for my exams. In fact I got a Double Fourth, an almost unknown degree—like two outers on the dart board.

Q: But once you moved away from Oxford and London, didn't you miss the chance to talk to people like Graves and Masefield about your work?

Hughes: When we first married, in the early thirties, we lived in South Wales, at Laugharne. Dylan Thomas was just beginning to write then, and shortly after we went to Laugharne he came and lived there—at times, with us. I saw a great deal of him and his friends. So at any rate during that time there was no lack of colleagues to talk to.

Q: Was *High Wind in Jamaica* affected in any way by this?

Hughes: High Wind in Jamaica was written long before! I finished that in the States in '28 and it was published in '29. I started it on an Adriatic island, did a bit more in London, a bit more in North Wales, and finished it in Connecticut: that is why it was published in America before it was published in England.

Q: Did you feel a need to talk about what you were doing when you were writing *High Wind in Jamaica*?

Hughes: It's difficult to think back all that time. Perhaps to some extent I did. And great friends were the Williams-Ellises, Clough and his wife Annabel who lived about five miles over that way. (*pointing out of the window*) She was then literary editor of the *Spectator*.

Q: Was this also the case with *Fox in the Attic*? I notice at the end of *Fox in the Attic* you have a note thanking a number of people for reading the manuscript. Was this simply a perfunctory reading, or was it real criticism?

Hughes: Well, that was largely, of course—since it is a historical novel—to check up on a lot of historical details. But, oh, various people read earlier drafts and commented usefully, particularly our eldest daughter.

Q: But you didn't discuss it in quite the same way as, say, you discussed your early work with Graves or Masefield?

Hughes: Well no, because when one is maturer one doesn't need to do that quite so much. I mean, what you really need is a reader's-eye view of it; and that is almost better got from a nonwriter than from a writer. I've always taken the opportunity of getting somebody intelligent who isn't himself a writer to say how my early drafts strike them.

Q: When *Fox in the Attic* appeared in 1961 there was a good deal of comment about your returning once more to the novel. *In Hazard* had been published in 1938: why did you cease writing novels for so long a period of time?

Hughes: Well, there was a war . . . I'd finished *High Wind in Jamaica* in '28; my second novel came out in '38 (it took me about five years to write, but there had been an aborted one in between, which I scrapped). Then came the war. During the war I was seized by a very strong conviction that to live through those times and not make them my main theme was—rather wasteful. But of course I had to let it recede into perspective and not start writing about it at once. In fact I waited ten years. Meanwhile, however, my pen had got so rusty during the war that I started off as in the beginning again by doing book reviews: then took to filmscript writing for Ealing Studios (which I enjoyed enormously). I actually started writing *Fox in the Attic* about '54, I think it was. I soon found that, whereas I'd originally intended simply to write a novel about the war, I needed to go back to the very beginnings of Nazism: thus as it progressed I came to realize that my project as a whole must turn into a very long book indeed. My two previous novels had been very short, but this one would have to be published volume by volume. *Fox in the Attic* came out in '61, and I've been working on the second volume, *The Wooden Shepherdess*, ever since. I've done about two-thirds of it now.*

Q: Do you work according to a time schedule of some sort?

Hughes: Well, let's see. I begin after breakfast and go on till I'm tired, not always stopping for lunch. Then I generally go out for a couple of hours, come back, and do a bit more. But I only do a six-day week: I always take Sunday off, because if I don't I'm not much good the next week.

Q: Do you do a great deal of revision on the manuscript?

Hughes: A tremendous lot. And I do it as I go along. I always feel I've got to get a chapter into more or less final shape before I can really know what the next chapter ought to be.

Q: Did you have the whole of *The Human Condition* plotted out when you began *Fox in the Attic*?

Hughes: Absolutely not. I'm tied to historical events, on that side of it; but on the fictional side I never know from one chapter to the next what's going to happen. The most unexpected things can happen. That's one reason why I've got to get a chapter more or less final before I can go on to the next one.

Q: How do you fix on your characters? The Welsh characters, or the German characters?

Hughes: They grow. I started writing that first page of *Fox in the Attic* while sitting in the garden of an inn in Spain. It was a very hot

*The Wooden Shepherdess was published in 1973. (Ed.)

day, so I started writing about cool Welsh weather. Then I saw those two figures approaching and suddenly realized with considerable shock that one of them was carrying a dead child. The whole story just sort of grew from that. I didn't know who the two figures were, as I saw them approaching! I had no idea that one of them was going to become my central character.

Q: Is this the way you normally approach a story, eidetically? *High Wind in Jamaica* as well?

Hughes: Yes. For instance, in *High Wind in Jamaica* I wrote a scene where the children are up in a warehouse watching a cow being hauled up for a nativity play. Then I stuck. The boy was at a window, looking out. For three weeks I couldn't write a word. Then I sat down—and he fell out the window. Some critics said how cleverly I'd kept the surprise—no wonder, for it had surprised me! (*laughter*) Likewise in the volume I'm writing now I've described a slightly farcical hunting scene, during a Boxing Day Meet—you know, not for serious hunting so much as for everybody to go out and try and follow. And somebody breaks her neck. I hadn't been expecting this to happen at all; but looking at it now, it seems to come just right after that particular slightly satirical description.

Q: Does this come to you as you're writing, or as you're walking and thinking?

Hughes: No, as I'm writing.

Q: When you walk, do you think out scenes in advance?

Hughes: No. No, it's all still going on of course in the bottom of one's mind, but mostly below the conscious level.

Q: So you try to put it out of your mind once you leave your desk?

Hughes: I don't *try* to put it out of my mind. What I'm mostly thinking about at the conscious level is revision. Yes, it's revision I'm thinking of, not ahead to new stuff.

Q: How far forward do you project *The Human Condition*?

Hughes: It will end with the end of the war. But at my present rate of progress I'll be about a hundred and twenty-two when I get there.

Q: Do you expect the second and third volumes to be about the same length as *Fox in the Attic*?

Hughes: Well, the second volume certainly will be. And there certainly will also be a fourth, there won't only be three.

Q: Do you plan to develop the German characters who appear in your first volume?

Hughes: Oh, yes.

Q: Did you find it difficult to describe a society that is not your own? Was it a particularly difficult problem to write about the German aristocracy at the end of the First World War?

Hughes: Well, in some ways I think it's easier if you don't know it too well.

Q: Are these characters that you had met at any point yourself?

Hughes: No. No, there is only one character in the whole of *Fox in the Attic* who was done from life, and that was the old coroner Dr. Brinley. I'd known him in South Wales before the war. He was an old man then and perpetually drunk: so by 1960 I thought he would have been long buried. When the book was already printed but not yet published, I went down there and asked someone and was told, "Oh no, he's still going strong." This gave me a frightful scare because the portrait was much too recognizable. So I dashed off down to the part where he lived, and found that fortunately he had died two years before at the age of ninety-four. *(laughter)* But he's the only one who was drawn from the life.

Q: Then you don't generally work from people that you have known yourself?

Hughes: No, I can't do that at all. After all, they've got their own life outside the novel—and you can't go altering that.

The Writer's Place

Q: What about autobiographical elements?

Hughes: Well, it is true that I make the central character exactly my own age; but then that is only because I wanted him to have been at the Oxford I knew myself. In general, when I'm remembering the atmosphere of a particular period, it's easier to remember it as seen by somebody of my own age during that period.

Q: So Augustine is not intended as an autobiographical character at all?

Hughes: I'm not and never have been a hereditary landowner.

Q: When you began writing at Oxford, you must have wondered if you could keep yourself alive by writing. Did this daunt you?

Hughes: Well, you see, I'd always known I must be a writer from when I was about six years old. I used to dictate little poems to my mother and make her write them down even before I could hold a pen myself. Short stories. When I reached my teens, however, everyone said that I'd never be able to make a living by writing. Of all things, I thought I'd be an Egyptologist for my bread and butter! But by the time I left Oxford, I was already making about 200 pounds a year out of writing. That seemed okay provided I kept down my standard of living. If you did that you were a free man: the gravest mistake I could commit would be to sell a story for a vast sum to some popular magazine and allow this to jack up my standard of living, thereby making myself the slave of my paymasters. So I settled in a primitive cottage in the Welsh hills where I could manage very reasonably on that couple of hundred: no water laid on, no drainage, no road even—but my rent was five pounds a year, home-cured bacon about one-and-sixpence a pound and farmhouse butter much the same price, while eggs were a shilling a dozen. What else did I need?

Q: So your choice of Wales as your domicile was dictated by economic considerations?

Hughes: That's putting the economic cart before the emotional

Richard Hughes

horse. I was of Welsh extraction. Though born and educated in England, ever since childhood I had felt a visit to Wales was coming *home*: at school it was Wales I was homesick for, never Surrey, and my greatest ambition was to settle in Wales as soon as I was a free agent. I must have been a kind of throwback: in spite of my upbringing and in spite of much English blood in my veins, in spite of English being my mother tongue and the language I wrote in, I felt I was Welsh to the fingertips. Then I got involved with A. O. Roberts (also just down from Oxford) in founding "The Portmadoc Players," a local dramatic company we hoped might prove the germ one day of a Welsh Abbey Theatre. Our first production was a triple bill with one play by A. O. Roberts, one by J. O. Francis, and one of my own. We were only amateurs, but Nigel Playfair happened to see the performance and offered us the Lyric Theatre Hammersmith for a series of matinees before London audiences—at a time when Londoners knew more about Zulus than they knew about Welshmen. However, I gave up playwriting altogether when I was twenty-four.

Q: Why?

Hughes: Several reasons. One was shyness: I was scared stiff by the extrovert manners of stage people. Again, you may make a fortune by playwriting but you can't make a living. More fundamentally, I wanted direct contact with my audience instead of having to pierce the barrier of a cast of actors. Moreover I was beginning to feel mature enough to attempt writing novels—something inadvisable when you are very young and you yourself are changing so fast that anything taking so long to write as a novel is bound to lack consistency. I had forbidden myself to attempt a novel till I was at least twenty-five—and in fact *High Wind in Jamaica* took three years to write. When that appeared it was an immediate success in Europe: much more immediate than in America, where it was a slow starter, though by now it has sold three-quarters of a million copies there.

Q: You mentioned earlier that you enjoyed writing film scripts. Did you find this at all similar to writing for the theatre?

191

Hughes: Yes. Oh yes, it was using that same sort of dormant faculty, I suppose. But the sad thing in the end was that I spent two years working on a script which I had written from the word go—I mean, it was my own theme and everything, they'd simply allotted a producer and a director to it and we worked together on it. Then Ealing Studios went bust just when it was ready to go into production, so it's never been produced.

Q: Have you tried to market it elsewhere?

Hughes: The rights are theirs. And the studios, as buildings, were sold to the BBC.

Q: Has the BBC approached you about it?

Hughes: Well, it was a satirical farce with a political background: it would date very much. It was an anti-planning film, rather in the same spirit as *Passport to Pimlico*.

Q: Was writing a film script anything at all like writing a novel? Can the film do things that the novel cannot? I'm thinking, for example, of the very visual quality of the opening section of *The Fox in the Attic*.

Hughes: Yes, but in that case you're saying that the novelist *can* do it. In fact he can do it much more as he wants than the scriptwriter can.

Q: You don't see the film or television then as media that threaten the existence of the novel?

Hughes: I've never written for television. I used to write broadcast plays quite a lot, for radio—in fact I wrote the first radio play in the world. Six months later I tried to market it in New York. They said that the whole idea of plays which couldn't be seen might do for the English public, but the American public would never take to them. (*laughter*) No, that was a thing that the BBC was ahead of the States with.

Q: You wouldn't agree, then, with Marshall McLuhan, who sees a

Richard Hughes

nonliterary, not to say illiterate, age coming when books will be forgotten entirely?

Hughes: Well, I suppose that day may come. Still, I think that some of these revolutions don't turn out quite so revolutionary as they looked in the beginning. No doubt the McLuhans in the Homeric age were saying that the tribal bard declaiming aloud was finished and that in future everything would be written down. But the *Iliad* and *Odyssey* have survived nonetheless.

Q: Still, no new *Iliad*s and *Odyssey*s are being written. Isn't the novel in danger of becoming a monument; a very imposing monument perhaps, but not a living thing?

Hughes: Well, there's one thing which fiction can do, socially and psychologically, which no other form of writing can. That is to get inside somebody else and look out through his eyes. You can't do that in real life—even in married life. You can never become self-conscious with the other partner's own "I-ness." No other form of writing than the novel or the short story can do that. I admit that to some extent in watching a film or a play the audience may feel themselves inside a character, but not to anything like the extent as when one is reading a novel. This makes the novel socially very important because, whereas the humanist or the preacher can *tell* you that other people are persons and not things, they can't make you *experience* it. Only reading novels can make you experience it as a fact which gets down deep inside you: the others can only convey a rational conviction, psychologically superficial.

Q: You don't think that the film can convey it the same way fiction can?

Hughes: I don't think it can to the same extent. Look at the period of the great social reforms in the nineteenth century—the abolition of slavery, the revised penal code, all obviously fruits of the dawning recognition that other people were persons and not things: it's no accident that this was a period when more novels

193

were written and read than any other kind of book. Whereas now, of course, fiction is only one-fifth of the books published. I see that as a danger sign—even one marking the road to the gas ovens! The archetypal nonreader of fiction was Hitler.

Q: And yet he seemed to live in those vast fictions of his own?

Hughes: But that's a different thing; that's lies, not fiction. He certainly didn't read novels. The essence of tyranny is to treat people as things and not as persons: therefore the first thing it has to do is to chain up the novel, because its victims have got to learn to think of themselves as things and not as persons.

Q: Then what would you say of writers like Joyce Cary or Georges Simenon who claimed that they—at least in later life—had stopped reading novels altogether?

Hughes: Ah, but they were still writing them. It's the novelist who first gets inside the character: his aim is then to induce that same condition in the reader.

Q: Why does there have to be action in novels? Why do we need to have things happen? Why can't we just have a long series of reflections on a problem?

Hughes: You mean like Virginia Woolf? Forster complains about this, complains about having to have a story. Well, I think there are few questions that there's any one answer to. One answer perhaps is that nobody lives entirely in an intellectual vacuum: people are involved in action all their lives—I mean, at least as much action as you'll get in Jane Austen, let's say. Another is that the novel has got to interest the reader and I don't think the average reader would be held by something which was a purely philosophical discourse, by something like the dialogues of Plato.

Q: Well, this is Ortega y Gasset's argument, as well as Forster's. I guess what they're saying is: "Look what's happening to the novel. The really interesting novels seem suddenly to have lost all sense of action. What are the really interesting novels? Thomas Mann, Proust, Joyce. There isn't much action in these novels. If you look at *Zauberberg* there isn't much that's happened in it: long discourses on time, on disease, on aesthetic questions, on spiritualism. Or look at Dostoevsky for that matter."

Hughes: You can't say that there's no action in Dostoevsky's novels.

Q: But already less than, say, in Tolstoy.

Hughes: About Tolstoy, of course, people complain of the opposite: his digressions. Again I don't agree with that. No, you can't measure action entirely in terms of violence and sudden death. In a novel there's always action: it's simply that the scale of the action is different—it's in a different key, that's what changes. Personally, I'm always glad to use action. I think that anything which is going to be read by a large number of people has got to be like a club sandwich: there must be something to satisfy every taste if you bite through far enough. The continued popularity of Shakespeare doesn't mean that everybody in the audience is seeing at all the same play: it's a quite false assumption that there's some kind of common denominator which everybody likes in a Shakespeare play. *Hamlet* for instance. One boy sees a nice lot of stabbings and murders, royalty stomping about, grand clothes; Viennese professors see a subtle psychological dilemma; somebody else hears beautiful language beautifully spoken. And yet they're all watching the same play, *Hamlet*. I think the key to Shakespeare's universal appeal is that. Rather than any common denominator it's just the thickness and the variety of the sandwich.

Q: Do you find yourself deliberately making this kind of sandwich, with different ingredients for various possible readers?

Hughes: No, I don't think I would ever do these things consciously: for that always shows.

Q: You don't have any reader in mind then when you write, except yourself?

Hughes: No. As I have said, I get very different people to read my drafts; but that's more to tell me whether I have put the thing clearly or not.

Q: Have you changed anything that you considered significant because of a reader?

Hughes: Oh, yes. But nearly always the shape and the order in which passages come, that kind of thing—and particularly of course if they say, "This page is boring." Then I try to condense it a bit further.

Q: What do you think of so-called experimental novels which consciously avoid the concept of being boring, entertainment or non-entertainment? Are these novels under false pretenses?

Hughes: No. I don't think the fact of consciously avoiding it makes much difference: either it *is* boring, or it *isn't.* Indeed somebody may set out to be boring and yet be interesting—he's just deceiving himself, if he thinks he'll succeed in boring you. But I'm afraid it's much more often the other way around. Our youngest son, Owain, is more of an experimental novelist in your sense (he's just got his second book coming out this July, and is already busy on his third and fourth).

Q: The writer then has a duty to attempt to entertain as well as to instruct?

Hughes: Well, I don't think he has a "duty" to do either. I mean, you're making it all sound too conscious. You might say a hen has a "duty" to lay an egg; it just lays the egg, it doesn't do it as a matter of duty. It does it because it's got an uncomfortable feeling inside, which can best be relieved by extruding the uncomfortable object. And that's how writers work, surely—though perhaps the writer is a little more like a cuckoo than a hen, because he has to consider whether or not he can persuade some other bird to accept and hatch his egg.

Q: You implied earlier that if you write novels you needn't also read them. Could you elaborate on that?

Richard Hughes

Hughes: I don't see how anybody's got time to be a writer and also to be "well read." I mean the only well-read people, the really well-read ones, never have time to write a word, and vice versa.

Q: Do you try to keep up with new novels?

Hughes: I don't try to keep up. At the moment I'm reading *The Golden Bowl*. And the last book I read before that, I think, was the *Odyssey*. Before that some Proust.

Q: What fiction still interests you?

Hughes: Certainly Homer. Tolstoy, Stendhal, Murasaki—she was a most extraordinary phenomenon, I think.

Q: Have these works influenced your own writing?

Hughes: Well, I don't consciously try to imitate them, which would be rather hubristic anyway. But they've certainly had a great unconscious influence on me.

Q: In *The Fox in the Attic* you're setting out almost to draw a portrait of an age. Is there a literary background to that?

Hughes: Well, of course, the reviewers mostly mentioned Tolstoy.

Q: In what sense do you think that the novel can or should make use of history?

Hughes: The novel's attitude to reality is entirely different. History is a diagram of the interaction of objects: biography is a perspective portrait of one such separate object. Thus often both are abstractions from life: the novel is far nearer to life-as-it-is than either of them can get.

Q: And yet it's not "real," in the sense that it has not actually been lived. Did you find yourself, for example, in dealing with Hitler—at least according to the note at the end of the novel, where you mention Bullock and other historians—do you find that you're doing something in these passages that the historian can't?

The Writer's Place

Hughes: Well you see, in the passages where I've got him after the failure of the 1923 Munich Putsch, where I've got him hiding in a cottage with a dislocated shoulder, I've tried to get *inside* him just as much as I would with a purely fictional character. A biographer who did that would just not be writing biography, he'd be digressing into fiction. In Murasaki's *Tale of Genji* there's a discussion at one point about what the novelist can do that the historian can't. I haven't read it for years, but as I remember it was more or less the idea that the historian sets out events in an abstract diagrammatic form, whereas the novelist is moved by a conviction—I think I'm quoting rightly—that "the time must never come when people don't know that this is how things were." Only the novelist can do this, not the historian.

Q: Has your own work been influenced in any way by reviews?

Hughes: You mean by the reviews I got, or reviews I wrote?

Q: Both, possibly. And what do you think of the way reviewing is done nowadays in England?

Hughes: Reviewing at the present time is very much better in America. Much more thoughtful. Reviewing always suffers from a deadline. I found that even more true after the war than in the twenties: I'd be sent a book and given three days to read it, write on it, and get my finished copy in. Indeed I was lucky if I got three days; it might be twenty-four hours. Certain practiced reviewers can do this; their minds work very quickly: I can't, I am slow in arriving at a considered judgment, like with people; in the course of my life, everybody who's become a really close friend later on was somebody I disliked at first sight—perhaps it took a year before I could see any good in them at all. I think in the same way my first judgment of a book is all too likely to be a wrong one.

Q: Is your son having an easier time making a reputation than you did?

Hughes: No, I think he's having a more difficult time. But then I had made a certain reputation while I was still an undergraduate, so by the time *High Wind* came out editors in England—literary editors—would know my name and probably see that the book got reviewed. There isn't that sort of opportunity at Oxford now. Owain wrote his first novel when he was still at Oxford (though it didn't come out until after he went down): he knew no editors and had published nothing in magazines. He's now living in Paris and works three weeks in the month setting up exhibitions for a mobile sculptor—the kind who work largely in neon lighting and so on. Owain goes all over the world setting up these exhibitions for him, he's a very successful sculptor. Sorry, I said three weeks: he spends *one* week in the month doing that and makes enough money in that one week to live on for the rest of the month, and write.

Q: Judging from your own experience and that of your son, how would you compare the difficulties standing in the way of a beginning writer then and now?

Hughes: It was easier then, in the sense of there being recognized stages in the acquisition of a reputation in the twenties. Today, if a book comes out by somebody quite unknown, it's absolute touch and go whether it will get any reviews at all, or suddenly hit the jackpot. But in the past—well, take Dylan Thomas. He used to publish his poems in Geoffrey Grigson's *New Verse*, which made the reputation of Auden and Spender as well as Dylan Thomas and several others. Anybody who was interested in contemporary poetry always read the *New Verse*: so when a volume by any of the New Verse poets was announced those same people would buy it—if they liked that particular poet.

Q: There's nothing of the sort now?

Hughes: Well, yes. There is. This is poetry I'm talking about now. Yes, there's *Agenda*, and there's always *Encounter*, of course. *London Magazine* is more for short stories.

Q: Pamela Hansford Johnson said that back in the twenties and thirties a writer was known to the literary world in London even before he began to publish his first volume of verse or whatever.

199

Hughes: Yes. But that was largely *because* he would probably already have published verse in small wildcat magazines.

Q: Wasn't the judgment of the literary society a very personal one, not necessarily based on his work, but on other factors—on the promise that he showed as a person, perhaps, more than the promise of his work?

Hughes: Well, there were people one liked a lot better than one liked their work: this certainly didn't mean that therefore you would give them a good book review! On the other hand, you might get to know somebody well enough to think, "This is obviously a late developer. He's going to write good books one day: this first book of his really doesn't do him justice." At least to that extent the personal judgments could affect literary ones.

Q: What I meant more is that people knew him, and that therefore the chances of his work being reviewed were much better.

Hughes: I'd agree that his chances of being *considered* for review were better. While still at Oxford I succeeded Walter de la Mare as sole poetry reviewer on the *Saturday Westminster Gazette*: I'd be sent some thirty books every week, and only expected to review four or five of them. Naturally if I found a name I knew I looked at that one first. There were some you could almost tell by the smell they weren't going to be any good, but I never failed to read at least a few pages of each one of them—and the ones I chose out for review I read from cover to cover. But then, that editor didn't mind if I spent a fortnight over my article.

Q: Did any editor help you significantly when you were beginning?

Hughes: Yes. Desmond MacCarthy did. He was a most admirable editor and critic; he had that peculiar power of reading and writing quickly and apparently giving mature, informed judgments in about twenty-four hours. And he was tremendously helpful to any young person he thought promising. He gave up a whole issue of his magazine to publishing *High Wind in Jamaica* almost complete, and to have a well-known literary magazine suddenly drop all its usual features to produce just a single novel like that—well, it hit the public in the eye. I think that's one of the main reasons why the book was a best seller from the word go in England.

Q: Does the decay of the sense of place concern you? That novels now can and do take place anywhere, and that it seems impossible for someone to write a novel about England in the way that Dickens did in the *Pickwick Papers* and be taken seriously?

Hughes: Well, personally, I can't read Dickens. Never have been able to. I can't stand the unchanging characters: once a Dickens character has come on the stage and said his bit you know exactly what he's going to do and say on his next appearance. There's some brilliant writing in Dickens, but I can never get through a whole book for that reason. As for regionalism—I can't see how the subject or the milieu can either make or mar a novel by themselves.

Q: What about the growing nationalist, regionalist interest right here in Wales? Do you share this?

Hughes: In a way this isn't new: it's nostalgia for something that they've been losing over the last half-century. When I was a boy the central government didn't much affect people's lives here—the real government in Wales was the local chapel; the deacons of the local chapel could make or mar the lives of people in their congregations. They could also control county council elections. There was a very strong Puritan feeling in those days. When the Graveses first came to Harlech, back in the nineties, and bathed in the sea on a Sunday, the villagers threw stones at them as they came out of the water—and again, even in the twenties and thirties no Welsh farmer would get his hay in on a Sunday. It might be the only fine day of the week, but he wouldn't touch it. As I say, that was self-government, really. But beginning with the First World War the returning soldiers were not willing to put themselves so completely under the thumb of the local chapel any more and this progress has gone on progressing, of course, much more again after the Second War. Meanwhile the long arm of Westminster has got longer and longer and poked its interfering fingers further and further. So that really what they're trying for now is to get back something that they've been losing, not to get something new.

Q: You don't share the sense of belonging to Wales or the Welsh nationalist movement?

Hughes: I do, though, alas, it's only the English who call me Welsh, while the Welsh call me English. I'm disowned by both. (*laughter*)

Q: Do you think of yourself as a Welsh writer?

Hughes: Yes—or rather, what they call an Anglo-Welsh writer. That is, a Welshman writing in the English language—like Dylan Thomas, for instance.

Q: Can Anglo-Welsh writing be distinguished from English writing, or is that merely an artificial, self-conscious difference?

Hughes: What matters is what's under your skin. Writing is something that comes out of your whole personality: your personality is colored by your nationality. That's what makes the difference, not your subject. I used to be thought of as an entirely Anglo-Welsh writer because when I was writing plays, they all had a Welsh background: now in my novels there's been very little Welsh background, but I think that temperamentally there's a very Welsh feeling in them.

Q: Do you participate in any Welsh literary societies? Do you attempt to foster Anglo-Welsh writing?

Hughes: Well, I belong to the CYMMRODORION and I've joined an Anglo-Welsh branch of the Welsh Academy they've started: though I can't say I've been very active in either of them. I doubt if institutions can help much. There was once a very strong local Welsh culture, which with the best intentions in the world I think

202

has already been killed by the BBC. Before there was any BBC, people had to do everything themselves, and it was taken for granted that everybody could sing in parts unaccompanied. On the farm, when they were engaging a farmhand, one of the questions they'd ask him was whether he was a tenor or a bass, according to what they needed for the farm quartet. I can remember as a child waiting at a railway station for three hours for a train, and somebody simply walked up to the passengers waiting on the platform, asked them what their voices were, and got them in a line. They just sang part songs without music and unaccompanied until the train arrived—nearly missing it when it did come because they hadn't finished the verse.

Q: How do Welsh writers feel about Anglo-Welsh ones?

Hughes: I'm afraid the writers who write in Welsh tend to despise the Anglo-Welsh ones. There's been an attempt to break that down, but I think they feel that their own motives are pure because, after all, writing in Welsh is writing for a very small public—that Welshmen who write in English are doing it simply because they can make more money that way. I don't think it's a fair charge, but it's the way they're inclined to look at it.

Q: Is there any contact between the two groups?

Hughes: That's one of the reasons why the Welsh Academy set up a section for Anglo-Welsh writers as well as for Welsh ones. As I understood it, they were going to try to get them together more: but I don't know if anything much has happened so far. You see, Welsh is probably the oldest as well as the finest surviving literary language in Europe, with a continuous literature from the fifth century which has never been interrupted. You still get novels published in Welsh, but nobody, of course, makes very much money out of them and indeed the Welshman's main interest is in poetry, which follows very strict rules of what they call "tongue-music." Welsh poetry had reached a climax by the time of Chaucer: it would have either gone downhill from there or had to go out into new fields and so it invented this tongue-music, which I don't think any other language has. It's a very elaborate system of alliteration and assonance. So that even if you don't understand a word it *is* like listening to a piece of music. Nowadays of course Welsh poets use "free" meters too and thereby have achieved a quite outstanding new brilliance.

The Welsh have an astonishingly retentive cultural memory. There's a stone in the churchyard here with an inscription in Latin on it, the gravestone of the mother of the man who built the church before the Norman conquest of Wales. When I was young, there was an astonishing kind of folk-memory. I'd been to Italy, and an old woman when I got back said to me, "Did you go to Rome?" I said, yes. "Are they still as unkind to the Welsh there as they used to be?" I said I didn't think I'd been discriminated against for being Welsh. Then she grew very very dramatic, pointing to a certain road up in the hills and saying, "You know that old road up there? They built that road." I said, yes, it looked like a Roman road. "No, they did *not* build the road. They made *us* build the road and they have not yet paid us our wages." That's quite a time to remember a thing like that! Another time when I'd been down to Pembroke she said, "Oh yes, some of my mother's family have gone to live there." I said to her, oh, when did they go? "Oh, about the twelfth century." This keeping of pedigrees was tied up with the system of land tenure. Ours was originally a tribal society, and land was originally—before the Normans—held in common: the nominal owner was the prince but he redistributed it every twenty-five years. Any member of the tribe was entitled to five acres on which to build a house, and that would be freehold. He was entitled also to as much other land as he needed and could work, according to the size of his family. After twenty-five years that would all be reshuffled. But his five acres and his house would remain: he could sell that, but only to another member of the tribe—he couldn't sell it to a foreigner. So it became extremely important to be able to prove tribal descent. That's why they at first kept their pedigrees, and once having kept them they went on with it: so you get these thousand-year pedigrees at all levels of society.

Richard Hughes

Q: One of the striking things about modern British literature is its rootlessness, its desire, almost, to remove itself from Britain. Think of Lawrence, Huxley, Auden, Graves, Durrell, Nigel Dennis, or Anthony Burgess. Does the quality of the expatriate's writing suffer from the fact that he doesn't live in the home country anymore—that he can't dip his feet into the home water, so to speak?

Hughes: I don't see why it should, necessarily. Indeed it can be easier to write about some place one has never been to at all.

Q: Why?

Hughes: Because you've got to make it vivid to yourself first. You do that largely—at any rate, mentally—through language: so you're already half way toward making it vivid to your readers. Think of two old clubmen talking together, and one says, "Do you remember that night with old Charlie?" They both go off into fits of laughter. He hasn't said anything funny, and it's very boring for anybody overhearing it: for them it's amusing simply because they both knew old Charlie and how funny that night was. Likewise, if you know a country well, you think you can mention some place-name that conjures up something very vivid to yourself and that it's going to do the same for the reader who's never been there: whereas if you haven't been there either, you find out about the place and what is vivid about it; you have to make it vivid for yourself, and therefore, more easily I think, make it vivid to the reader. I'd never been to Jamaica when I wrote *High Wind in Jamaica*—just as I'd never been a little girl, which was equally important so far as that book was concerned.

Q: Of course, that's also a different period.

Hughes: Exactly. If I had been to Jamaica in my own lifetime I'd have committed more anachronisms.

Q: On the other hand, you had been to Germany when you wrote *The Fox in the Attic.*

The Writer's Place

Hughes: Germany I went to solely for the purpose of writing about it.

Q: So you had not been in Germany in the twenties or the thirties?

Hughes: Only once, for a few days: just driving through from Holland to Klagenfurt. I'd been in Central Europe, though: I'd been in the early twenties through Austria, and paddled a dinghy down the Danube from Vienna to Budapest.

Q: You don't agree, then, with the usual cliché that one has to write about one's own soul, about what one knows.

Hughes: As I said before, I think that writing comes from under the skin, not from what's under your nose.

Q: You think then that modern literature is essentially international, not regional?

Hughes: Well, it's regional in the sense that you yourself were born a regional chap. What is under your skin must be regional, and you won't alter that fact simply by traveling abroad.

Q: Is there anything else you can recall that helped you get started as a young writer?

Hughes: Not long after I left Oxford, a London publisher offered me a small fixed income provided he could have my first novel whenever it appeared. Then I fell ill, and wasn't able to work for some time: so actually that first novel was *High Wind in Jamaica*, which he didn't get until seven or eight years later. But he was quite calm and happy about it, and I'm glad to think it paid him in the end.

Q: That subsidy was enough to keep you?

Hughes: Along with what I was already making through book reviewing and amateur play royalties and so on.

Q: Do you subsidize your novels nowadays through articles and reviews?

Hughes: No, I don't write anything else now at all. I did that during the period just after the war simply in order to get the rust off my pen; but now—well, I've spent a couple of months writing an address which I had to give in New York,* but otherwise I've refused everything.

Q: Can one still make a living by writing novels exclusively?

Hughes: It would be a much better one if I wrote them a little faster. All three of my novels have never gone out of print, either in America or in England: the old ones still bring in small amounts, in addition to advances on the next one.

Q: In other words, one can still be a novelist without having to worry about writing for the films or TV?

Hughes: I should have thought so, *if* you keep down your standard of living. I've probably let mine get much higher than I should have, that's the only trouble.

Q: Would you have been grateful in the twenties for a British Arts Council grant, if those grants had existed?

Hughes: No, you see, the publisher then was the equivalent—though it was a debt against future royalties, of course. In those days publishers depended much more on their backlists than they do today. Chatto & Windus owned some of Stevenson and Ouida, and a number of other valuable "backlist" properties which just went on bringing in income for the publisher without the publisher having to do much about it. Charles Prentice, who was the head of the firm then, had the sound idea of investing some of the "backlist" income in new writers in the hope that they too would become his backlist one day. If he lost on some of them, he lost on some of them—that was part of the game. But publishers' backlists aren't anything like as valuable now, though I think it's partly the publishers' own fault in that they now concentrate their advertising always on this being the newest and the latest masterpiece, until they've gradually got the public to thinking that only new books should be read.

*To the American Academy of Arts and Letters. (Ed.)

They've killed their own goose with the golden eggs thereby.

Q: In the United States the universities, by requiring certain books in courses, say, on modern literature, do keep a great many older works selling in large quantities.

Hughes: Yes, it's frightening: I was very, very alarmed when I first found my books being used as set-books in examinations. There's nothing that can more put the reader against them for the rest of his life than that!

Q: Thank you, Mr. Hughes.

Pamela Hansford Johnson

PAMELA HANSFORD JOHNSON was born in London in 1912 and educated at the Clapham County Secondary School. She has been married twice: to Gordon Stewart, with whom she had two children; and to the novelist C. P. Snow, with whom she has one son. Aside from writing plays, novels, criticism, and sociology, she has done journalism and, occasionally, taught as a visiting professor of English. Among her best known novels are *This Bed Thy Centre* (1935), *A Summer to Decide* (1948), *An Impossible Marriage* (1954), *Night and Silence, Who Is Here?* (1963), and *The Honours Board* (1970).

The interview took place at Miss Johnson's home in London.

Q: What are some of the differences between the literary situation now, generally speaking, and that of the thirties and forties when you made your reputation?

Johnson: Well, back in the thirties it was very much easier for a first novelist to get going. I wouldn't like to be starting a writing career today. For one thing, the publisher's got to get back far more before he can really make a start at all. I know in the thirties, if you were a first novelist and you sold fifteen hundred copies, then your publisher was delighted with you. Well, he wouldn't be now. The publishers will tell you they want four thousand copies to get away. Personally I think that's a slight exaggeration, but it's very difficult indeed. There is such a flood of books. Very few have enough success to make a living at it, so more of them do something auxiliary, like writing for radio or television or working as journalists.

Q: Could one at that time actually make a living from selling fifteen hundred copies?

Johnson: Well, no, but it could keep you going. There was a sporting chance that you'd get known rather more easily, and with any luck you did make a living after a time.

Q: How many copies would one have to have sold in order to make a living? Were you able to manage?

Johnson: Well, I just scratched a living. I was very poor, but I just did do that. If you managed to sell about four thousand copies, you could live on it.

Q: Were there also other means of making yourself known then than there are now? I'm thinking, say, of the remains of the Bloomsbury circle.

Johnson: Yes, I'm inclined to think there were far more literary circles, not organized ones, but just young, aspiring writers getting together in the same pubs. And yes, they did know each other in very large groups, which I should say is far less common today. But of course there was the disadvantage that in those days you didn't have the benefit of getting known by television, which provides a new possibility of getting publicity. As for radio publicity, I haven't regarded that as particularly valuable at any time: in one ear and out the other.

Q: You haven't noticed any increase in sales following a radio broadcast?

Johnson: Well, I really can speak with some authority about that because I used to do a good deal of radio broadcasting about books. It struck me that even though I was bursting with enthusiasm I hardly sold a copy. I once said to one publisher that I liked a particular book very much and was going to give it all I had the following week and would he see what happened? When I rang him up he said nothing had happened. The only time I knew anything to happen was when I was reviewing a novel which dealt with deafness. That got an immense amount of interest because it was a special subject which interested many people. That did boost the book, but only because of the subject.

Q: Do you think that the possibility of talking about your own work in a circle, or talking about literary work in general, helped you in your own writing?

Johnson: Oh no, not a bit; or only as much as it helped me because I came to be known by people. I was known around in the way a lot of people got to be known around. Dylan Thomas was enormously known around before he was barely published. But talking to anybody about writing never did anybody any good. I never talk about mine, not if I can possibly avoid it. I just give my publisher a brief sketch of what I'm doing, and then I'm quiet. A lot of people, of course, exist on talking about the writing they never do.

We used to like to talk about other people's work, and then of course we were very serious. We'd sit down and have an enormous discussion about Blake or Pound. We'd have evenings on writers who were chosen sometimes deliberately, and at other times would arise fairly spontaneously. That was instructive and pleasant, but, as for being a help in one's own work, I don't think so.

Q: Do you regret the absence of this kind of literary circle today?

Johnson: Well, in the coarse-fibered terms of publicity they were very good indeed. I don't know whether they were in other terms. But the salons certainly did get names known, and devoted people like Lady Ottoline Morrell would see people got known. There's no doubt about that. Even Lawrence, who declared he couldn't stand the sight of her, was helped a great deal.

Q: What besides television and radio are, in your view, the means whereby writers get to be known now?

211

The Writer's Place

Johnson: Oh, all kinds of publicity: journalism on quite a wide scale. You see writers absolutely rushing to give their views on anything. They sign things; not that we didn't sign things enough all the way through the thirties, but that was when the political wave had got so strong that with most young people nothing could withstand it. I was quite as bad, or I'd rather say quite as good as anyone else.

Q: Do you feel that TV and radio are depriving the novel of good writers who might have otherwise gone into it?

Johnson: Yes, they are, just as the whole medium is undermining the reading of novels. It's taken a very long time to happen, you realize. When we first heard about radio and television, we all thought the novel would die and nobody would read again. Well to a surprising extent they provided a stimulus to the novel, and it didn't die. It went on. But now I think we are seeing the effects of less reading. There are enormous numbers of books published and very little seems to be read.

Q: Would you agree that the novel is reacting to the challenge of television on the one hand by becoming very intellectual, very consciously nonvisual, and on the other by trying to compete on the same terms as television, but with even more violence and pure narrative?

Johnson: Well, it's possible to say that both things do happen. There's a trend of writing novels with as little sensational content as possible, in which the interest is almost purely verbal. And then there's the other novel which apes TV and film, because the greater the sensation that's poured out, the more people really seem to need or to expect. I've seen a lot of writers whose names I won't mention, who have simply been ruined by attempting to follow this trend. Every time there's a new gust of violence they think they've got to be violent. So you get both things happening, with more success I should say for the ones who go the way of television and film.

212

Pamela Hansford Johnson

Q: In *On Iniquity* you deal with some of these problems. Did you at any time conceive of taking this material and putting it into a novel instead?

Johnson: No.

Q: Why not?

Johnson: Well, it would have been a revolting novel, since this is probably the most revolting case in English criminal history to begin with. A novel *was* written about it, by Emlyn Williams, extremely well done, in fact, though a little early in the day. But I wouldn't have thought of turning this into fiction, since I couldn't have made the social reflection I wanted to make. And I didn't want to write more about the case itself than was strictly necessary for the purposes of the book. I thought it would be very off-putting to a lot of people who I wanted to read my small book. Indeed, some people found it almost intolerable as it was.

Q: You don't think that the novel, then, can perform this kind of social function?

Johnson: Well, it can, of course. It can and it has all the way from Upton Sinclair's *Jungle* to thousands of others I could think of. But it all depends on what and for what purpose. You could take a case like that, you could write a novel that really did expose all the forces behind, as far as one knows them in a crime of this order. You could make it a valuable social document. Or you could use it for sensation's sake and make it a very nasty job of work. It depends which attitude you're going to take toward it.

In *On Iniquity* I wanted to ask a lot of questions and I wanted not to give answers. I was very particular about that. I wanted to ask if there is anything in the climate of our society that is driving certain people to act in this way, or making it more likely that they should, or even dictating or directing the manner in which they carry out what they want to do. I was just asking questions because I thought they were questions that needed answering. One can't do that in a novel.

213

The Writer's Place

Q: Have you always seen yourself as a writer who has a social function to perform?

Johnson: Only inasmuch as I believe in drawing character against the background of society, and not character in a vacuum. I don't want a character called K whom you know nothing about moving along in a sort of a fog without the reader knowing where it is or what it is. The social background is very important to me, but I wouldn't call myself a social novelist in that sense. I haven't always got an axe to grind, at least not a social axe to grind. If there are any axes, I hope they'll arrive out of the background quite naturally, almost without me thinking it through.

Q: In the last volume of the Dorothy Merlin series, you do deal with some of these same questions.

Johnson: Oh, I had an axe to grind there. I was dealing with the theatre of violence and just how revolting and absurd you can possibly get before somebody got up and thought it was time to stop. Certainly I had an axe. I made myself damned unpopular with it too.

Q: Is this the direction that you see yourself moving into, using the novel as social commentary?

Johnson: I suppose I am inclining that way, but without trying to give answers, or writing anything as violent as *Cork Street* is. I know it's quite a violent comedy. In my last book, *The Survival of the Fittest*, the social background was extremely important. There I wasn't attempting to give any answers; I was trying to say, this is what happens, and no more than that, trying to do it rather as Balzac did, by putting it all down and leaving the reader to find his conclusions. It's very interesting to think of Balzac, a right-wing Royalist, being enormously popular with Lenin and Marx—just for telling the truth. What I want to do is tell the truth, as far as I'm trying to write about society.

Q: What kind of novels do you read, and would you classify these novels generally as novels of social analysis or criticism? Would you agree with a definition of the novelist as a social analyst?

Johnson: Oh no, there's no compulsion for him to be anything of the sort, just to tell the truth. I love Proust more than any novelist who's ever written, but I regard him as so valuable, so compelling because he does give the effect of man on society and society on man. He does that all the time, representing their interaction, without which I don't feel a novel is of any great value.

Q: What truth do you think that the novel as a form can tell that other forms cannot?

Johnson: Well, the novel can tell the truth, the play can tell the truth, poetry can tell the truth—within its own framework—but biography really can't. The biographer has not got the liberty the novelist has, to try and look into people's minds. Or he's a bad biographer if he does. He's got to conjecture so much from the facts that he's tremendously bound down. Nothing is worse than the sort of novelist-biographer who's half a novelist and does the guesswork. Hence the novelist has much more chance of telling the truth about things, because he can invent them. After all, he's really only inventing from what he knows about himself in all kinds of phases. It's impossible to draw a character who's of any use if there isn't something of him in you. You can't invent outside yourself, or beyond your psychological potentialities, even though these may be things you would never do.

Q: Who would you say are the interesting novelists now?

Johnson: I can never answer a question like that very readily. It's such a very personal business, since there are obviously people who are "interesting" whom I can't stand. I don't think, however, that this is a great age of the novel. It obviously isn't like the mid-nineteenth century or even the beginning of this century. But then one must never expect art to be like that. Art goes in great big jumps, without consecutive history. You see it in painting, where Flemish painting collapsed and just went into the swamp, and now hardly exists. The same thing happened in Italy after the Renaissance, but it lasted very much longer there. Well, the same happens in the novel. I don't think myself that the eighteenth century in the novel was all that good a period. The novel, in my view, really began at the beginning of the nineteenth century.

Among the interesting novelists right now, there are, oddly enough, a lot of women. Margaret Drabble is an excellent writer, very intimate, with a very small range to which I think she's very wise to stick. I hope nobody's going to lead her off the path and tell her that she simply must write enormous set pieces. They won't suit her any more than they did Jane Austen. Iris Murdoch is an original *fantasiste*. Muriel Spark is still writing well. Olivia Manning continues to be grossly underrated.

But that's all I can say. I don't read—here I must be honest—anything like as many novels as I did. That's because I'm writing hard and I'm no longer a book reviewer. I was for seventeen years, and of course then I had to read and know everything. Then I could have given you a fluent answer at once, but now I have to cast around.

Q: Why do you think there has been this sudden influx of women writers?

Johnson: There's less prejudice against them in this art than in any other art at all. It's still residual a bit in some of the other arts, though not of course in acting or anything like that. The woman novelist has been free for so long. It's something they're in the habit of doing, and it doesn't seem peculiar. It's still peculiar for a woman to paint, and I'm rather inclined to think that though we have some admirable women painters, there isn't very much history behind them. You see, we weren't even allowed to go to life classes in the Academy schools until the latter half of the nineteenth century. The same I'm afraid must account for the extraordinary fact that women don't seem to write music. There's no reason why they shouldn't, but they don't or very few do. But they can and do write novels; it's just one of the feminine things, among others. Though there's no need for them to write particularly feminine books. I don't.

Q: Were you very conscious of the obstacles facing a woman when you began writing?

Johnson: Well, I don't think there ought to be any. Disregarding the so-called women's novels which are meant purely for women to read, I think that when a woman writer gets it well into her head that differences do not extend really to the emotions between the sexes, that everybody loves in the same way and hates in the same way, and is ambitious and nasty and hypocritical in exactly the same way, then I do not see any difficulty in making sex changes. In fact, nobody seems at all puzzled when men write beautifully about women. Why are they so puzzled when women write beautifully about men? Olivia Manning, for example, writes admirably about men. I write about men a lot; I write even through the eyes of men. I think this is all right: they don't turn out to be feminine creations.

Q: Do you feel that you met with practical obstacles that you might not have encountered as a male writer?

Johnson: Not really, at least very serious ones. Men do tend to congregate together more, so there may be a slight advantage in that. Women are not clubbable, for example; they're the most unclubbable of creatures, and all their clubs fail. But no, I shouldn't say I've been held back.

Q: What do you think of writers being more or less maintained by universities and using universities as their primary settings?

Johnson: I'm getting dreadfully tired of it. I don't think novels should be written for academics or that writers should write for writers; it makes it too narrow. But America has been awfully lucky to have patronage through the academies, awfully lucky. I've done some of this work myself in America. Americans are very generous in looking after their writers. We haven't done so at all, or only on a very small scale and that's why we're really down to BBC television and journalism. It would be very valuable to a lot of writers here if they had more university patronage. Whether it would drive them back on writing about university life the whole time, I don't know. I rather doubt it. Doing it rather reminds me of the very young writer who writes books entirely about himself and his years at school, and his family, and his first years at college, which they all do. Because they don't know anything else and they've nothing to write about. But it seems to me an odd thing to do persistently when you're a mature person, even if you do live on a campus. I know I did write a novel about a campus after I'd been on one, but whether I should continue to do that forever if I were always sitting on campuses I can't tell you. I doubt it.

Q: What is your opinion of the work of the British Arts Council?

Johnson: Oh, it's done some very valuable work indeed. Of course, one always has reservations and thinks sometimes it's done foolish things, but it has been extremely good in general, and the number of writers who pretty well owe their lives to the Arts Council is considerable. I know of one particularly grave case that I think the Arts Council's going to help—a poet who really is in desperate straits because of ill health. But of course the Arts Council is pretty small beer in comparison with what the universities can do for writers in the United States.

Q: What changes would you suggest society should adopt in supporting serious writers?

Johnson: Well, this is very unpopular, but I would advocate that society not concentrate on the very young writer too much. After all, they have got to make their own way to some extent, and they've got to prove that they've got more than one book in them. I'm very much against paying people for work that hasn't been started or for a finished half work, and I think it's probably dangerous to extend large bursaries to free writers from any other kind of work. Historically it's simply not true that a writer must devote himself exclusively to his craft. Dickens was doing plenty of other work when he started, Fielding was a J.P., Chaucer was comptroller of the Port of London, and Trollope, of course, worked in the post office most of his life. It is possible in one's young years to do this when one is still fresh and has the strength for it. It's also frightfully important, because if you're sent off to live only with other writers, then you get dreadfully ingrown, and the next thing you know you're writing books about writers. That is almost always fatal. Therefore I would be careful about dishing out too much to people who've only just begun to show themselves at all. On the other hand, I would help elderly writers who've done a lifetime's honorable work and obviously can't write any more. They do, to be sure, already get some help from the Arts Council and from the Royal Literary Fund, but we haven't anything like the money to help as we ought. Furthermore, I would also want to help writers in mid-career who have really produced several books and are now under a certain amount of strain; they could and should be released from this strain. I'd like to see more of that. But I'm really not for traveling scholarships to very young writers. Travel's broadening to the mind, perhaps, but it does nothing for literature.

Q: Do you think that the character of English literature in general has changed because of so many writers leaving England? For tax and other reasons? That the very English themes such as you find in Dickens's or Trollope's novels have disappeared from English literature altogether?

Johnson: I wouldn't say they had disappeared altogether. A lot of writers are still writing about the English scene: Angus Wilson conspicuously, who just stays here and does write about the English scene very interestingly. Margaret Drabble is, of course; Iris Murdoch is still writing about the English scene more or less. I don't think we tend to cut ourselves off, as you seem to think.

Q: Is writing about English people quite a different thing for you than writing about American people?

Johnson: Oh, it's terribly different, yes. I've only written one book set in the United States, and I was careful then to have it seen through the eyes of an Englishman; and I was also careful to have every bit of dialogue checked and double-checked by Americans. Our ears are not as good as we think they are, and there is the language difficulty. For example, there's the curious way that we'll use prepositions—quite differently. And then you suddenly find out, if you're an English writer, that no American really says "shall" and "should." These words seem to have left the language. There are all these difficulties which have to be checked. I would never write a novel seen through the eyes of someone whose nationality was not mine. If I were writing a novel about Belgium, and I know Belgium extremely well, I would never write it through the eyes of a Belgian, or I wouldn't write a novel seen through the eyes of an American. I'd be terrified I'd get it wrong.

Q: Do you think that the business of reviewing has changed appreciably since you stopped doing reviews regularly?

Johnson: Yes, it has. There have been very, very wide changes. For example, an awful lot of reviewing is now done fortnightly. Reviewers don't do it week after week after week for years, as they used to do. Well, it's very hard to get up any charisma if you do it intermittently like that. There isn't now any English reviewer with the ability to get a book going all on his own. Nobody. Not as Arnold Bennett used to do, or later and to a lesser extent, Howard Spring. This is partially because nobody really sits down to the job of novel reviewing as anything other than a chore. It's no longer regarded as a vocation, which to an extent it used to be, in Bennett's day certainly.

Q: Do reviews help the sales of books?

Johnson: Well they do—in a sense they do. If they all come together, they help very much indeed. If they're lengthy they help immensely. If they're good ones, so much the better. But even length is better than nothing. If a book is published on Thursday, it can be reviewed in all the weekend papers. By the time Monday comes your agony is pretty well over. You've got your reviews in, that is, if you're a writer whom one would review naturally when your book came out in any case. But one swallow won't make a summer; one brilliant review without a follow-up won't do the trick. Of course reviews help to sell. Somebody's got to direct people to the bookshop or the library.

Q: Are they the primary means of getting a book into the hands of readers?

Johnson: Oh yes. They're still the primary means. That's why they're still so important. One dreads them so much, and dreads their neglect more than anything.

Q: Do writers in England still know each other personally by and large?

Johnson: Oh, yes. It's very difficult to be writing long in this country and not know pretty well every other writer in it. There are disadvantages in this: it makes for a rather inbred literary society. It would be impossible at one time to go to the parties which the American cultural attaché used to give without meeting everybody you knew. Then of course you swap opinions, and if you meet your worst enemy you pretend you don't know him. We are very inbred. This has been seriously harmful in some ways. For instance, we've never been able to have a provincial literature, not really. There are perhaps a few books still being written about the provinces by people who've had the courage to live there. But, normally, when anyone does that and they get successful they're up to London as fast as their legs will carry them.

Q: You mentioned earlier that Dylan Thomas was already known in London before he had published poetry. Could you be more specific about that?

Johnson: He was very widely known in literary circles there when he had barely published anything. His extraordinary personality made him very rapidly known indeed.

Q: How does this work with a writer like Thomas coming from the provinces to London? How does he nose out the literary circles?

Johnson: Well, it was me in a sense to begin with, because I liked a poem he wrote, and wrote to him and said I liked it. So we had a friendship on paper for quite some time. Then he came up and stayed with us and gradually began to meet other people. Then he branched out and met still other people and so on. It's like throwing a pebble into the water.

Q: Is this generally, you think, the way a writer's reputation is made?

Johnson: It's the way it's done usually. You really have got to know people.

Q: Thank you, Miss Johnson.

Melvin Lasky

Melvin Lasky was born in New York City in 1920 and educated at the City College of New York and the University of Michigan. He is married to Brigitte Newiger and has two children. After serving during the war with the U.S. Army, he worked as a journalist and editor, first for the German literary monthly *Der Monat*, which he published and edited between 1946 and 1958, and then for *Encounter*, which he has co-edited since. His publications (in both German and English) reveal a remarkable range of interests: history, literature, travel, and sociology.

The interview took place in the editorial offices of *Encounter* in London.

Q: To begin with, how do you go about gathering and selecting what you print? Why, for example, do you solicit, as I assume you do, an essay on some subject or other from John Wain rather than from someone else?

Lasky: Well, obviously every intellectual or literary review has a circle of friends and regular contributors. Some of them may well be accidental. One hates to concede it, but it may well be because a man is your neighbor that he's appearing so often in the magazine. One likes to think, however, that there's an elective affinity of mind. There was a time when I didn't know John Wain. I had read a few reviews in the papers, looked at some of his poetry, read a book of his essays. At one time he was editing an

223

The Writer's Place

international literary annual, which was full of ideas and energy. It appeared to be competition as a rival publication; but instead of "beating" him, we "joined." He's been doing some of his best things for us, and I like to think it's because, like some other writers, he matches up with a certain atmosphere in the magazine. Lots of writers have to do casual journalism; but for a monthly review, where they can have four to six thousand words and where they know what they write isn't going to become a yellowed clipping—people can very easily consult it, go back five or ten years—they try to do their best.

What happens is that these people drop into the office; or we have a meal together; or we chat at a party. He tells me what's on his mind, I tell him what's on mine. Perhaps an idea or a suggestion emerges. We "solicit," I'd say, articles from Wain, but if I try to steer him on to something that he doesn't want to go into, of course, he'll say, "No, sorry, not for me." As a result, the magazine is 90 percent "solicited articles," in that sense: not one-way suggestions. They tell me what they're working on. I say fine: "Could we have it done this way rather than another way?" By that I don't mean altering the thesis or the argument; that's up to the author. I mean whether it should be a review article or whether he should scrap the idea of mentioning a lot of recent literature on the subject and simply expound his own views; they'll be relevant enough to what's being published. Possibly 10 percent of our articles come in casually. This manuscript here, for example. But from the pile on my desk, you can see we're absolutely overwhelmed.

As a little magazine, we only have a few offices, as you see, a couple of editors, a couple of assistant editors. Obviously there comes a point when you're absolutely all snarled up. We can handle twenty phone calls a day, thirty-five letters, and fifteen manuscripts. But if it turns out to be forty-five letters and eighteen manuscripts and thirty-two phone calls, well, then nothing ever gets done. Nevertheless, you have an obligation to read all of these things, a moral obligation. Otherwise you shouldn't be an editor, and you're being irresponsible to the

224

intellectual life. So you've got to read it all, and then of course you might always find a nugget. It's that old panhandle philosophy of '49. Who knows? Some great poet is not going to send four glittering lines. You don't find much gold. But you find funny people, you find interesting short story writers, and, occasionally, a young film critic or sharp-witted novel reviewer. You don't find them in the mature intellectual fields. You don't often find a philosophical article coming in from someone you've never heard of before.

Q: Do you send out these articles, or do you read them yourself? Or does an assistant editor?

Lasky: Well, everybody takes a crack at it. I'm a little tired by now, so I get it only if somebody else is really enthusiastic. All the stuff by somebody we know or on some subject we're terribly interested in—we'll all read that: my co-editor (Frank Kermode or Nigel Dennis or whoever it happens to be), myself, Goronwy Rees, and John Hall (our business manager who is a good poet and reads most of the poetry that comes in). Just yesterday a short story writer sent us a contribution which I thought was absolutely fascinating.

Q: Unsolicited?

Lasky: Yes, we once published something from him, so he had in that sense a standing invitation—every time he wanted to write something like this or something that would interest us, why, to send it along. Which he did. Well, anyway, this is a typical example of editorial policy. I just wrote a little note on it saying, "I found this like his previous story in *Encounter*, cryptically fascinating, full of satanic, if non-laughable jokes. I'm all for it. Very good to get away from straight old-style narrative." And Nigel Dennis said, "No. Try it on Goronwy Rees. Not my cup of tea. I feel there's a lot of this studied, modish form of melodrama floating about. Sort of dissociated pornography. But see what Rees thinks." The third comment is Rees's: "I'm for it." There's a feeling of "two to one" and now we'll go back to Nigel Dennis. If

The Writer's Place

he thinks this is against all principles and he wouldn't want to be associated with this story in the magazine, why we'll simply say, "Sorry, we can't publish it." In that sense, we don't work democratically, that two to one will carry the day. But he'll feel that if the two of us are for it, and he's against it, and he doesn't have violent feelings that this will disgrace literary standards, corrupt the young, and set Shakespeare spinning in his grave, why then we'll publish it.

Q: How active is Nigel Dennis in *Encounter*?

Lasky: He reads all the manuscripts, but doesn't commission as much as I do.

Q: But he lives in Malta, doesn't he?

Lasky: He's in Malta at the present moment, but he comes back and lives here. Last year he was here about six months; he comes into the office fairly regularly, and reads manuscripts, edits. He's a very professional editor; he can take a manuscript which is unreadable—and I can hardly believe my eyes, but by very careful cutting he transforms it. He worked for a long time in New York with *Time* magazine; he spent some fifteen years in America, I think.

Q: In *Sprightly Running*, John Wain talks about writing for *The Observer* and mentions that they cut out about one hundred words, crucial ones, from his article on the Soviet Union. Does *Encounter* ever do that kind of editing?

Lasky: In principle, I would say no. We'll argue about certain things, but I don't recall where, for that kind of political purpose, we ever made cuts. Wain went to the Soviet Union, and it was a very simple case of an ideological falling out. He's not a very political person—a warm, gay, funny, roustabout kind of fellow. He was horrified by the conversations which he had, found he was talking to gramophone records, and this was a great shock to him. He wanted to keep the experience as recorded, close to the way it was experienced. *The Observer* felt it was a bit too sharp and there

226

was the usual liberal-left dilemma about sounding reactionary or something of that kind. I remember how incensed he was.

No, I don't think we've ever had any such case. We get accused a lot of times of slanting. Many people say, "Oh, well, you don't have to cut anything out. You make sure you only get the writers that would never even think of writing a paragraph which you may want to cut out." Well, this is a hell of a joke, really, because we publish so many writers and so many different points of view. You can't tell these days whether somebody's going to be on the left of you or the right of you, whether he's going to be very political, very cynical, or whether he's going to be for the students, or down with the twentieth century. A man who had one point of view five, six, nine years ago might be changing that almost day to day in these turbulent times.

Q: Does *Encounter* have a recognizable political leaning?

Lasky: Yes, we definitely have political leanings, but we're interested in controversy. We're interested in debate. I published an article by a young Oxford don, Robert Skidelsky, some time ago. At dinner one evening, a friend of mine, who's a splendid, reactionary Tory, the deputy editor of the *Daily Telegraph*, a man who makes Gladstone and Disraeli look as if they were revolutionaries of the twenty-first century, told me he wanted to reply to it. Well, obviously, I gave him his two or three thousand words. We don't want to say we dissociate ourselves from that. There doesn't have to be that kind of giving-the-opposition-an-obvious-chance-to-come-back. In the present issue we have an article by an MP, a young Labour, socialist representative, a former don at an English university, quite intelligent; he's done a couple of pieces for us before, and this is a fairly wild piece. There must be a dozen things in it with which I not only violently disagree, but which I think are ridiculous—actually illogical and absurd. Especially in view of what he wrote just a paragraph before, which was also wild and ridiculous but in another sense. But, you see, the government and the party and he are presently in a great period of stress. If I'm going to get an article from him commenting on the London scene, I take it to be a documentation of this confusion. Anybody reading this will say (if he has my view of it), "Now I've got a real sense of how distressed and in what panic and disarray so many people are over the continuing series of blunders and especially the political unpopularity of a movement which had an overwhelming majority two or three years ago."

I remember the late Robert Oppenheimer, whose essays we often published, once sent me a manuscript. I was about to dispatch it to the printer, but there were half a dozen passages in it which struck me as excessive. He had a tendency—it gave him a very special, almost unearthly atmosphere and a certain obscurity—toward mystical eloquence. I thought he overdid it. And so three pieces of obscurity I cut out and left five others in. Six repetitions I cut out and left three in. So if someone were to come up and say, I think the author is really an obscure and sometimes repetitious, mystical writer, he could legitimately conclude that. But if I cut them all out, which I obviously couldn't do without the permission of the author, I'd be falsifying a document. People would conclude, "He's not at all obscure and repetitious. I've read many articles of his. He's clear as the sunlight in June." And that, of course, would be mistaken. So you must do a little "editing." But, without making it into a Hippocratic oath of fidelity, you try to help the author say what he wants to say, in the way that he wants to say it. The one rule we do have is never to change anything without the permission of an author. We never rewrite anything without checking it back to the author. Then of course you have the usual reactions that you'd get in a football team, or an orchestra, or a ladies' sewing club. Somebody will say, "Thank you very much; you were very helpful. I'll go along with you." And somebody will say, "Monstrous!" I remember I once got a terrifying cable from Colin McInnes, the novelist, when he saw his proof. It was one of the first articles I edited when I came to *Encounter* in 1958. He said, "REMOVE YOUR FLABBY SEMICOLONS. RESTORE MY SPLENDID

DASHES." The thing was full of dashes, all over. I thought semicolons would serve just as well.

We've lost some friendships. There is a distinguished man who's very close to the magazine, has written for us for years. A book of his comes out and you give it to some reviewer. You think maybe he'll be friendly, maybe he wouldn't be. He's an able, sensible fellow, he's not vicious, but he's not sycophantic either. He's a thoughtful person, let him do it. Let the dice roll, let the chips fall where they may. And he comes back, he's been in a foul mood, and he's done a review that's particularly nasty. Mr. So-and-so, the distinguished novelist, who has given and should be able to take, can't take. He doesn't talk to you for two years. This happens. I recall once having protested, "But our duty is to tens of thousands of readers out there, not to one author—not to any one author." Because once you get into that position of being cowardly, and start to trim, then it's an endless road to perdition. Then you're afraid of every telephone call, and you're afraid of every phrase you publish. You've got to let all your friends know—and everybody out there—that nobody is sacrosanct. If our review turns out to be hostile, you'll just have to grin and bear it. You'll have your chance to come back if you want to. Our pages are always open.

Q: Does the editorial staff on *Encounter* share a generally similar political view?

Lasky: Well, there aren't enough of us really. Actively involved here are Dennis, Goronwy Rees, and myself. I would say that Rees and I probably on politics are a bit closer to each other than to Nigel. We still have some good words to say for the socialist movement. I don't vote in this country, but Rees voted for the Labour party and has been a traditional Labour party supporter, albeit a very critical one. I've been close to the socialist movements, the social democratic movement of Germany, of France, such as it is in the United States, and especially here, the British Labour party. I would say that, along with most of my friends, the role we've always thought of ourselves as playing is to the left of center, and therefore closer to the Labour party than Nigel would be. This is also true of Professor Frank Kermode when he was here. Nigel, I would say, is more conservative than that, but he's not explicitly and ideologically political. His politics come out more in irony and indirection, rather than in frontal attacks. As for the contributors, it's difficult to say. I think most of them are somewhere a little to the left of center. Maurice Cranston does a lot of articles for us; he's liberal left, ethically liberal left. Under the pressure of the Maoist student revolt at the LSE, he's rapidly moving to what is called the right. Dennis Brogan, I suppose, would also be on the liberal left.

Q: Instead of publishing Cranston's essay on Marcuse, or Michael Beloff's essay on the LSE revolt, would you have considered bringing out an extremely left-wing account of what went on at LSE, or a favorable analysis of Marcuse?

Lasky: Probably not to begin with, no. We don't think that would constitute a sound, accurate, and truthful view of ideas and events, of what's going on. Whether I would be against publishing a critique from some revolutionary from the LSE to match Michael Beloff's on that—that's another question. I'd be very happy to have Mr. Robin Blackburn, who's been sacked from the LSE, who is a revolutionary Che Guevera–Castroite leader on the campus (no, not campus, but the asphalt jungle just around the corner). If he wanted to write a reply, we would never turn the piece down. We'd accept it. In fact, we sought that: equal time. That kind of principle is involved. But to initiate the thing, no; there are plenty of other journals where people can do their new left thing. I myself am critical of Marcuse's work. Most of our editors and contributors think of it as faddish, modish nonsense, and, sometimes, a fad and a mode which is thirty or forty years old. It's all very much like German Hegelian-Marxist philosophy of about 1930. Alas, American minds currently feel that that Weimar philosophy was great stuff.

Q: But you yourself would only criticize it?

Melvin Lasky

Lasky: Yes. We would only do a critique of this nonsense. There's no sense pretending, for all our open-mindedness, that we have no convictions whatsoever and are just interested in publishing "good stuff." On things on which we have less of an overview—say, an interpretation of some historical event—I would still read that with open eyes, on whether the work of Georges Lefebvre on the French Revolution represents the greatest achievement since Aulard and Mathiez, or whether it's merely the last dying embers of the great tradition. The French Revolution has to be completely reevaluated. Where there is no clear ideological principle, obviously one can be vaguer; one can be looser, more flexible. One hates to feel that one is superimposing any kind of a line, although one knows that one is if one's a little self-critical. That is, if I were to do an article on R. D. Laing, I know it would be a critical article. And if I were going to do an article on Michael Foucault, it would have to be a critical article. Why? It's less the political implications, I think. This tends to be a new orthodoxy; these tend to be the new idols of the marketplace. These are the new fads, and all the modishness goes to reading the latest Penguin by Laing on psychiatry, or Marcuse on sociology and philosophy, or Foucault (to the extent that he's being translated) on madness. All of that begins to take on a kind of a new closed system—which cries out for the reintroduction of a little critical controversy. And I think I would need to swim against the current. You know, somebody once did an analysis, a Ph.D. or a master's thesis, of the magazines that I've been editing over the last twenty years. That is, monthly magazines with eighty thousand words of all kinds of articles, and he discovered a very peculiar triad. He saw what I didn't quite realize, that I often had three different authors at three different times with three completely different approaches. He told me: The pattern is that on almost every subject and every important thinker it is as if you said, "First article, let's build him up—second article, let's tear him down—and the third article, let's reevaluate him." In a way I think that might well be the ideal intellectual approach, over a long period of time.

231

The Writer's Place

Q: Would it be fair to describe *Encounter* as having at one time been in the forefront of liberal journals, and now finding itself somehow left lagging behind by changing sentiment, which has moved much further to the left or the right? That now *Encounter* is in a place where it never expected to be, in the middle?

Lasky: Well, I don't like the word *behind*, because I don't think we move ahead and then get "behind." I don't think the history of our intellectual life moves in that linear way. To be in the middle somewhere, I think, is probably the most admirable place to be, particularly if you define the middle as the high ground. And what happens is that away from the high ground, both to the left and to the right, you move down into the swampland. This is what is happening at the moment. We're in an expansion of the intellectual swamps. With the cult of irrationality, with the cult of sloganeering, many people simply do not want to consider a problem. I can watch today gigantic parades and demonstrations which were inconceivable, especially in this moderate country, five or ten years ago. Ten thousand, twenty thousand kids marching up and down, past Marble Arch, all yelling, "*Revv-oh-loo-shun, Revv-oh-loo-shun.*" You know the scene. "Capitalism Means War," and all the rest. Well, I don't want to challenge completely the thesis that capitalism means war—capitalism does often mean war. But socialism often means war, communism often means war. If one's going to try to struggle for peace and prevent the world from blowing itself up, the first intellectual recognition has to be that there's just as much danger of war between the Soviet Union and Communist China as there is between the bourgeois West and the so-called socialist countries. There *was* just as much of a possible conflict between Albania and Yugoslavia, or Yugoslavia and all the rest of the Eastern bloc. This seems to me so elementary. What then, is the point of going around saying, "Capitalism Means War"? Or that the transcendence of capitalism is going to solve the problems of the alienation of work, of a class culture, of a stagnant economy? Well, it might and it might not. But certainly if you

232

argue rationally on the basis of evidence, you'd soon discover that we're living in a swampland of sloganeering. If the thing is going to be argued out, we want to play our role in the process of intellectual clarification. What's become old-fashioned is to think that the question is open, to try to marshal arguments while not screaming at the top of your voice, and not simply offering self-certifying theories and builtin systems for the analysis of society, aesthetics, and all the rest of it.

No doubt about it: there's been a tremendous move toward a recrudescence of Marxism, a reactivation of militance, a revival of the so-called New Left, although it's really an old left. If you're going to come out and wave red flags, and sing the International, and shout slogans in the most simple-minded way, like "*Ho-Ho-Ho Chi Minh!*" raise your hand in a clenched fist, then what else is it but old old left?

Q: Of course, it's Mao's Left.

Lasky: Yes, to some extent it's a Maoist Left. Well, when I was lecturing recently at the University of Chicago, I met a lot of the New Left fellows, at a very early stage of the SDS. They struck me as very bright, and very hopeful at the time. They gave me the Port Huron statement to read and I found it extremely interesting. For the first time, they were trying to look beyond certain shibboleths and trying to revivify older types of radical social analysis. I don't know how it happened, but that just disappeared somewhere along the line. They became infatuated with a certain cultural mode of action, a myth of violence. Possibly Georges Sorel's writings suggested the myth of the general strike on the campus. And with that new technology of protest, of seizing buildings and hoisting up flags, and changing the name of the Goethe University in Frankfurt to Karl Marx University, they think they've achieved something. They've achieved nothing. It's all a very strange world of symbolic action. But that means that there has been a tremendous loss of intellectuality. So far, I haven't seen any interesting books come out of it, I haven't seen any good poetry come out of it. Robert Lowell is a fine poet, but he doesn't write great poems on the subject of the causes for which he's been marching.

Q: But in some sense *Encounter* has participated in the politicalization of literature. *Encounter*, after all, has a mix of articles of social and political analysis, of fiction and literary criticism. Are these two groups kept distinct in *Encounter*, or do they wash over, the one into the other?

Lasky: Well, it all depends on whom I'm co-editing with. We all commission and we all take a look at the poetry, and the short stories, and the literary articles together. I've been over on the heavier side, the sociology, the philosophy, the politics, the world-wide reportage. Generally speaking, I think that we do want to have a common taste interfuse. So that if somebody's going to write an article on politics, it has to have a certain literary distinction, it has to have a certain intellectual character. You wouldn't want to have a dull deadhead article on some subject and to have the people who read you for your literary criticism say, "Is this the way they write about political and world affairs?" B. H. Haggin used to refer to music for the man who reads Hamlet. In *Encounter* it's got to be politics for the man who reads Hamlet, or a criticism of Shakespeare, for the man who knows Karl Marx and Nietzsche. This doesn't really signify politicalization of the literary intellegentsia; or if it has been that, the opposite process is equally discernible: that there has been an aesthetization of the political intelligentsia. And, of course, that only happens with the intellectuals in the middle of the spectrum. On the one side, there are the readers who are just interested in the literary articles and the abstruse essays and the philosophical material. They would love an article like the one on Wittgenstein, which was a tremendous success, although every reader must have had enormous difficulty following it; and it did take two or three readings on my part to know what every point really meant. On the other side, there are the people who would read us for a discussion of the Middle East, for a discussion of Soviet or Chinese foreign policy, for an article like Professor Nat Glazer's on the black dilemma in the United States, and would pay little attention to the others. I imagine they're in a 20 to 30 percent extreme, and in the middle there are the people who are interested in both. The extension of that middle ground is what one wants, but it would be Utopian to believe one will ever get an end to our own little "two-culture" problem. One of our distinguished political writers once came to me and said, "You're always talking about Henry James. I've never read a novel of his. Should I read one?" And, of course, in the old avantgarde days I would have thrown up my hands in horror. Here is a man whom I admire and he's never even read James, or Proust, or Kafka.

Q: Do you allow your reviewers to choose their books?

Lasky: We don't really review enough books, and we just do it on the basis of enthusiasm for something; then we'll come in and praise it. We won't do any logrolling for a friend. If the reviewer hates a book, he'll come in and say, I think this is being widely praised everywhere else, but it's a horrible or stupid or vicious book that will turn back the clock of human reason for fifty years. Well, then, go to it, go to it! But then, once again, I'm fairly confident he's not suggesting it to do somebody in, to play the old nasty literary game.

Q: Encounter, you would say, has a fundamentally rationalist, humanist, eighteenth-century approach to issues?

Lasky: If I may say so, I think it's Socratic; I think it's Athenian. This book which I have just ordered here: it's a great book which I read the other day; I just had to have it, the *History of the Royal Society* written in 1667, after the Royal Society was one year old. They consisted of some fifteen to twenty English intellectuals in London, who finally decided that Reason and Evidence were profoundly important. It was necessary to experiment (as Robert Boyle among them knew), to be inspired, to try to combine ideas with some imagination. But *reason* and *evidence* were going to be the new light of day. Subject every question to scrutiny, but don't come in with fancy and unsubstantiated conjectures—and apocalyptic passions, of which the world has had enough. Well, that was in the seventeenth century. And I think it's an ethos for all centuries. Some critics have said that we go in for the old writers, we don't go in for the new. But we don't make a fetish out of the new. I've often felt that if John Stuart Mill were still living up here in London, aged 143, and said, "Would you like an article next month?" why, I would say, "Fine, Mr. Mill. Any time at all." Would I care about his age—if he could still write the way he used to write for the *Westminster Review* a hundred, a hundred and twenty-five years ago? Those articles are just as fresh as any being written today.

Q: Does *Encounter*, in your view, exist in, as it were, a lonely splendor of the middle, or are there competing journals performing something of the same function? For example, the *TLS*, the *Observer*?

Lasky: No, here I think we're fairly much alone, because *TLS* is a book-reviewing journal, and a very good one. Most of its articles are anonymous, and therefore you get a kind of vague sense, and a very contradictory one, of the whole intellectual picture. On any one specific issue you'll get three violent judgments, all depending on who the anonymous reviewer happens to be, whether he's in this faction, or in that coterie. That makes it democratically eclectic; but it doesn't give a kind of general thrust, a general direction to the paper. The *Observer* is a Sunday newspaper; it runs two very good pages of literary book reviews, but it doesn't have a general view, which I think we attempt to have. In the United States, there are comparable journals.

Q: The *New York Review of Books*?

Lasky: Yes, the *New York Review of Books*, *Commentary*, *Partisan Review*. *Partisan Review* is the old mentor of us all, but it remained a little magazine of four or five thousand circulation, with very good pieces on Henry James, or Proust, or aspects of Negro history, or Camp, or what have you, but necessarily limited in its range. *Commentary* is also a general magazine, but its special interest in Jewish questions, being published by the American Jewish Committee, limits it a bit. Half an issue may be devoted to articles on problems on which you've already read thirty other articles and don't want to go ahead. But under Norman Podhoretz, and before him under Elliot Cohen, I think it has been brilliantly edited and is an excellent journal. The *New York Reivew of Books* is closer to what we were and probably are, given differences of political and literary politics. There's political politics, and literary politics, and of course, editorial politics, and all of the other attitudinizing to which the intelligentsia is addicted. Many people try to put it down by saying that they are publishing today what *Encounter* was doing ten or fifteen years ago. There's a long article by Isaiah Berlin on Herzen, and there's a long diary of Stravinsky, and the latest poems of Lowell and Auden: all things which we did, but they're very good things to do. If they want to do them, well, bless them. There's plenty of room for everybody. I would think that they're rougher and tougher. And I think—given our penchant for civility—we wouldn't want to be like that.

Q: They seem to be further left, too.

Lasky: Politically I would say they have been allying themselves in most cases with the New Left forces. But there's been a mass movement that way in the United States, whereas there hasn't been over here. We have no differences on the Negro issue. They'll have kinder words to say about Black Power militants, I think, than we would have to say about them. We didn't conduct any "campaign" on the matter, although we were critical of the Vietnam War; we published three or four articles on the subject, and, if you want to, left it at that. Privately, a man can go out and demonstrate, write to his senator, or his prime minister. That would be the difference, I think, of thrust, style, and type of writers. That's always been the case. In France there are people who want the *Nouvelle revue française*; there are people who used

The Writer's Place

to read nothing but Mauriac's *Table ronde*; and there are still people who go along with Sartre's *Temps modernes*. In Germany, too, there are excellent reviews—fine weekly reviews which fill pretty much the space that we want to.

Q: Would you compare yourself to something like *Die Zeit*?

Lasky: Die Zeit is probably closest to what we would be if they were a monthly; or if we were a weekly. That would be the type of thing closest to *Encounter*. In general, the international, liberal, humanist approach to issues of public interest.

Q: How many copies do you print?

Lasky: Well, we print something between thirty and forty thousand, depending on extra orders, and we sell roughly that—thirty-seven, thirty-eight thousand, with two or three thousand left over which get gobbled up by back number requests. And it sells out at that point at the end of the year, or at the end of a year and a half.

Q: Who do you think your readers are?

Lasky: Well, whoever is considered "intellectual." I imagine half of them are in the academic world and the other half in the journalistic world.

Q: How much of your printing is sent out to the United States?

Lasky: About a quarter. We're a very prominent little magazine in the United States. We sell on the average more than ten thousand copies every single month, which is more than most native little literary magazines.

Q: Academics buy most of these?

Lasky: Well yes, a great many copies go to the universities, but beyond that to architects, engineers, scientists. We once conducted a poll. It was an enormous scattering of 6 percents, 8 percents, 11 percents.

Q: How many members of Parliament read it?

Lasky: I would say there's a corps of several hundred.

Q: Does *Encounter* exercise an influence on the literary scene as well as on the political scene?

Lasky: Well, as Professor C. D. Broad used to say, it all depends. If a writer publishes an article in *Encounter*, he's likely to get—if it's outstanding—five or six letters from publishers who want to have books from him. He's likely to get an offer from a television studio to follow it up one way or another. He's likely to get a literary agent coming along with an offer. Not every article; but enough happens every single month that way. So you know that the journal is *seen*. If Michael Beloff does an article, he gets three or four requests from other editors. This becomes, then, a professional journal for the editors, and just as we are trying to meet, on a high-brow level, forty thousand readers, the people who have reviews for three hundred thousand or eight hundred thousand readers see this as a kind of an arsenal of ideas. This is the replacement depot, so to say, of the next wave of ideas. They go around picking things up. Obviously that's what I'm here for, that's what we're here for. We read the other papers and people come up and say, "Well, why haven't you published an article on this or that subject?" Well, the reason why we haven't is that the rest of the papers were full of it. There was nothing left to be said about certain issues. What's there left to be said? "Well, you have to do something about having a letter about de Gaulle or from Paris." What's left to be said about de Gaulle, after all the experts have ploughed the field? Who can still think up a profound remark? Just to waste another ten pages on "whither France?" and "what's going to happen now?" would seem to be a little silly. So we just eliminate a great many subjects that everybody else has to waste space on—other weeklies and dailies and other reviews, the *New Statesman* and whatnot—and just pick out those themes that we think are especially important, and have been neglected, or haven't been presented in this way before. In that sense, I do think we have influence. We also try to pick up crucial, underlying issues. I myself think that academic freedom in the universities in

The Writer's Place

most of the Western world is under siege. A word not merely for
the faculty but also for the overwhelming majority of the students
is needed. The so-called student movement is only a minority of
the students, and even in that minority there's a smaller minority
which is composed of ideological fanatics.

Q: One could say that for any movement, couldn't one? It's always
a minority.

Lasky: Yes, it's always a minority, but there are certain activities
which the minority legitimately engages in. If they're democratic
activities, they can be approved by other people. But if they're
faits accomplis, if they're acts of violence, then what can be done?
If sixty kids can close down the LSE and close out three thousand
students, well, you can always say, "Get the three thousand
students out and let them vote on this matter." But there's a
certain amount of inertia in society, and among young people
even greater than before; you just don't get three thousand
people coming out there. At Harvard you don't even get the full
faculty voting; you only get 40 or 50 percent. So minorities can act
in a civilizing and constructive fashion, and minorities can act in a
destructive fashion. I do think the accent now is on the
destructive. In my view we've had an influence in half a dozen
universities, because we were the only ones, now, for the last two
years, who have emphasized the international aspects of this
whole problem. You can't know what is happening in Columbia if
you don't know what's happening in Berlin. You can't
understand what Nanterre was all about, or what the LSE is all
about, if you don't see it in terms of the ideology, the slogans, the
arguments of the New Left. Every vice-chancellor and every
professor just begins to think about this problem when it hits his
own academic doorstep. He has precious little intellectual, or
international, curiosity. We have published reports from France,
from Italy, from Berlin, not once but a dozen times, in the last
years, keeping people up with it and giving people cross
references and, therefore, trying to extend their experience in

240

the hope that they'll be able to deal with this thing in a wiser, more intelligent, more humane way if they have their eyes and ears and minds open—instead of being narrow little administrators, who think the world is coming to an end. It might well be. But it's not coming to an end just because they think it is. And they think it is, if they get into a little spot of local trouble.

We've received a great amount of mail on these articles. On each one the bulk has been from educators and from professors and from university chancellors and presidents. I received one just now, from the vice-chancellor of a leading English university—and another from the president of an important American university—and both were saying that they have been going through our series of articles on the various aspects of the subject and, for the first time, they are beginning to comprehend what the phenomenon is really about.

Q: Is this particularly so because *Encounter* draws its writers so much from the universities? That it's the university mind speaking to the university mind?

Lasky: No. I wouldn't think so. Quite the contrary. I mean the best contributions were done by people outside the universities. The article we had on Columbia University last month was written by Arnold Beichman, who is really an outsider. True, he's been studying at the university; at the age of fifty he's gone back as a student to get a Ph.D. But he's a man of outside experience and looks at the academic crisis without having been a professor all his life. He sees these professors trying to struggle with a dilemma, and he says, "Well, can't you see the nose? It's plainly on your face." It is also my own feeling that one has to live these days in more than one country. One has to participate in the political and the literary and the cultural events of more than one country.

Q: To get a perspective?

Lasky: To get a perspective, not to become provincial, not to become narrow. In no matter what country it is. We Americans

241

still remain very, very provincial and narrow. It used to be said that everybody has two countries: France and his own. But very few people from the United States live in France, or in Germany, or in England. They don't really participate in that type of cosmopolitanism. Well, occasionally there's something. I hear that *Le Monde* has had a good sale in the United States. But I try to take a French paper, and a Swiss paper, and a German paper, an American paper, and half a dozen English papers, each day. I try to see the *Spiegel*, *L'Express*, the *New Republic*. So you feel what's really "new" and you don't simply turn to your *Oshkosh News Enquirer*. You feel, "Oh, my God, Günter Grass has gone off the deep end in a speech yesterday in Frankfurt."

Q: Yes, but you're describing an extraordinary man, not someone who restricts his intellectual horizon to Oshkosh.

Lasky: Oh, yes, well, I'd never expect that and I wouldn't want it. When I was a young cosmopolitan, I thought the whole world should be that way. Now I think it hasn't made me all that wise, tranquil, or happy; and I haven't been a very thoroughgoing cosmopolitan anyway. But I do think that in the intellectual life at least, there should be a strong current of cosmopolitanism. It should not be overwhelming; I've lost my fanaticism on that score. I do think that by becoming a cosmopolitan, what Goethe called "a citizen of the world," you do become a little rootless—in the old phrase of being a "rootless cosmopolitan"—and that there should be *another* tradition which just believes in paying attention to the little flowers in one's own backyard. A poet can be just as good if he's a Wordsworth looking at the countryside than if he's a Goethe, worried about the whole state of world culture as a new world citizen. Both can be poets, depending on temperament and talent. It is unfortunate if it becomes all cosmopolitan, or becomes all provincial. But I do think as far as the intellectual life is concerned, for the people who are in political, academic, cultural life, in book publishing and so forth, that it's important for them to have some more informed, some more world-wide and hu-

242

mane view of what is going on. I do not mean just the faddishness, which says there's a new best seller over in France, let's get it translated and publish it immediately. It is a matter of living *urbi et orbi* in our time.

Q: Thank you, Mr. Lasky.

Thomas Michael Maschler

THOMAS MICHAEL MASCHLER was born in 1933 and educated at the Leighton Park School. He is married to Fay Coventry and has two daughters. Before joining Cape in 1960, he worked for MacGibbon & Kee and for Penguin Books (as fiction editor). In 1970 he was appointed chairman of Jonathan Cape Ltd. He has edited a well-known collection of position statements by various "Angries," *Declarations* (1957), as well as the *New English Dramatists Series* (1959–63).

The interview took place in the Bloomsbury offices of Jonathan Cape.

Q: What is your policy on new fiction?

Maschler: Well, firstly, I should say that at Cape we attempt to publish fiction with the passion it deserves. I don't take the line that a lot of publishers take that fiction is a terrible problem, that it's a luxury one can't afford. We not only care about our fiction list but we really try to find new ways to make fiction sell. Now, the average sale of a first novel in this country at the moment is probably something like 1400 copies, maybe only 1200, of which perhaps as many as 90 percent are sold to the libraries. That's the *average*. Cape sells a great deal more than the average, but we too have novels that sell as few as 1700 copies, sometimes even fewer. But if one takes enough care in promoting a new novel, there is a market to be reached.

By this I mean that we are consciously trying to be the most aggressive literary (*very* literary) publishing house in the country. We very rarely publish purely commercial fiction. That's not to say that we don't publish profitable fiction. We do; and of course we make a profit out of publishing Edna O'Brien and John Fowles, for example, but these are writers to be taken seriously. We publish no one of the ilk of Irving Wallace. We used to publish Rona Jaffe, but I turned down her new book because I really couldn't stomach it. Now there's a writer on whom we could make a profit of a couple of thousand pounds for each book we published.

If you go through our list you will occasionally find a book that's obviously going to be a commercial success. For example, we are publishing a novel that is also about to come out in America; in fact it should be out just about now: *The Andromeda Strain* by Michael Creighton. It's a novel about a strain from outer space that threatens to destroy the world. I assure you it's going to be one of the most successful novels published in America this year; it isn't literature with a capital "L," but it is extremely well written and there's nothing vulgar or meretricious about it. We also publish thrillers, as I said, where the standard is much lower, obviously; although here again we attempt to find the best in the genre. For example, we published all of Ian Fleming's books and we now publish Len Deighton. We have a policy of not publishing thrillers that have no literary merit whatever—even though I do regard them as a slightly separate category.

I should perhaps say that being a publisher is not a question of working to any specific set of rules. It's more a question of personal taste. If I truly enjoyed block-busting commercial novels, then I have no doubt that I would publish them with zeal, but the fact is that they bore me. I don't regard my taste, in other words, as being the result of any special virtue.

Q: How much of your list is fiction?

Maschler: I should say about 50 percent of the total.

Q: And of these how many are first novels?

245

The Writer's Place

Maschler: Well, here's the problem: I joined Cape eight years ago. The previous editorial head, Jonathan Cape himself, was then aged eighty, so that inevitably there were very few young writers. We took on a lot of new writers and quickly had some substantial successes. For example, we published *Catch 22* when nobody had heard of it and it sold extremely well. We made quite a big success of Edna O'Brien and John Fowles. Last year we published *Figures in a Landscape* by Barry England, again an outstanding first novel, and quite recently we published a small, very beautiful, almost perfect first novel called *At the Jerusalem* by Paul Bailey, a novel that I'm convinced is as fine as *Memento Mori*, better perhaps even than Muriel Spark's book, because it's got real feeling to it and she's as cold as ice. I admire her work but this book has qualities hers doesn't.

If you take on quite a few first novels you soon find that (a) your standards go up and (b) you attract good authors who are unhappy with other publishers. For example, Anthony Burgess came to us. Now Anthony Burgess is obviously one of the most original English novelists of our time and you simply *have* to publish him. In a relatively short time, then, you find yourself with a large fiction list and a lot of established names. Inevitably—and this is the tragedy—you take on fewer first novels. Whereas once we used to publish as many as six first novels a year, we may now take on only two a year, simply because we've got so many other commitments. I very much regret this trend and I am trying to figure out some way of publishing more first novels, but I'm afraid there aren't any easy answers. We don't want, of course, to publish fiction exclusively: 50 percent seems to me the maximum we should do. Not for any economic reasons, but because the house would otherwise lose its balance.

We also publish quite a number of translations, particularly of South American writers. We published Carlos Fuentes, for example—who does not sell well in this country, by the way—as well as Mario Vargas Llosa and Marquez. We're also publishing a number of South American poets— Neruda, Parra and Paz. The best and most vigorous writing of the present time, it seems to me, is coming out of South America.

My own literary roots are in Europe and the novelists who interest me most are Mann, Kafka, Camus, Musil . . . Now, this is precisely the sort of fiction that is least appreciated in England. Even Kafka doesn't sell here. Nor for that matter does Günter Grass, whom I don't publish but would like to. He sells a tenth of the number of copies here—not that he does in Germany, which would be understandable—but that he does in France, in America, or in Italy. Grass is a strange beast to the English. It is the *English* English writers who do well here, people like Iris Murdoch or Alan Sillitoe.

Q: You said earlier that you don't recruit authors according to any specific criteria, yet here you have outlined a clear set of preferences which is reflected in your publishing list. How do you get at the kind of writer you want?

Maschler: It's hard to explain. Vague though it may sound, books do have a way of coming to you through the people you know. I mean, publishing isn't a nine-to-five job; it's a way of life, and if you're a real publisher, you're a publisher all the time.

And, of course, one must point to the fact that more and more books are agented nowadays. If you get a reputation for promoting books imaginatively and for doing something significant, then you'll soon catch the eye of the people in the trade: namely, the agents. Agents now handle, I think, 80 to 90 percent of all important authors, or of all published ones anyway. Inevitably, if you're producing a particular kind of book well, the agents will be attracted to your house and will recommend it to their authors.

Q: What happens to a manuscript when it first comes into your office?

Maschler: The system we have here is this: if the manuscript is addressed to me personally, it comes to me. Manuscripts that are addressed to the firm go onto a shelf in the readers' room. We don't have a full-time staff who sit at a desk reading five days a week, because I think anyone who does that will surely lose his sense of judgment. Nor do we ever send our books out, except where we think specialist advice is required. Most of the readers, in fact, are women who have children and can't take on a full-time job. I can assure you that all the fiction that comes in receives at least one reliable reading.

Q: How do you select your readers?

Maschler: Well, you try them out first with a few manuscripts in order to get a sense of their judgment. Frankly, it doesn't matter much whether you agree with them a lot of the time. I almost think it's more interesting if you don't. What's important is that they should not let some important book which they have a prejudice against get by without saying, "This is not for me but someone else should look at it." When the reader's finished the book, he does a report on it. If the report is at all favorable, we get a second report. And then all the reports go into a folder.

Q: All of these are reports from the same type of reader?

Maschler: Yes, initially. Once a week we have an editorial meeting—that is, of the directors and readers—and there each of us has a complete list of the books under consideration, even the ones we are dismissing. We go through our list and discuss each case—I mean, those that are worth discussing. We then decide whether to accept a book or to give it another reading. I myself read every novel that we are seriously considering. When a number of people are for something that I'm not keen on, we may take it on, but if I *really* hated it, then I'd probably try to change their minds. In point of fact, this has never happened.

So each book really does circulate through everybody, even if it ends up only with a two-line dismissal. In the case of books we decline, I write personally to everyone who has written to me personally. For others, someone else writes a nice letter if the manuscript has some quality. I don't believe in rejection slips; it seems to me that if a man has spent a couple of years writing a book, he deserves more than a rejection slip.

Q: What's your policy on continuing to publish an author if he doesn't pay?

Maschler: That's quite irrelevant. You just go on publishing him if you care about his work. An author not paying simply means the book doesn't sell. So what? It's only when you don't really like a book and it's not selling that the operation becomes pointless. It just depends, you see, on how *much* you like it. I could imagine—though I haven't been here long enough to have done it—but I could imagine publishing ten books of an author, every one of which lost money, and then going on and publishing another ten. It's unlikely to happen, however, because if someone is good enough for me to want to publish ten books, even though we lost money on each one, then there's got to be some way of building up his sales. Sooner or later you'd certainly work up some sort of excitement.

Often there's a delayed reaction. To cite one instance, we published a quite extraordinary first novel called *The Sun's Attendant*, by Charles Haldeman, a boy I'd met in Greece, an American actually whom we published before the Americans did. Now, I really loved that book and made a considerable song and dance about it. I sold the rights for 2000 dollars to France and, I think, for the same amount to Italy. These are very large sums from France and Italy for a first novel that we hadn't even published yet. People were really excited about it and considered it a major work. It failed dismally here. It failed in most other places as well. We had treated it like a really important first novel and it didn't sell. Now, I thought Haldeman's second book, *The Snowman*, rather less good, and we didn't make a song and dance about it. Yet when we published it, it got lead reviews and people said things like, "Here is the long awaited second novel by the author of that brilliant book, *The Sun's Attendant*." The papers that were saying this, such as the *Sunday Times*, had totally dismissed *The Sun's Attendant*. So that something of what we had done had somehow, somewhere filtered through to somebody.

Do you know the critic George Steiner? Well, for example, the day before we published *The Sun's Attendant*—it was on a Monday—all three Sunday papers had reviewed it, which is something. I mean they don't usually do that, so it's clear we had made an impression. But it was reviewed as the last novel down, the fifth novel in the column, in every one of those papers. I hadn't met Steiner then but I had sent him a copy of the book and had received no reply. Well, on Monday I got a phone call from Cambridge and a voice said, "A crime has been perpetrated!" and I said, "Excuse me, what did you say?" and he said, "This is George Steiner. *The Sun's Attendant* is an extraordinary book, a great book." So that's one nice thing that happened. Later he was reviewing another book in the *Sunday Times* and spent half the review (since he couldn't very well rereview the book) talking about *The Sun's Attendant*.

Q: You said you made "a song and dance." Could you be more specific?

Maschler: Well, what you try to do is build up some sort of network for the book by sending it to people who you have reason to believe will read it and like it. You try to get the book talked about in a very narrow circle. It's extraordinary how if fifty persons in London admire a book four months before publication you can bet that something's going to happen.

Q: How do you get in touch with that small circle?

Maschler: Well, it's complicated. You really don't even get hold of fifty people; you get hold of five people, and then you get them to get hold of some more.

Q: There's no special influence here? No clique?

Maschler: No, not really. It's just a process of sending a book to various people and talking about it. I don't go to all that many literary cocktail parties, but I do go to some; and there I talk about my current enthusiasms. I might say to somebody, "We are publishing X, which I think is a masterpiece." If you say that fairly forcefully, that person will at least remember the title; and somebody else will sooner or later ask him, "Have you read any exciting new books?" and he will say, "No, but Cape have got this extraordinary book called . . ." Sometimes I get people who ring me up and ask, "What's that book you were telling so and so about? Do you think it might be suitable for serialization or something?" I know perfectly well they're not going to serialize it, but at least they've heard of it. That's how it works.

It's not just me, me, me—it's the whole place. Naturally, I spend a lot of time trying to get everyone inside the organization excited about a book. Those who don't like it probably won't be persuaded but if there are five or six people here who are really excited about it, then they'll tell their friends and it'll spread from there. Then things begin to happen.

Q: How do you select your senior editors?

Maschler: We don't have the American editorial system. Until two years ago, I was "editing" ninety books a year. And I was promoting them as well, doing the jackets and the advertising. By "doing" I don't mean commissioning art work; I mean taking an active interest in what's being done, approving the jacket or rejecting it, perhaps showing it to the author. And ditto the copy, though only occasionally do I write copy myself for the ads. Usually I'll just discuss it with the advertising director. Now we have another man here at my kind of level, Ed Victor, who is very good, does half the work, and is bringing in a lot of things of his own.

Q: And just how do you do that? Sorry, if I'm harping too much on the same point.

Maschler: Well, as I said, most of what we get comes in through agents. But you also run across writers and ideas for books in the newspapers and in literary magazines. Nonfiction, of course, is easier to find than fiction. You can't go up to someone and say—at least this is precisely what we don't do—why don't you write a novel? That's the quickest way to court disaster. But with nonfiction it's possible to write to someone who has published an interesting article and say, "Have you thought about writing a book on the same or some related subject?"

Q: What if you should happen on a short story which really intrigues you in, say, the *London Magazine*? Would you follow it up?

Maschler: Yes, I might write to the author and say, "Have you ever thought of writing a novel or are you by any chance writing one; and if so, do send me a part of it." So you start getting involved. Friends ring you up and say, "Do you mind if I bring over so and so?" And authors who like the way you publish inevitably know other authors and recommend their work.

Q: Has anything worthwhile ever issued from casual contacts of this sort?

Maschler: Oh, endlessly. For example, Paul Bailey. His first novel, *At the Jerusalem*, won the Somerset Maugham award—probably the most significant literary award in Britain—and he also won a 1000-pound bursary from the Arts Council for the best first novel in three years. It didn't sell wildly because it was about an old people's home and that's not the most commercial of subjects.

Now, this is how that book came to Cape. I met Caspar Wrede—who is a television and stage director—at a party and I asked him what he was working on. He told me that he had just read a play by a writer called Paul Bailey and then added, "Incidentally, I think he's writing a novel. He really is a very interesting television writer. I have a feeling that he's serious about his work. You should write to him." So I wrote and he sent me sixty pages of his novel. I was so knocked out by them that I offered him a contract at once. That's something I very rarely do on the basis of just a few pages. Usually I'd just write back and make encouraging or discouraging noises. But Paul Bailey's book was very special.

Q: Do you give an advance in a case like this?

Maschler: Yes, certainly. Not a big one but perhaps a total of 200 pounds: fifty on signature, fifty on completion, and a hundred on publication; or a hundred on completion and fifty on publication. If we sign a contract, we always pay an advance.

Q: Are large advances more common now than a few years ago?

Maschler: Well, yes, but not for first novels. We pay various amounts up to several thousand pounds. The highest advance I can recall paying for a novel is 8000 pounds. Naturally the advance relates to what the book's commercial possibilities are, including the paperback rights. This is, incidentally, another way of helping a writer—by selling the paperback rights. And that's something which is relatively easy for a publishing house like ours to do. I would argue that for a problem novel—for one that's apparently unsalable—we are more likely to sell the paperback rights than another publisher. Not than *any* other publisher, but than publisher *X*, because the paperback house may feel that publisher *X* won't do anything for the book, so that by the time they get around to publishing it two years later nobody will have heard of it. Whereas with us, paperback publishers tend to feel that sooner or later that writer is going to be worth having, if we are passionate about him. We never pretend to be passionate about a book unless we really feel it. One can only go flat out for five or six novels a year.

Q: How large a printing did you make of the Bailey book?

Maschler: Of Paul's book, because we felt it was especially good, we printed 5000 copies, of which we've sold 4000 by now. That's a remarkably good sale; it's simply impossible to sell more than 5000 copies of a book of this kind.

Q: How large a printing do you normally make of a first novel?

The Writer's Place

Maschler: About 3000, on the off-chance that we're going to sell them. It really depends on what kind of a first novel it is. Sometimes you can print more, as in the case of Barry England's first novel, *Figures in a Landscape.* I was very much involved in setting up a literary prize recently, the Booker Prize for fiction, the biggest award of its kind in Britain: worth 5000 pounds. Rebecca West, Stephen Spender, and Frank Kermode are on the panel of judges. In addition to awarding the prize, we decided that it would be a good idea to name six books as candidates, in order to generate speculation and excitement about which one would win. Barry England was one of the six and in fact almost everybody thought he'd win, but he didn't.

Figures in a Landscape works on two levels. It's a variant of an escape story but at the same time it has a man-versus-machinery theme, almost a *Lord of the Flies* feeling to it. That's the type of novel of which, because of its high literary quality, we would print 3000 copies, but because it is also an escape story, we can sell more, so in fact we printed 8000 and have sold pretty close to that number.

Q: How did you promote England's book?

Maschler: By the methods I've talked about. Also we produced posters and advertised in the national newspapers—though that kind of advertising is a terrible waste of money. It's good for the reputation of the publishing house, but I don't think it sells books. Trade press advertising, on the other hand, does sell books. We sell to the bookshops and not to the public. It's ironic, I know, but you cannot really afford to reach the public. It's different in America, of course.

Q: And yet you regularly take large columns in the newspapers.

Maschler: Certainly we do, because everybody else takes large columns. The authors get upset if you don't. When I say it's a waste of money, I don't mean that you don't get *any* return. I mean that we don't get back the money that we spend or anything like it. I would estimate it's about 80 percent down the drain.

Thomas Michael Maschler

Q: Do you believe that reviews really make or break a book?

Maschler: They certainly play a part, but the biggest factor is word of mouth. That's even more important than the reviews. John Fowles' last novel, *The French Lieutenant's Woman*, did not get good reviews. It's an infinitely better book than the reviews said and I'm sure it will sell far more copies than you'd expect on the basis of such reviews.

Q: Now that you've merged with Chatto & Windus, do you expect the character of Cape's publishing to change?

Maschler: Absolutely not. The idea behind this merger is precisely to assure that the opposite takes place. We are doing extremely well and so, for that matter, are they, but they don't happen to have much young blood there at the moment. This merger will act as a financial umbrella for both of us, an insurance policy against possible bad times. Editorially we will remain entirely separate. In fact, I would like to see them compete against us for the best books.

Q: How much do you think Chatto differs from you in literary taste?

Maschler: Well, there is a flashy, satirical, clever kind of novel which I can't imagine Chatto publishing. *Catch 22* would be an example. Nor can I see Chatto publishing someone like Kurt Vonnegut. They tend to publish a slightly quieter, though not boring type of fiction. And they do a great deal more literary criticism than we do.

They would not, I think, publish a book like *The Naked Ape*. Desmond Morris had written several books prior to this one and none had ever sold more than 4000 copies. *The Naked Ape* sold in the millions and was translated into every imaginable language.

Q: How did you get this book for Cape?

Maschler: By meeting the author at a cocktail party. It was obvious, after talking to Morris, that here was a man who had an extraordinary book in him. He had written a book called *Biology of*

Art about a chimpanzee he'd taught to paint, and I happened to have read it. It hadn't sold, needless to say, but it had interested me. It took me three years after that meeting to persuade him to sign a contract and four more years to get him to deliver.

Q: Would you say that at Cape you're performing a function that differs considerably from other publishers?

Maschler: Yes, I would, especially with regard to poetry. Take Charles Olson, for example. His poetry had not even been published in England when we took on his *Call Me Ishmael*, which is an essay about *Moby Dick*, for our "Cape Editions" series. It's one of the most exciting pieces of modern criticism, though slightly obscure. Who else would have published it? In that series we have also brought out two essays by Roland Barthes, a play by Havel, and poetry by Hikmet, the latter probably the greatest Turkish poet of the twentieth century. Malcolm Lowry's *Lunar Caustic* was an obvious choice, since it had not appeared previously in book form. His *Under the Volcano* is, in my view, the best novel Cape has ever published.

Every single volume in this series—and there are forty—is a gem of some kind: poetry, literary criticism, science, where science verges on literature. Who else can say that of a series? Penguin can't. We can't about fiction, for that matter. But we put no book in that series for even the *least* commercial reason.

We also publish the "Cape Goliard" series in which Olson's *Maximus* appeared—the original publication, mind you. Into that series we've also put Louis Zukovsky's translation of Catullus, and as a result of our publishing *All*, he was nominated for the National Book Award, though before he had been relatively unknown in America. We took both books before any American publisher did. I do think we are performing a special function. We even do our own printing for this series.

Q: How long have you been publishing poetry on this scale?

Maschler: About two years. We joined forces with a printer who published books part time. He had done six books and we liked them, so we decided to pool Cape's resources and his talents. We now publish about twenty books of poetry under the Cape Goliard imprint alone. Along with Cape Editions and with the poetry we publish at Cape, we probably publish thirty-odd volumes altogether in a year. I doubt whether there is another general publisher in the whole world who publishes more poetry.

Q: Thank you, Mr. Maschler.

Charles Osborne

CHARLES OSBORNE was born in Brisbane, Australia, in 1927 and educated at Queensland University. He is married to Maria Korbelarova and has one daughter. After coming to England in 1953, he worked as assistant editor for the *London Magazine*, leaving it to join the British Arts Council in 1966. In 1972 he was appointed literature director. He has published books of criticism, biography, poetry, and musical history, including *Kafka* (1967), *Swansong* (1968), *The Complete Operas of Verdi* (1969), and *Ned Kelly* (1970).

The interview took place in the London offices of the British Arts Council.

Q: Very briefly, what is the historical background of the Arts Council?

Osborne: The Council grew out of an organization called CEMA (Council for the Encouragement of Music and the Arts) which was set up during the war to encourage and help the continuance of concerts and theatre performances under wartime conditions. It seemed natural at the end of the war that out of this some body should emerge which would go on giving such support. Although state subsidy was then a fairly new thing here, it was something which people seemed to accept, even rather enthusiastically, from the beginning. When the war came to an end there was a change of government, with a Labour government coming to power and it was under their auspices that the Council really got under way.

Nevertheless, I think it's true to say that over the years its development has continued without special reference to which political party was in power. It has never been a question of Party A being generous and in favor of state subsidy, and Party B preferring private enterprise and the arts paying for themselves. One might think so, from looking at our two big political parties, but experience really doesn't bear this out at all—possibly because the amount of money involved is still, in terms of government expenditure, relatively small.

Q: How much?

Osborne: It's approximately twenty million pounds.

Q: How much of this is devoted to literature?

Osborne: A very small amount indeed. The Literature Department—to come to my own province—is the most recently set up of the Arts Council departments. It only came into being six or seven years ago. Prior to that there were three specialist departments, dealing with art (by which was meant the visual arts), music, and drama.

Q: Literature, then, was not supported at all until about 1966?

Osborne: Well, that's not strictly true. Though there was no Literature Department, it had been vaguely accepted that there ought to be a little money available for poetry.

Q: Meaning direct subsidies to individual poets?

Osborne: Yes, that's what it amounted to. There were a few thousand pounds—ten thousand at the very most—looked after by a member of the staff, the assistant secretary of the Arts Council at the time. Then the Council rather belatedly decided that literature was also an art, set up a department, and made the then assistant secretary, Eric Walter White, its first literature director. The department at that time wasn't considered important enough to require a full-time director, so he still did a lot of administrative work for the Arts Council.

The Writer's Place

Q: Why was he chosen in particular?

Osborne: I imagine because, amongst the Council's existing staff, he was—I won't say the most literate, which would appear to reflect badly on the others—but the one most interested in literature and poetry. It was an appropriate appointment if you weren't going to bring in an outsider. The feeling at the time was, I believe, that the department ought to be given a year or two to run before it was decided whether or not to establish it on a more ambitious basis. But it proved necessary almost immediately for him to have an assistant and this is where I come into the picture.

Q: Were you with the Council before?

Osborne: No, I came into the Council from eight years of helping to edit the *London Magazine.* And when Eric White retired two years ago, I replaced him. It wasn't quite as cut-and-dried a thing as all that: the Council has to advertise jobs over a certain level of seniority and they received a number of applications. It was by no means certain at all that I should take Eric's place. But of course one does have a certain advantage in being the chap inside who's been helping to do the job.

Q: Who was responsible for the selection?

Osborne: A committee of the Arts Council, consisting of its chairman, then Lord Goodman, and three or four members of the Council itself—the unpaid body of distinguished people involved in the arts.

Q: The same procedure was also followed in the case of Mr. White, earlier on?

Osborne: Yes, it would have been. Anyway, that is how the department has developed. Although we still deal with a quite small percentage of the Arts Council's money, it has increased enormously over the years. For instance, during my first years here as Eric White's assistant—between 1965 and 1971—the literature subsidy went up fairly slowly from 63,000 to 85,000 pounds. It was my contention that the former figure was initially plucked out of the air in an ad hoc manner. It didn't really relate to anything very much at all. You could have set up the department on 20,000 pounds or on 2,000,000 pounds, and it certainly did not seem to me that 63,000 pounds was a very meaningful figure. It ought to be either much less or much more. So one of my first concerns when I became director was to try to get the figure much higher. And it is now much higher; it passed the 100,000-pound mark immediately and in the current year I have 150,000 pounds. We know almost three years in advance roughly what our subsidy from the government will be, and I know that it will go up to about 175,000 or 180,000 pounds next year, and to about 200,000 pounds the year after that. When it gets up to about 250,000 pounds, if it does, about the year after that again, I feel it will be at about the right level. I know it's a small amount in comparison with the other arts, and a lot of people from outside the Council do look on it in that way; they say, "How unfair! Literature gets only 1 percent of the Arts Council's grant." It seems to me that isn't the proper way of looking at it. It's a question of what needs to be done and how much money is required to do it. Sometimes people outside the Council try to play off one art form at the expense of another; they ask me, don't I think it's monstrous that the Royal Opera House should get nearly two million pounds while my entire department has only 150,000 pounds? No, of course I don't think it's monstrous. If you're going to have opera on a national scale, it costs a certain amount to do. If you're going to have a national theatre, it's also going to cost a lot of money.

It's not, of course, as easy as all that, because the business of subsidizing literature is not cut-and-dried. If you want to subsidize opera houses and symphony orchestras, you know roughly what it costs and you do it. If you want to subsidize National Theatre and repertory theatres and summer stock up and down the country, you know how to do it and you know roughly what it's going to cost. But what does subsidizing literature mean? Almost everybody who has a theory about it has a different theory. I've certainly got my own.

261

The Writer's Place

Q: Yes, but of course you're sitting in the seat of authority, so it's your theory that counts.

Osborne: My feeling is that there are three places where one can legitimately subsidize literature: the point at which it's being written; the point at which it's being published; and the point at which it's being bought and sold in the shops. At the moment we're in the first two fields and are not really doing very much in the third. I don't say that we're completely adequately dealing with those first two fields, but we are dealing with them; and I suppose we're most adequately dealing with the first of them: that is, the point at which books are written. We give grants to individual writers and translators to enable them, literally, to buy the time to work.

Q: But they must first be recommended by a publisher, isn't that right?

Osborne: No, not necessarily a publisher; the writer can be recommended by his agent or a literary editor or reviewer or by some other writer. The sponsorship device is there because it's useful to have someone between you and the applicant, someone to whom you can refer for information and who can give you an opinion about the writer. Also, if you had a free-for-all application system, I would think that there's hardly a literate man or woman in the country who hasn't got a book of poems or a novel hidden away in a bottom drawer somewhere. How do you define a writer? Someone who writes? Well, if so, we could find ourselves swamped with applications from several hundreds of thousands of people. That may seem a rather flippant reason for not allowing it to happen, but we haven't got the staff to deal with it. One has to thin the ranks somehow. The very fact that someone can persuade someone else that he or she is a writer to be taken seriously helps.

Q: How many applications do you in fact get?

Osborne: I would say roughly about one hundred and fifty a year.

262

Q: And how many awards do you make?

Osborne: About one in three, about fifty. We could, of course, if we had more money—and it might not be all that difficult to get the extra money—give many more than that, or we could give considerably fewer, as we used to do when we first started out. At the time I first came here, we called our grants bursaries and we invited people to apply. We would give these out just once a year and have a kind of competition. Our panel of literary advisers would simply vote on the applicants, and the top fifty got the fifty grants and the other hundred or so were disappointed. That seemed to me manifestly unfair. I thought that the applicants really ought not to be contesting each other; we ought to be able to look at each writer on his own merits. That was one of the reasons I wanted to get more money, so as to have enough—and we do at the moment have enough in this particular field—to deal with the general volume of applications. If I found there were several more good ones whom we wanted to give grants, I would press the Council to give me more money and I would, I think, have a reasonable expectation of getting it.

Q: You could potentially go up to a hundred awards?

Osborne: Yes, I think so. The reason we give these individual grants, as I'm sure you're well aware, is that with very few exceptions the writer's profession is just not an economically viable one, given the way we run our economy. These matters seem to be much better organized in the communist countries—but then, of course, there is a very high price to pay for that. In our kind of mixed economy, where publishers, it seems, can stay alive more easily than authors, we do find it necessary to help the writer while he's at work. The provision is that the writer has to be at work or about to begin work on some literary project.

Q: You do, however, tend to favor younger writers, don't you?

Osborne: Yes, that is true, though we have given grants to quite elderly writers as well, the condition being that they are still active and at work. We have nothing against older writers, but we're certainly not in the business of giving grants merely to recognize or reward past achievement. That would not be doing what, according to our charter, we're supposed to do, to increase the accessibility and to improve the standard of the arts in this country. It's very proper that there should be help for older writers who may have fallen on hard times, and there is an organization designed to provide this, the Royal Literary Fund. It has a reasonable amount of money at its disposal and it does a lot of good work. It also, quite rightly, doesn't concern itself with the question of literary standards. The writer is a person who has written books, and if you've written fifty books and you're in need of money now, you've got a good claim on the Royal Literary Fund. But it would be wrong for the Arts Council to take that strictly charitable view.

Q: How has the Council, or your department specifically, come to grips with the question of literary standards?

Osborne: The only way you can, it seems to me, is to rely on the people who are advising you. We have in each department our advisory panels, and we try to ensure that as wide a range of opinion as possible is represented on these panels.

Q: How do you do that?

Osborne: One tries to choose young people to put forward the younger generation's viewpoint, to choose middle-aged and middle-of-the-road people, to choose one or two conservative people, so that we're not actually biased against any particular kind of literature. That's the theory at any rate. I know that we fall short of it almost continually, but this is what we're aiming for.

Q: How large is the panel?

Osborne: About sixteen or seventeen people. The term of appointment is three years and sometimes, if we think we can squeeze an extra two years of service out of them after that, we do so. It's so arranged that about a third or a quarter of the panel is retiring at the end of every calendar year and new people are coming on, so it isn't a static body by any means, dictating who should be given grants. The only constant figure is the paid official, myself. But we do quite seriously try to see that most kinds of taste are represented, and not only taste, but also that all elements of the literary field are represented. For instance, I have four or five novelists on the panel, two or three poets, a couple of publishers, a literary agent, a librarian. Among the novelists there is a youngish experimental novelist, a middle-of-the-road novelist, a science fiction novelist, and so on.

Q: Do they get paid for being on the panel?

Osborne: No. This is one of the strengths—and one of the weaknesses—of the system under which we operate, by which we make a great deal of use of unpaid advisers. We're very fortunate: people seem very willing to give this kind of public service. I'm increasingly conscious, however, of the fact that we do make very great demands on them, particularly in the literature panel where I'm continually asking them to read books—which take up a fair amount of time, after all—and to come along to more and more meetings every year. They're not paid, but if they come from outside London to meetings, then of course they get their travel expenses reimbursed.

Q: How successful do you think the Literature Department has been in the seven years you've been in it?

Osborne: That's not an easy question to answer. One could point to a number of books published with Arts Council assistance which would presumably not have been published otherwise; one could point to an even larger number of novels and books of poetry, of general books—criticism, biography, and so on—which have been written with the aid of grants, and while most of these would probably have been written without these grants, they would not have been so easily written. They might have taken longer to write, some might not have been completed. A number of books

The Writer's Place

have been translated with Arts Council help, which in most cases would not have been published without it; or if they had been published, would have needed to be published at a much higher price and therefore would have sold fewer copies. Ours is not the kind of achievement which can be neatly totaled up in the way the program of a national theatre or an opera house might be. It's a very complicated area and I'm very conscious of the danger of making too many claims for what we've done.

Q: Do you think you've given voice, as it were, to any mute inglorious Miltons? That you've provided writers with an opportunity which they would otherwise not have had to succeed in more than a merely financial way?

Osborne: There are certainly young novelists and poets who have been helped by the Council, possibly after producing their first novel. They've been nursed through the most difficult stage of producing second and third books.

Q: Have any of these people won major literary prizes?

Osborne: Yes, they have gone on to win major literary prizes. V. S. Naipaul is one; Hugo Williams, the poet, is another; Paul Bailey, the novelist, is yet another. It does happen. And of course, I must say, we've helped a few lame ducks. It's always difficult to know in advance whether the project you're helping is going to come out well or not. The fact that someone has written a good novel doesn't necessarily mean that his next novel will be good. But if you're in the business of subsidizing writers and you have faith in a writer, then you have to help him or her write the novel. Even if it turns out to be a critical failure—I was almost going to say a commercial failure, but then there's no way of evaluating that except to say that most novels are commercial failures—then, it seems to me, you've still got to take a chance and go on for another book or so before possibly deciding that it's not going to work.

We haven't really been in the business long enough to point confidently to any of the emerging novelists and say, "This is one of our great successes and this is one of our failures."

266

Q: If you once support a writer, does that disqualify him from further support?

Osborne: No. We do try to spread the jam on the bread rather widely, but if a writer has had a grant and his sponsor comes to us and tells us he's been working on his book the past year and is still working on it, and shows us what he's done, then we might very well continue to give help. But for the most part we try to avoid helping the same writers two or three years running. What doesn't seem to have happened—and this is worth mentioning as a kind of negative success—is that a writer will win a grant and then spend it drinking himself into a stupor or going off somewhere and failing to write the book. That has happened, to my certain knowledge, only once. The books do almost all get written, though whether they're all worth writing is not so easy to decide.

Q: Would you agree that the Council tends to support "experimental" writers who are unlikely to get advances from publishers?

Osborne: Yes, that's generally true, although we do also support the more conventional writer whose publisher would claim that he's being given a reasonable advance. But what publishers think of a reasonable advance—well, it just isn't possible to live on that. An English publisher will think nothing of offering a novelist—on the basis of seeing and approving perhaps two or three chapters—an advance of 250 pounds to go away and write the novel. How long they expect the novelist to live on that 250 pounds, I can't imagine. So what does he do? If he's a full-time writer, he either has to support himself by doing other free-lance jobs, reviewing, or doing a little extra work somewhere else. This is where we come in, giving him perhaps another 500 or 750 pounds or as much as 1000 pounds, so that he can live, even if not very comfortably, and put away other chores while he concentrates on writing his book.

The writer, of course, does not have to be destitute. For

The Writer's Place

instance, he might be an academic who can take a year off without salary, so we make his salary up while he writes his book. It is true that the Council does tend to subsidize the younger and more experimental writer. It does so not merely by way of direct grants, but by grants to literary magazines and to little presses. There are magazines and presses which publish work by younger writers. The little presses not only publish poetry which the bigger publishers mightn't consider sufficiently commercial, but also nowadays they publish experimental novels. The little presses, of course, have an obvious advantage over the big commercial publishers: they can publish four or five books of poetry at a print run of only 250 copies each; and their overhead is so minimal that they can do quite well out of that, or at any rate they'll make a profit. They perform, as you can see, a particularly useful function and we give grants to a number of them.

Q: Is there infighting among these small presses and magazines regarding who will receive grants? Jealousy that one should be getting more than another, and therefore pressure of some sort exerted on you to make changes?

Osborne: Yes, occasionally. These are the consequences of any system of grant giving. "Why did he get it and not I? Why did that magazine get it, when mine is so much better?" One really has to steer a path between complacency on the one hand and becoming too neurotically affected by that kind of criticism on the other. So long as one knows that one is trying to be as fair as possible, that one is taking as wide a range of advice as possible, that is the best one can do. If there are genuine complaints, one must always be willing to listen and to look again at particular cases. But there really isn't a great deal of criticism of this kind, because over the years I've found it possible to get more and more money for these various allocations, so that we're not squeezing any magazine or any little press out through lack of funds. Therefore they know that it isn't a question that only four could have got it and "I wasn't one of the lucky four." The reason any particular one didn't get it is that the Arts Council didn't think they were good enough.

268

And of course we do so much else besides subsidizing writers and magazines and little presses. Without being at all against giving grants, I like very much the idea of paying the writer for a service rather than giving him a handout to help him write. We engage writers to undertake talks in schools and to undertake tours in the provinces, and we pay them quite well for this.

Q: This is in lieu of grants?

Osborne: No, in addition. Some of the writers who have gone on these tours may be writers who have had grants or might get grants in the future. Others are writers who are far too successful—Angus Wilson is a case that immediately comes to mind—ever to want a grant from the Arts Council. We try to engage writers who we think are good writers and who are also articulate. The two don't always necessarily go together; some people, after all, write in order not to talk. The tours last usually a week and we pay about 150 pounds. Some people think that's very generous; I think it's just reasonable, though it's certainly as much as many of them will earn in six months from the novel that they may be taking that week off from.

Another indirect means of subsidizing writers that we employ is to buy their manuscripts.

Q: To prevent the Americans from doing it?

Osborne: Exactly. We came to this rather late in the day and I'm afraid most of the English manuscripts that we might have wanted are safely resting in Texas. We have a committee which encourages the national and the university libraries and the British Museum to add to or to build up manuscript collections of writers of some particular interest to them, perhaps writers of local significance—say D. H. Lawrence in Nottingham. We encourage libraries to buy, while they can still get them reasonably cheaply, manuscript material by the writers of tomorrow, so to speak: the people who are being published today but who are not yet being chased after by the big universities and foundations in the States and elsewhere.

269

The Writer's Place

This is rather an uphill task because many of the libraries, while they'll jump at the manuscripts of the dead—even the recently dead—are a little more suspicious of the living. They will take manuscripts of the distinguished elderly living, but ask them to interest themselves in the work of a novelist who everybody might clearly agree is going to be the D. H. Lawrence of the 1990s and they don't want to take that kind of chance. To overcome that resistance, we give grants toward the purchase of manuscripts of living writers.

Q: But you won't pay for the entire cost of the manuscript?

Osborne: Until very recently we did not, but since I've found it a rather slow business to get the libraries to buy the younger writers, I recently received the Council's agreement to use some of the money I had for this purpose to buy material directly which will then become the property of the Arts Council. This means that we can get money to younger writers who can use it; and also, if I play the market rightly, it may well mean that in generations to come the Arts Council may be able to make quite a good profit by selling this material to the libraries when they *do* want it!

Q: Is your object here mainly to avoid the aura of patronage associated with direct grants?

Osborne: Yes, exactly. I don't think we're ever going to avoid that completely in the foreseeable future, but the more methods I can devise of paying the writer for something—whether for his services or the contents of his wastepaper basket—the better. For example, we also give grants to some literary organizations, like the Poetry Book Society, which is a book club; the National Book League, which is a kind of public relations organization for publishing generally. Now in doing so, I'm conscious of the fact that we're possibly indirectly helping something which it's really no business of ours to help. This doesn't worry me unduly. The borderline between the word used for art and the word used for commerce is often blurred. We could say that we're only interested in literature as an art—which is strictly true—therefore

270

we are duly subsidizing novelists and poets. And of course books of criticism about literature and, by extension, about the arts are something we ought to be helping too. But in giving money to the National Book League, for example, which is concerned with helping publishers sell books, and not just books of literary interest, but books about beekeeping and so forth, I realize that some of our money is spilling over into other areas.

Then we also help the Poetry Society, which puts on readings up and down the country and at its premises here in London. We subsidize it to quite a large extent every year. There aren't really very many of these organizations. This is another way in which we differ from the other departments: there is no big national organization for us to subsidize. Of course there could be. In fact, that's something I think about fairly consistently, that there should be a literary equivalent of the National Theatre. Once one says that, people think one's talking about a state publishing house, and they see it as some grim, gray Eastern European monolithic state agency which will swallow up all the commercial publishers and only publish literature that is agreeable to the state. That, I dare say, roughly describes the situation in the Eastern part of the world, but that's not what I mean at all. The National Theatre coexists fairly happily with the commercial theatres; both are now strong and flourishing. If anything, the National Theatre may have helped to improve the standards of the West End theatre by giving them a little competition. The same thing could happen in publishing if we had a national publishing house. It doesn't have to have a name like "State Publishing House" or "Her Majesty's Publishing House"; it might be called something very gay and zippy. But it could be a publishing house which is completely subsidized, which is a nonprofit distributing organization, and which therefore does not have to take into account the profit motive in the books it publishes. It could begin in a fairly small way, publishing forty or fifty books a year of interest to the arts and literature which had failed to get a publisher elsewhere. These books do exist and at the moment we help them in a different way, because the publisher comes to us and says, "I will only do this book, which I'm sure you, the Arts Council, would like me to do, if you'll give me a grant to do it, since otherwise I'm sure to lose money by it." So we give publishers grants—we call them grants, though in fact they are really loans or guarantees against loss. Since the publishing houses are commercial organizations and we're dealing with public money which we can't just hand over to private companies, we give them grants on condition that they do separate profit and loss accounting for those particular books. And we have the right to see these accounts when we wish. If the book makes a profit, then we get that part of our grant back.

That's how we do it at the moment, but I find this rather unsatisfactory. If we could have such books published by a subsidized company—in the way that plays are put on by the subsidized National Theatre—it would be a neater operation. Such a company could perhaps also publish a first-rate international literary magazine, a magazine of the arts, which doesn't really exist at the moment. We have, to be sure, one or two good literary magazines, but they're either like the *London Magazine*, which I used to work for, as I said, for many years and which represents, rather quirkily, one man's taste; or like the *TLS*. We don't have anything like, say, the *Nouvelle revue française*. This is one of the things I keep banging on about, and I hope the opposition is slowly being worn down. There is a certain amount of feeling here against this kind of project.

Q: What do you make of the reaction of some former recipients of Arts Council grants that their very acceptance of such assistance has in some way compromised them, that they have become part of the establishment?

Osborne: I don't think that particular reaction is very widespread, but I do recognize the syndrome. It is a difficulty, though I don't really see what one can do about it. Writers of a certain temperament will just not apply for our grants for that reason; they would rather retain their independence, even if their lives are made more difficult. Others won't feel threatened at all by it and will quite cheerfully accept grants. A third category will, as you suggest, accept the grant but then feel compromised by it in some way. But I don't really see what we can do about it. We do what we can by attaching as few strings as possible to our grants: we don't look over the writer's shoulder, and we certainly try not to make him feel that in accepting this money he's really got to knuckle down and do that book or else there'll be a moral, if not legal, commitment for him to return the money. We really fall over backward in making him *not* feel that way about it.

Q: It's surely a problem for the kind of writer who feels that he must be free to criticize his society at any time and at any place.

Osborne: I see your point. However, the kind of writers we breed don't seem to have that problem. I've had occasion to point out to some semi-underground or way-out writers who are busily criticizing the Arts Council in very vitriolic terms in their magazines—not recently, but there was a spurt of it three or four years ago—that they're only able to do it because we're paying the bill for them.

Q: Have you yourself been the target of attacks?

Osborne: Not so much recently, but it has happened.

Q: From people who have not received grants?

Osborne: Yes, usually. There was one instance some years ago when outside my window a group of poets organized a burning of books of those poets who had been given grants that year. When I looked out of my window, I was very upset to find the book burners included and indeed were headed by two or three poets who had been given grants the year before. That seemed to me to show a very mean attitude indeed. "I had it last year, but thou shalt not have it this year."

The thing to do is to learn to live with these attacks and not to be too sensitive to them—once again, without assuming a kind of Olympian detachment in which one feels one is above criticism. It's difficult to walk that path and I'm not sure I always manage it, but at least it's what I bear in mind. And I think also that as I've gone on doing the job and more and more people have got to know me, they can see that at least I'm sympathetic and reasonably open-minded and willing to discuss grievances. I may not have the friendship of the fringe element, but I do have at least their knowledge that I have no axes to grind, that I'm not against any particular faction of writers or for any other. Of course, I've got my own tastes and opinions in literature and my own feelings about a great deal of what the Arts Council subsidizes, but I try not to let that interfere with the way I do the job. In any case, with our system of advisory panels—by no means composed of yes men—my power to influence the course of events is severely limited.

Q: Do you find pressure coming at you from the other end, not merely from frustrated poets perhaps, but from, say, public groups which are unhappy about the kind of writers you are supporting? Political pressure groups?

Osborne: We've been completely free of political pressure. The principle seems to be accepted that the government of the day attaches no political strings to the money that it gives to this quasi-independent body, the Arts Council; that, while the Council remains a responsible body of people, it must be left alone to do that job as it sees fit.

Occasionally, of course, some pressure groups and some writers will get together and suggest one thing or another. I always consider whatever suggestions come in on their merits and put them to the panel and to the Council. I don't think that there's really a strong feeling among any section of writers against the Arts Council—maybe a certain amount of skepticism among the very young and way-out. But there the Council has tried to be especially helpful. It set up a special Experimental Project Committee, literally in order to be able to give money to more way-out events that the specialist panel possibly might have been too conservative to deal with.

Q: How do you think the public at large reacts to this kind of support of writers, especially the middle and lower class "average guy"? Are they even aware of what you're doing? Do you get letters complaining about this kind of use of public money?

Osborne: Yes, it's happened, but so rarely that it's quite remarkable. I suppose really that the great majority of the public does not care; it's as simple as that. Among those who do give the matter some thought, I think there's overwhelming agreement that it's a good thing to subsidize the arts in general and certainly literature in particular. People do appear to realize that it's not unfair to say that a great many writers who are very widely read can't live from their writing and should therefore be helped. One could count on the fingers, if not of one, then of two hands, the number of letters that have been written either to the press or to us here putting a violently contrary view. That doesn't seem to be one of our problems at all.

Q: Thank you, Mr. Osborne.

V. S. Pritchett

V. S. PRITCHETT was born in 1900 in Ipswich and educated at Alleyn's School. He is married to Dorothy Roberts and has two children. A distinguished man of letters, Pritchett has done a great deal of journalism and reviewing (notably for the *New Statesman*, of which he is also a director); and since the Second World War he has been visiting professor at a number of American universities, including Princeton and Berkeley. Aside from novels, travel, and criticism, he has published some of the most remarkable short stories of this century, partly represented in *Collected Stories* (1956). The first volume of his autobiography, *A Cab at the Door*, appeared in 1968; the second, *Midnight Oil*, in 1971.

The interview took place in Pritchett's apartment in London.

Q: Would you comment on the function of the British Arts Council and your own role in it?

Pritchett: I am no longer connected with it. I think the Arts Council is valuable. It's in an experimental stage; and it's a very difficult experiment. But for literature very little money is available. First of all, money was given to young people, particularly to poets. I can't tell you the amounts because I don't know, but anyway, quite decent sums. I'm not sure how successful the results were, but it was my feeling, and the feeling of some others, that it was about time we thought very much more about prose. We felt that the poet, unless he was writing "Hiawatha" or

Paradise Lost, did not need that degree of support, whereas a prose writer, turning out so many thousands of words a day, did need it. On the whole, the Arts Council hasn't done badly. I've no doubt there have been losses; that is to say, young writers who fail to come up to scratch; or older writers who hoped to revive their talents if they were given a little money, and have not revived their talents. But I think it has been a good thing. Literature can no longer be privately supported.

However, from the point of view of my generation, it's rather different. It was not—it has never been—very easy to earn one's own living as a writer, and indeed, until about 1940, it was extremely difficult. One lived in relative poverty. Things improved during the war because of government employment, and the BBC above all. The BBC employed a great many writers and represented a form of support for them. Most of the writers of my age have been through this mill, have managed to survive and produce a certain number of books.

Q: Do you think you yourself would have been helped?

Pritchett: If it had happened twenty years ago, yes. My own view is that no one really ought to have awards until they have a wife and three children and are about forty, which is a very crucial age for mature writers. The writer who has considerable family commitments and who has a certain body of work behind him, in order to earn his living, has to scatter his powers and this damages his best work. The middle period is the time when I think awards would be really valuable. Of course, money is more easily earned now than it used to be. Many writers are invited to America and are paid ten times the amount we ever earn here. But one would have to be a most unusual person, really, to stand the transition from one culture to another, except as a passing commentator.

Q: With some Americans it seemed to work the other way, Fitzgerald and Hemingway, for instance.

Pritchett: Yes, at certain times that's true. America at that time was starved of Europe which was at one of its splendid periods

The Writer's Place

culturally, say, between 1900 and 1930. It was a marvelous twilight; and anyone who saw it was enriched. I don't think any American writers who came to Europe *now* would get anything out of it beyond social amenity. London is one of the few remaining civilized cities in the West.

Q: Did you become a writer yourself by participating in a movement? A movement of some sort?

Pritchett: I never was self-consciously in any movement. I did not belong to Bloomsbury—the older generation of Forster, Virginia Woolf, and so on. I was brought up in the emerging lower middle class. I did not go to Oxford or Cambridge, nor even to the Red Bricks. So in that sense I wasn't influenced at all by that movement. I think I was certainly influenced by what went on in the thirties. I would describe it in this way: I'm a year younger than the century, and I grew up after the 1918 war. That meant that people of my generation were very much cut off from the people who were five years older than ourselves.

Q: Would you describe your early writing as socially committed?

Pritchett: I was only moderately "engagé," but I was attracted to realism, or some form of realism. Most of the stories I wrote during that period are all, generally, of lower middle class or working class life, as distinct from the educated upper class life. If my characters were tramps, they were real tramps; if it was a sailor, it was a real sailor; if it was a missionary, it was a real missionary.

Q: Do you think this change was brought about by a change in political atmosphere?

Pritchett: It was affected, of course, by politics, certainly by socialism and the Popular Front, and by the Spanish War. Those affected me very strongly. However, my intellect was not political. I disliked political, dogmatic Marxism, although I was interested in Marx. I couldn't possibly have become a card-carrying communist. I was a parliamentary democrat. Although I was very much in favor of the Republican side in the Spanish Civil War—I had lived in Spain long before the famous generation that went there to see the war—I saw at once that they had got Spain all wrong. I was distressed by the international interference and by the fact that Spain was being used. I knew that the Spaniards were in themselves so strange that they would soon "muck it up," which indeed they did very thoroughly.

Where the people of the Spender generation were disillusioned, I wasn't really disillusioned; I was only confirmed, so to speak, in what I had suspected was very liable to happen. I hadn't expected that degree of savagery, but I didn't think there would be any kind of union in the left-wing forces, and I was surprised to see it last so long in the right-wing forces.

Q: You have spent a considerable period of your life abroad. What impelled you to leave England? What has impelled so many writers of your generation to leave?

Pritchett: To speak generally, first of all, there was the influence of fashion. England is a tiny little island. You can drive across it, as you know very well, in a very few hours and fall into the sea if you drive too fast. Sooner or later, all island people feel claustrophobia. The fact that we do spend a lot of time on the continent means that we've grown indifferent to the separations of culture.

In my own case, I suppose such romantic motives also must have played a part. But there was another thing too. I come from a very poor family, and I had very little education, because I was brought up in the First World War. I resented this. I was very good at languages, so I thought the best thing to do, since I didn't appear to be on the right tramlines in England, was to go abroad. In that way, I would be able to build up something of my own. Whether it did me any good at all I don't know, except that I speak French and Spanish very well. (I spent a long time in Ireland, which was important for me too.) France was a form of education, and especially going to Spain. It was an education in history.

The Writer's Place

I got sick of it in the end. I spent about seven years outside England. The only way I could sustain myself was by newspaper journalism, and I began to think this was a cul-de-sac.

Q: You have been invited to American universities a number of times. What do you think of the growing habit of English writers associating themselves with universities, not merely in America, but here as well? I don't mean just as "creative writers," but also as lecturers of a more traditional stamp.

Pritchett: In theory, I am very suspicious of it; but on the other hand, I think it is true that certain kinds of writers profit by it. Nowadays a large number of critics are really academic critics. People who, when I was young, would have been writing long articles for serious reviews now teach in the universities, and write things from the university. In the old days, academic writers and critics often wrote very badly. If they submitted their work to, say, the *New Statesman* and such, they were turned down because they were unreadable. Now these young men write extremely well and are not turned down. I'm speaking particularly now of critics, though possibly it may apply to poets, I don't know. For prose writers, playwrights, novelists, I think the university is dangerous, because the university is a specialized community. It is quite unlike the outside world. In the outside world you are not among young people exclusively, nor are you dominated by their professors. It is an artificial world. The world around me is not full of young people; it's got a proportion of all ages. Artificial worlds have a sterilizing effect on writers. They begin to think of life in terms of specialized communities. There have, of course, been a number of rather good "academic" novels, though awfully small in their scope. The curse of academic life is the watchfulness of one academic upon another. Writers can be as bitchy as they like about one another, but they've got the whole of London or the whole of England or the whole of Europe to be bitchy in, and it does not really matter. But in academic life, the infighting goes on day-by-day, inch-by-inch, hour-by-hour. Their jobs depend upon it, the whole organization encloses them.

280

Q: You don't see the university taking over the nation's cultural life in England in the way it seems to in America?

Pritchett: Well, I'm afraid that it is going in the same way with us as in America. It frightens us because, by now, a great many of us have been to America, and, although we enjoy ourselves, we are not altogether happy about culture as industry. As John Gross remarks in his book, *The Rise and Fall of the Man of Letters,* how do you have time to read Wordsworth when you've got to read forty books on Wordsworth first? This is what is happening at the universities. There have been three books on Ford Madox Ford in the last eighteen months. They're good, but why three? I can't tell you how many books there are on Faulkner, you probably know better than I. At every college I've ever been to someone's written a book about Faulkner. That seems to me mad; and worse than mad. You know it's been done for a purpose; there's a compulsion: his status won't improve unless he has "published." He's got to publish something or die. But is it going to happen in England? I hope we can somehow avoid it, though I don't know whether we shall.

Q: Do you think that the British Arts Council is a way of staving it off?

Pritchett: Yes, and also we have one great advantage, though I don't know how long it is going to last. That is the BBC, which has a pretty high standard and has given quite a lot of writers perfectly honorable employment of some kind. I don't know if it's going to go on doing so successfully because there is always a tendency to try to popularize and to appeal to mass culture. However, the BBC has been a great help to English writers. After the war, when I was certainly well known but earned very little money, I used to support myself by writing short plays or doing broadcasts for serious programs on the Third Programme and so on. That can still happen, especially with playwrights.

Q: Do you feel that your own audience has changed in the last ten years or so? Do you feel you're writing now for a university-trained, university-oriented (perhaps even university-employed) audience? Is it an elite now, whereas earlier it was more broadly based? Who, for example, reads the *New Statesman* now?

Pritchett: The *New Statesman* was always read by people who were intellectually minded, and rather intellectually snobbish too. R. H. S. Crossman used to say it was read by the most snobbish girl in every street. I don't think the nature of its audience has changed very much, although the younger generation tend either to be revolutionary in politics or to be indifferent to them. I would have said in my case, my audience was certainly not a mass audience. However, I've just written an autobiographical volume and that has had a much wider audience than I have ever had before. It was read because the readers were about my age and they want to read about that period. Quite a number of young people have read it too, but it's because of the period really.

Q: Do you think that the writer in England can live from what he earns by writing?

Pritchett: Books? No, certainly not. There are only about six writers in England that can live solely by writing books. That is, of course, one of the reasons why the Arts Council exists.

Q: Do you think this is as it should be? Ought something to be done about it?

Pritchett: I think something ought to be done about it. Not necessarily by giving money, but there might very well be a much more sensible tax law, as I hear there is in France. For instance, my autobiography was a great success, and it made a lot of money. However, that put me up into such a high surtax bracket that I was no better off. I am a serious writer; I have a reputation. To be actually punished for having written a book which people admire seems to me idiotic.

Q: Have you been tempted to emigrate to Ireland to benefit from its new tax law?

Pritchett: I think I should go to sleep in Ireland. The climate is so relaxing. I don't think I would do that. Ireland is all over in about three weeks; it has told you everything, there's nothing more to be got for a foreigner. Nor, indeed, for an Irishman; they all leave.

Q: You agree then with James that a writer needs the thickness of society, the density of environment?

Pritchett: Absolutely! Absolutely yes, yes. I've often heard American writers complain that they feel so isolated, and that large portions of American society are so thin on the ground that you are confined to writing one or two brilliant books when you're very young and then there's nothing more. America is the country of brilliant first books.

Q: Are you tempted at all by the film, by TV, as alternatives to the novel?

Pritchett: If I were a young man nowadays, I think I probably would turn to the theatre or the film rather than to writing short stories, which is what I turned to originally—a kind of poetic, dramatic form in any case. And now the opportunities for doing that are far greater than they were in my youth. Now, the opportunities abound, especially in England where there's been a powerful movement in that direction. I've got rather set in my ways, and I suspect that the idiom of dramatic performance in TV or cinema or theatre has a very limited duration. The given idiom at any moment probably lasts about five or ten years at the very most, and then it's completely out of date, and no one understands what is being said anymore in that idiom. I think a writer gets fixed in the idiom in which he grew up, and that would become extremely noticeable if I wrote a play!

Q: Do you sense that the best talent in England is being swallowed up by TV and film?

Pritchett: First of all, I don't believe that anything that's been well done in the dramatic arts can be done without a great deal of writing. Things have to be written and rewritten, and they've been established before the drama has been extracted from them. If you were to go into the visual media without any sense of written literature, you would become as thin as many of the films have been. There are, of course, many extremely good films, done by very fine visual artists, but the majority of script writers are not like that. They deal in clichés, simply because the mind that has conceived them has not been a writing mind.

Q: What is your taste in fiction?

Pritchett: I don't read much current fiction. I enjoy reading the famous novels of the past. I enjoy reading certain American novels; I'm a great fan of Saul Bellow, and I am a great admirer of Malamud. I think American writers are much more interesting than contemporary British writers. However, I do read short stories quite a lot. I shall never give up that addiction. I do like books of travel which give me curious information. For me the whole business of the writer is learning how to write, and I am still learning and trying to find what to say and how to say it. I just write for my own sake. In a sheerly egotistic way, I simply hope that what I read will encourage me to write something else.

Q: Thank you, Mr. Pritchett.

William Sansom

WILLIAM SANSOM was born in 1912 in London and was educated at the Uppingham School. He is married to Ruth Grundy and 'has two children. Since the war he has published a novel or a book of stories almost every year; they include *Fireman Flower* (1944), *The Body* (1949), *A Contest of Ladies* (1956), *The Stories of William Sansom* (1963), *Goodbye* (1966), and *Hans Feet in Love* (1971).

The interview took place in Sansom's home in London.

Q: Is it possible to make a living as a writer in Britain today?

Sansom: I think so. It has been possible for me, whether I have been lucky or not I don't know. I'm a hard worker and I have written a lot of journalism, travel writing, that kind of thing—for *Holiday*, for instance. This, of course, pays very well. Then I've had a couple of prizes—a novel taken up by a book club, and so on. It all seems somehow to work without making you rich. But it is possible.

Q: Would you agree that it is the living one makes from journalism that allows one to write novels?

Sansom: Yes, in a way, but I very, very rarely review, and I only do the journalism that I want to, which is usually therapeutic to my other writing. That is to say, I've got such a sense of place that to be able to get it out of my system by writing travel articles gets it out of the novels. It does not fill them as it might otherwise. One novel of mine called *A Bed of Roses* has a Spanish background. I wrote that after I had been in Spain for a month or two, and it's far too full of Spanish background. If I had written it now I'd cut and cut and cut. So that this kind of journalism helps both financially and the writing itself.

Q: Could you make a living out of the novels alone?

Sansom: Only a very inadequate one. You see, it takes you at least a year and a half to write a novel, maybe two years. One took me four years to write. You may end up with fifteen hundred pounds from that, which isn't enough, and this includes translations and other fringe benefits. Unless it's taken up by a book club or becomes by luck a best seller; and it usually becomes a best seller for the wrong reasons. So you can't aim to make money from a novel. It can come from selling film rights, but of course it's death to any good writing if you start writing with the film in view. That's obvious.

Q: Would you say that your audience, or the audience in general for novels, has increased or changed in make-up?

Sansom: No. For mine, it has neither increased or decreased. Except when reproduced later in paperback or made into a film. What's happened generally, I don't know. The pace of writing has got so much quicker even in the last five years, let alone the last ten years. I think people are reading differently, they need much more action. In fact, life is very largely influenced nowadays by the image, the amount of stuff coming from the TV, from the film, from illustrations in the newspapers, and so on. The old pages of description very seldom work any more. It's got to *move* all the time.

Q: Do you find your own writing changing because of this?

Sansom: Yes, it's very much influenced by the film, particularly the film, with me. I like the cinema, the big dream-screen.

Q: But you're not tempted to write for the film?

286

Sansom: No, I don't think so. Or should I say, "perhaps." Provided the offer is good and leaves me my so-called freedom.

Q: Why?

Sansom: Because I prefer the autocracy of writing here when every word I write is likely to be published. No one can change a word. As soon as you start writing a film script, five dozen people put their fingers into it and change it and di-dah, di-dah . . . Now, this depends upon your character. A lot of people like the amount of talk that goes with the theatre and the film. I hate it. There are exceptions. Christopher Isherwood, for instance: he's a good novelist and yet has been writing scripts quite happily, I imagine.

Q: You don't consider the film or television a threat to your novel-reading audience?

Sansom: I think in the end perhaps it might be. It's very difficult to say. Take television, for instance; this is supposed to have stopped people reading, but it's also made a lot of other people read that never read before because they can't stand the damned thing on. They have to go into a room by themselves and do something. There is a privacy about reading which no big image purveyor will ever destroy. There will probably be changes in technique. Reading books may finish and you may end up with a microfilm and a little thing going flip-flap.

Q: You've written a great many short stories. One of the things that is usually said about short stories now is that there's practically no market for them any more. Has this been your experience?

Sansom: It's not true. I think that perhaps the large sums of money that used to be made out of them can't be made now, because most of the magazines are smaller and more literary, but you can always earn something. Very odd things happen: the glossy magazines change editors and they want to raise the level suddenly and you find yourself being offered quite a whacking sum for something you would otherwise be selling to a literary magazine. It's so variable, and of course it's easier when you've got a name. What is always a bad seller—and for very good reasons—is a book of short stories, because this is the wrong way to read them: each one cancels the other out. It's like going to an art exhibition and trying to see too many pictures at once. You simply forget the ones you started out to see. But digested individually, I think people like short stories.

Q: What are the usual outlets for short stories in England? Are British short story writers dependent on the American market?

Sansom: The American market has become much more formalized than it was fifteen to twenty years ago. I used to write a lot then for various magazines. Now, when I write an individualistic story without the usual formalized plot and so on, it just does not sell any more. So I can't remember when I last had a . . . well, I did have one published by *McCalls*, but this was possibly chancey in today's market. (Though recently they have inquired for the sight of another.) But twenty years ago, I could sell quite a lot. This is bearing in mind that I never write with an audience in mind. I always write for myself or the elected twelve envisioned critics whom one respects.

Q: How do you distinguish between writing a novel and writing a short story? Are you conscious that you are writing a novel rather than a short story?

Sansom: Well, I believe in keeping short stories short, and I know bloody well when I'm going to write a novel because it's going to be a stinking long job, inhuman. To me, writing a novel is like being a boardinghouse keeper where you've got the same characters, the same people to serve for a terrible long time: a year and a half to two years living with you. This does not happen in any other form of art, as far as I can see. We'll leave out the Sistine Chapel ceiling, perhaps. I don't know how long that took. On the whole, works of art are a damn sight quicker than a novel is.

William Sansom

Q: How do you distinguish in your own mind between a short story and a novel: the boardinghouse and, say, the hotel?

Sansom: The boardinghouse and a nice short holiday by the sea. I like writing them better than novels; I've come to that conclusion now. Although I'll probably write another novel simply because one likes to change what one is doing. It's because you can write at full steam for about three weeks with one picture in your mind. (I have a very visual mind because I'm a sort of painter manqué.) And also one philosophical theme or human action that you want to get at. It's conceivable that you could link a lot of short stories and make one picaresque novel with the same people, but it wouldn't truly be interlinked or flow like the ordinary novel. Or would it? In fact, I have now done it—a book called *Hans Feet in Love*. It got a mixed reception. Rotten reviews generally. But lovely letters of appreciation from readers I respect. I sit here, at least, with a little bit of fan mail. But with a novel, a "normal" novel, you must remember that, the human mind being what it is, after writing a hundred pages it's very likely you'll forget what the first pages were like and have to read the damned thing again.

Q: Do you plot a novel out in advance?

Sansom: Yes, but then it, well, always goes against the plot. It *should* do this, in fact, because only when the characters take on their own lives and use the author are they really living people.

Q: Does this happen with short stories as well?

Sansom: Much less, because of their nature, I think. Because you've got in mind what they are going to do. Still, it does a bit; it should. At least the first three or four pages of the short story are pretty fixed, whereas in the novel you might have to rewrite the beginning because the people in it have taken over.

Q: Where do you get your ideas for your short stories from versus the ideas you get for novels?

Sansom: Different ways, of course. One very odd way, I find. It doesn't happen every day, but I get a visionary, almost drunken feeling about a scene of some sort which suddenly flashes into my mind with great reality. It might be the most dull suburban street or anything. This remains fixed. I want to write about it and I wonder to myself what could happen there. At some other time I see a very strange human action in a hotel or park or something, and I set that in the scene. With the human action, I always think about it a great deal: why? and then I get a philosophical theme coming in. So there are three things: a visual and a human action and a reason for the thing to be. And it usually comes, with me, first from the human scene.

Q: How conscious are you of introducing the philosophical element?

Sansom: I like it to be implicit, not stated. But I know that it's there. I kind of hint at it. I think it's an awful bore if people write it all out.

Q: Do you have the philosophical theme in mind before you set pen to paper?

Sansom: Yes.

Q: Do you find that it changes as you get on with the story?

Sansom: Well, a case in point would be writing about sexual jealousy or romantic jealousy, love jealousy. You study the question, what people do under these circumstances, and you find in the end that if they discover by chance that they needn't have been jealous at all, then they find a need to be jealous. It's just like having an illness and when you've got rid of it you sort of need it. I mean you don't really want it back again, but there is a vacuum where something existed before. This is a strange quirk.

Q: What do you feel about the work of the British Arts Council?

Sansom: I think it's a very good thing. Obviously I do because I've been on the Literature Panel myself. And my main personal interest in being on the panel is giving away money to writers. We give away quite a fat sum every year. This goes in the form sometimes of prizes, sometimes of bursaries—they're called various different legal names, but the purpose of the money is to allow the writer to buy time. That's to say, most writers in England have another job of some sort, reviewing, or the BBC, or something like that; and the point is to give them the chance to have three years of paid leisure in which to write. That's obviously a good idea, as I can vouch from personal experience, because when I was very much younger, starting out to be a writer—quite late in life, when I was about thirty, I think—I was flat broke. It was just after the war, and I had saved up a little money from various things, but very, very little indeed. I was living on almost nothing. I never starved, but I was devoted to writing and that was all I could do. I couldn't get a job at night clubs or anything like that. That was out. And I got published in a few literary magazines. Marvelously through the post came anonymous checks from people who just liked the stuff and had heard that I was living on not much. This made a great deal of difference. It gave me both the knowledge that I was respected in some quarters and of course the cash to carry on, which was very important. If you've got a year's cash in hand, then you can really not worry about writing commercially. That's to say if you're unmarried and have no children, because as soon as you marry and have children the picture changes. And then I also got a couple of literary prizes and again this made a difference. I had the practical knowledge of what difference it did make at least to one person, and it made, as far as I can see, a great difference.

Q: How is it that a writer attracts public attention? Is it because he gets involved in a movement which then attracts the public eye and focuses it on the individual?

Sansom: I don't know. It's very difficult to say. I think myself it's a matter largely of luck. That the news needs something at that particular time. For instance, the Angry Young thing started with John Osborne's play. This provoked a controversy at that time. But had it been overshadowed by Churchill's death, or what have you, it might never have received such a degree of notice. I think news is largely a matter of luck. It is rather different in France, for instance, where professionally they go out to be cher maître or have this or that school of writing. But here it's all very individual and it happens by chance. Content has a great deal, of course, to do with it—the content of your work.

Q: What are your feelings about "movements" or groups of writers? Do you feel the need to talk to another writer about your work?

Sansom: Personally, I hate it because it has the effect upon me simply of talking out of me what I should be writing. But this is again a matter of individual character. Some people can talk all the time about it and still write like beautiful birds.

Q: Would you say that if, for example, you wanted to meet a particular writer who interested you, would it be possible for you to go to a café or go to a particular party and meet him, rather than just calling him up? Is there such a thing in London?

Sansom: Well, there is no café; there used to be, but it's finished. I think there may be—you see, now you've got to consider my age, I don't go out all that much now—but there are perhaps two or three pubs where you're more likely to meet people than elsewhere. Certainly there are literary parties given by publishers, which gather together a lot of writers and you meet them there. But, personally, what writers talk about mostly when they get together is money: royalties, and how awful the publishers are and so on and so on. This gets to be an awful bore, I think. I prefer, myself, talking with my raw material, just ordinary people, listening in to overheard conversations in buses and just being a general poke-nose. Also, I like people such as doctors and, say, sailors, because they've seen so much and are good storytellers.

Q: Who are the "important" people on the English literary scene right now? Where do you think English literature is moving, particularly the novel and the short story?

Sansom: That's a very difficult question, because I'm not a very eclectic reader. There are many writers who I'm sure are very good whom I cannot read for a moment. I tend to read over and over again things like Chekhov, whom I admire enormously, and Raymond Radiguet. Good masters are Maupassant and even Somerset Maugham as a raconteur, and in American terms Hemingway and Carson McCullers. I reread these over and over again, so I'm not very much up with present-day writing, although I'm a great admirer of a woman writing here called Jean Rhys. And a man still very much alive but who has ceased to write called Henry Green; and, since we're talking of "greenish things," Graham Greene can, I think, write well. But I couldn't pour out a proper list. Except—I forgot for a moment—a youngish Jewish writer called Michael Feld. And a number of others whose names I can't remember, because they seem to come and go. Where? What I think is happening is that a lot of good writers here are writing for television. There's a lot of good stuff coming out, and obviously someone was employed to do it.

Q: One last question. Do you feel that in your own writing you are performing something that might loosely be called a social function?

Sansom: In the very loosest form. That's to say, I hope to make people more interested in life. Now that's not saving anyone or politically training anything, but I think—and this is what I've been thankful for, have heard about once or twice, in fact quite a lot of times—that what a novelist does is to bring a realization of what the reader knew all the time, but has never been able to express to himself. And this throws a light on it. Forever afterwards they know. Whereas not having the observant eye or the capacity to retain an emotion and analyze it and so on, it's past them. It's kind of gone through—they've gone on to something else. So you make them, I think, more alive.

Q: Thank you, Mr. Sansom.

Anthony Thwaite

ANTHONY THWAITE was born in 1930 in Chester and educated at Kingswood School, Bath, and Christ Church College, Oxford. He is married to Ann Harrop and has four daughters. He has taught English at the universities of Tokyo (1955–57) and Libya (1965–68), worked as producer for the BBC (1957–62) and as literary editor for both the *Listener* (1962–65) and the *New Statesman* (1968–73). In 1965 he was awarded the Richard Hillary Prize. He has edited various collections of poetry, written books of travel, criticism, and poetry, including *Home Truths* (1957), *The Owl in the Tree* (1963), and *The Stones of Emptiness* (1967).

The interview took place in the London offices of the *New Statesman*.

Q: Is there a tendency, do you think, among editors of literary magazines to pick up an interesting young author, blow him up until he becomes fashionable, and then cut him down to size again? In other words, does the sale of literature require that there always be controversy about an author, that his reputation can never be stable?

Thwaite: I certainly wouldn't like to be responsible for such an atmosphere, but if it exists, I suppose we almost inevitably reflect it. I can't think of any recent examples of this kind of thing happening on the scale of Colin Wilson. When *The Outsider* was first published back in 1955 or 1956, he was widely praised—book reviews in the Sunday papers using words like "genius" and "highly original." Then a myth grew up about him, how he slept out in a sleeping bag on Hampstead Heath and went to the British Museum to read, how he was an autodidact, and all that. *The Outsider* became a best seller, though how many people who bought it actually read it is another matter. Then with succeeding books, the critics began to feel that they'd been taken in, until gradually it came to seem that Colin Wilson was not a serious figure at all. What has he been doing since? Writing—what could one call them?—intellectual thrillers and anthologies of murder, a kind of production that confirms the suspicion that he'd been a ludicrously overpraised figure.

Q: How do you choose your reviewers and what do you think of the present state of reviewing?

Thwaite: One of the bad things about the state of English reviewing at the moment is that the same people tend to get used over and over again by a fairly wide range of periodicals, in the *Sunday Times*, the *Observer*, the *New Statesman*, the *Listener*, the *Spectator*, the *Telegraph*, the *Times*. It would be better if each journal had a recognizably basic team of reviewers who would be committed to that journal and no one else. But that's economically very difficult to achieve. If one's using a free-lance reviewer and not an academic with a regular, salaried job, it's impossible to provide the money necessary to keep him going under a contractual arrangement. The Sunday papers do, however, manage to do this, with a small number of contracted people: Cyril Connolly and Raymond Mortimer on the *Sunday Times*, and Philip Toynbee on the *Observer*. On the *New Statesman* we're very lucky because we have V. S. Pritchett built into the system, as it were. His association with the *New Statesman* goes back to the thirties and he was himself for a short time its literary editor and is now a director. He has a contractual arrangement whereby he doesn't review for anybody else in England. This is a marvelous arrangement, because Pritchett is probably the outstanding man of letters in this country at the moment. He's one of the few remaining masters of the full-length essay-review.

The Writer's Place

We do have contractual arrangements, however, with reviewers of the arts, film, opera, theatre, painting, and so on.

Q: How are they selected?

Thwaite: Well, I've been on the *Statesman* for a year and two or three months, so I've inherited some people from my predecessors. I wasn't bound to keep them, but in fact they were on the whole good. The ones I didn't think were good were tapered off gradually and new ones were hired. How did I find them?—To be fair, it was not in all cases a feeling on my part that these contractual reviewers were bad; in the case of a theatre reviewer, for instance, he simply gave it up and went back to the BBC, where he'd been previously employed.

I did a great deal of asking round among people whose opinions I respected—looking for a theatre reviewer. Eventually I narrowed down to one choice and had him over to the office for a number of sessions. First I hired him as a sort of fill-in, while the regular reviewer was going on holiday, just to see what his stuff was like. I was pleased, so we made it a regular arrangement.

In general, however, with books which seem to need specialist reviewing, one looks for the specialist. In time, therefore, one builds up a team of specialist reviewers. With more general fields, with fiction for example, my feeling is that one can't use a fiction reviewer regularly for too long. I think Cyril Connolly says in one of his early essays that the ideal fiction reviewer should be under twenty-nine and have the hide of a rhinoceros. Here again I inherited a small team of reviewers. I kept one of them and let the others taper off. I kept those for about a year and just recently I've hired a new lot. Well, finding these is a matter again of asking round and reading—not just one's competitors, but the little magazines. For example, one of our reviewers, James Fenton, is still at Oxford; I picked him out of one of the little university magazines. I saw some things I liked and so I got in touch with him. I took him on on the basis that, if we didn't like his first piece, we would pay for it but we wouldn't go on. But we did like it. In other cases, we've in a sense poached on the *TLS*. If over a period I read fiction reviews there which strike me as good and I sense a distinct personality behind them, then I find out who is writing them and get in touch with them.

Q: How do you find out who wrote the article?

Thwaite: Well, I have my contacts. Are you going to the *TLS* after this? (*laughter*) Ideally, as I say, I would like to have a small, compact, loyal group of my own reviewers. At any rate, during my editorship here I've avoided as much as possible repeating the same names. Of course, some of our reviewers also get poached by other papers—the *Observer*, for instance. Since we can't afford to offer a firm, well-paid contract, there's no way to prevent that in most cases.

Q: What would you say is your policy on reviewing—or do you have a coherent policy?

Thwaite: Well, I hope we have some sort of coherent policy. I hope that it reflects my taste to some extent, though I'd be very surprised if we were terribly consistent. I think there's a sort of lazy myth that the books and arts character of the *New Statesman* is such and such, as distinguished from the *Spectator*, which is such and such. One feels as if these people haven't read us for some time, perhaps five years. Occasionally I get letters from people, picking up something they've read in the *New Statesman* and dragging in with it a whole barrage of extraneous criticism: why, for example, do you use that dreadful woman Brigid Brophy? In fact, Brigid Brophy hasn't written for the *New Statesman* for about four years; and I wouldn't employ her if she paid me. People get a fixed idea of what a paper is like and don't bother to see what changes have been made.

Leavis is guilty of this kind of attack, for example in the last *TLS* where he has a go not only at us, but at the Sunday papers, at Lord Annan, Lord Robbins, the BBC. Well, I'd very much like to know when Leavis last read the *New Statesman*. His idea of it dates from a good many years back and even then, I suspect, was not based on too firm a bedrock of fact. Of course, over a period of time a paper does build up an image for itself. For example, in the thirties the character of the front of the paper and the back of the paper was markedly different. The front was radical and represented everything Kingsley Martin stood for, and the back, edited for most of the period by Raymond Mortimer, represented something quite different, with the Bloomsbury values and imagining that everyone had a country house and went to France. It's very difficult right now, on the spot, as it were, to characterize the paper as a whole, except that, as I say, I hope that the back part reflects my tastes. That doesn't mean, of course, that every book which is dealt with there is one which I have read or have knowledge of or even have opinions about. But over the years, as a literary editor (or go-between, which is what one essentially is), one develops an instinct about which books are worth doing. A great deal of this job is sniffing and tasting.

Q: When John Gross's book came in, for example, did you ask Pritchett to review it or did he ask for it?

Thwaite: No, I asked him. I've known about that book for quite a long time, and so has Pritchett. We agreed months and months ago that when it came out, he would do it. Both of us read it in proof, we discussed it and agreed that it should be our lead review, about eighteen hundred to two thousand words. Our lead reviews vary in length, with the minimum about thirteen hundred and the maximum something over two thousand.

Q: How do you decide what's going to be in the lead position? Do you try to vary it, have fiction one week, criticism the next, history, and so on?

Thwaite: Yes, although one might very well have three political books done in a row. The lead, of course, is fixed a little way ahead; it's the most important thing, to get that right. And then, throughout the rest of that particular issue, one tries to get a balance of subject. The only thing that is absolutely consistent is that we do review new fiction every week. At the moment we have four fiction reviewers. I also try to get a poem in every week.

Anthony Thwaite

Q: How do you select the poem?

Thwaite: We get about three hundred poems a week, unsolicited ones that is. About once every ten days I get down to reading them. The great majority of them—80 to 90 percent—I read very quickly, just enough to recognize that they're amateurish or highly derivative. The rest I read over again, though most of these too will be rejected because we just don't have the space. I accept a poem if I think it's good, even though I realize it won't go into the paper for quite a long time. Length, within reasonable limits, has nothing to do with my choice—of course, if it's as long as *The Faerie Queene*, then the poet would have to go elsewhere. But the common notion among poets, that all that literary editors want is little two-inch things to shove in at the bottom when the review falls short, is quite mistaken. Though, of course, it's useful to have such little things around to buttress the prose, but that's not why I choose them. Being a poet myself, I can see the thing from both ends.

Q: Are you at liberty to make space available for a larger poem?

Thwaite: Yes, that's entirely up to me. My responsibility begins with the books and goes right on from there up to our competition. For this we get a very large entry. One has the feeling that perhaps the majority of the readers of the *New Statesman*, certainly in this country, will turn first to "This England," then to the competition, then perhaps to the letters, then to the small ads to see what nonsense is about in the way of little meetings on obscure topics in obscure places, and only after that will they begin to read the "hard" stuff in the rest of the paper.

Q: Does the dichotomy between front and back parts of the paper still exist?

Thwaite: There's less now than there used to be. Not that I think it was a bad thing. It was interesting to have this two-backed beast prowling about. And I find room in the back for people who would be hardly suitable for the front part. For example, in the next issue the lead review is by Robert Conquest who is regarded by many left-wing people as a fascist monster. That's neither here nor there, though I wouldn't get Robert Conquest to review a book on Vietnam, because I don't agree with his views on Vietnam. But it seems to me nevertheless that on a whole range of topics he is a very interesting and expert writer. People have a right to see what he's up to. We haven't got a narrow political line at the back of the paper. But then I don't think that's really true of the front either. The social-democrat line it believes in is as broad as the Church of England.

Q: So there's no political overflow from the front part to the back?

Thwaite: No, there's never been any interference at all with my policies or actions at the back of the paper.

Q: What you said about your readers' probable reaction to Conquest just a moment ago seems to imply that you have an idea of what your audience is like. Could you elaborate on that?

Thwaite: Very difficult. When I used to work for the *Listener*, which I did for three and a half years, I used to have a definite notion of the *Listener* reader. He was a lecturer in the extramural department of a northern university and in his mid-forties. But I haven't got such a clear picture of *New Statesman* readers, because the range of appeal, I think, is a great deal wider here. A lot of people buy the *New Statesman* not for political reasons but in order to read what we have to say on the arts.

Q: Do you do market research on your readership?

Thwaite: Well, there was a full-scale reader survey in 1962, but nothing like that since. But there is, I think, a constant review by our advertising people of the readership.

Q: To backtrack for a moment: how did William Trevor get to review Margaret Drabble's last novel?

Thwaite: Well, I admire Trevor's novels and he's someone who used to review for me on the *Listener* when he was much less well known than he is now. On one of his visits to London we had lunch together and I mentioned that the Margaret Drabble proof had just come in. I asked him about his feelings about Margaret Drabble's earlier books and when he said he liked them, I asked him if he'd be interested in doing this one. I then read it in proof, thought it was her best book, rang him and told him I was sending it off. He liked it too, but if in fact he had taken against it, that would have gone in. We agreed, after he'd read *The Waterfall*, on the length. Certainly I wanted it done by itself, but it was a matter of whether it should be eight hundred words or the fourteen hundred it finally turned out to be.

But I did try to establish first of all, you see, whether in fact he felt in sympathy with Margaret Drabble's earlier work and whether he'd read all the novels.

Q: How do you select among new novels which to review?

Thwaite: I leave that very much to the individual fiction reviewer. At the moment we have a rota of four reviewers. That means that each reviewer in his week, as it were, gets every work of new fiction that comes into the office—unless I've pulled one out to be done by itself. I prefer the reviewer to do four or five or even six of the weekly batch. All I do is put a slip in the parcel that goes off almost every day to these people, to the effect that X or Y or Z may deserve special attention. But after they've had a look at X, Y, and Z and don't feel they can say anything, that's their business. It's up to them. That's not, I think, general policy with literary editors in this country. Some literary editors are very selective about which novels get reviewed. That seems to me unfair, because what happens very often is that the promising first novel gets passed over. If you leave it to the reviewer, he'll do his own sniffing and tasting, whereas the literary editor inevitably tends to rely on names and sells the rest off to some bookseller who specializes in review copies.

Q: As literary editor for the *New Statesman*, what special or perhaps unique contribution do you think your paper makes? That other comparable papers don't?

The Writer's Place

Thwaite: Well, it's difficult to say. I try to have standards of excellence in choosing books and reviewers, and in seeing to it that what we publish is stylistically of good quality. I'm against the increasing use of the little one-inch review which one finds in the *Observer*, the *Sunday Times*, and elsewhere. That was also creeping in a bit with the *New Statesman* before my time. That's all very well for some people, but that's not our function. If a book is worth doing, then it's worth doing at reasonable length. So I'm inclining toward the kind of *New York Review of Books* style, with enormously long reviews of selected books. I don't think we'll ever reach that stage: that isn't our function either. But fewer and longer reviews is, generally speaking, my aim. Also the poetry is important. There's no other weekly review that gives quite the space to poetry that we do. The *Listener's* policy is good, but not as consistent as ours. That's part of our duty, to keep poetry healthy. It can't just exist in the world of the little magazine.

I do think it's healthy to have several weeklies competing. I would hate to see the *Spectator* or the *Listener* vanish, because we're all good for one another as long as we avoid taking in each other's washing, as it were.

Q: The attitude of writers—at any rate those I've spoken to—has been by and large that reviews have not made all that much difference to their sales and their reputations. As a poet yourself and as a literary editor, how do you feel about that?

Thwaite: I think that's true. But after all, we're not publishing reviews primarily for the sake of the authors of the books. That's not what the whole exercise is about. Kingsley Amis's reaction to reviews is probably the right one: a bad review might put him off his breakfast, but it won't put him off his lunch. I don't think it's our job to hector and berate authors for their own sakes.

Q: How much do you keep in touch with what other literary reviews are doing? If, say, one week the *Observer* reviews a particular book in an important way, does that mean you might change your emphasis?

302

Anthony Thwaite

Thwaite: No, not really. These decisions are made much earlier. Of course, I do read all the book pages of other papers, but I don't copy from them. Practically every British publication comes out on either a Monday or a Thursday. In the case of a Thursday publication, we very often beat the Sunday papers because we're on the streets by late Thursday afternoon. In the case of a Monday publication, we're behind. But I don't let the others influence me—though I'm sometimes worried if I see them attach a great deal of importance to something I haven't even sent out.

Q: In other words, there's nothing approximating a literary stock market?

Thwaite: Yes, I know one hears whispers about this sort of thing, though generally not from literary people. At a party someone, a solicitor perhaps, may ask me, "Why do you people always review the same books?" As if there were a cabal of literary editors meeting together on a Tuesday or something to decide who was going to be put in and who left out. We do in fact meet at literary parties, but it's very rare to find anyone saying what they're going to do next week or what they're going to do with a particular book.

Q: Thank you, Mr. Thwaite.

William Trevor

WILLIAM TREVOR (COX) was born in 1928 and educated at St. Columba's College and Trinity College, Dublin. He is married to Jane Ryan and has two sons. Abandoning a career of sculpting in the early sixties, he made a considerable splash with his satirical novel *The Old Boys* (1964). Aside from writing stories and more novels, Trevor has also done a number of plays, especially for TV.

The interview took place in Trevor's suburban London apartment.

Q: Does the American market at all interest you as a British writer?

Trevor: The American market is certainly helpful. It's another source of income which is, so to speak, automatically there, along with television and radio.

Q: Does one have to be consciously popular in one's writing in order to succeed?

Trevor: No, I don't think so. I myself couldn't write in a way which I thought would make money, because I know instinctively that if I tried that I wouldn't make money. But there are some writers who can, because they have the talent for it.

Q: Does this apply to television and radio as well?

Trevor: Oh yes, very much so: potboiling for television would be grim. As for radio, I write mainly for BBC-3—hardly popular stuff.

Q: Is there a smaller payment for BBC-3 than for the others?

Trevor: No, curiously enough I don't believe there is. But of course there is a difference between radio and television fees, although not all that much. My plays for radio are usually repeated and also translated. Well, when you add all that up, you're almost in the television class where fees are concerned.

Q: What about repeats on TV?

Trevor: Yes, there are repeats. But if you want to look at the situation in economic terms, take my stories: I might write a short story and publish it some place, and then even have it anthologized, perhaps, before it goes into a collection of my own. But the same short story I tend to turn into something else, a television or radio play. Most of my television plays have been based on short stories.

Q: How do you think of the transformation aesthetically? Is the short story the primary, serious medium for you, the play secondary?

Trevor: No, I don't think of it in those terms. What interests me in turning the story into a play is changing the characters around and getting to know them. You go into the thing in greater depth than you've gone into it in the first place. The characters, of course, can't become different characters, but you've got to force them to say in their own ways what you've said in several paragraphs. In this respect I'm very fond of the discipline of the radio: the listener has to get the feeling of, say, a room with the white carpet, an archway, etc., purely through the dialogue.

Q: Don't you feel you're losing control over the story when you have other people entering into it, the actors?

Trevor: Well, you do take that risk every time you do anything

The Writer's Place

that's dramatic. That's even more the case with a television play or an ordinary play. The risk is slighter in radio. I have had plays of mine on television which I didn't like at all—you know, they've exaggerated some point which I'd exaggerated enough. In the end, as far as I'm concerned, everything I do for radio and television comes back to the short story. I love the genre and I love going back to it, though I admit I like the large audience.

Q: Was your leaving Ireland a conscious choice to leave a country where there was no large audience?

Trevor: No, because when I left Ireland I wasn't writing at all. In fact, I was a sculptor. The reason I left Ireland is purely economic: in those days there was very little work for people like me. I don't think that's true now. Now I find myself more interested in Ireland, from a literary point of view, than I've ever been. My novel *Mrs. Eckdorf in O'Neill's Hotel* is set in Dublin and is a purely Irish novel, and increasingly I'm writing short stories about Ireland.

I've always thought that writing books about this country and especially a book like *The Old Boys*, which is a very English kind of book, is being like a photographer and looking at a world from the outside. To me, England was an amazing and strange place. I'd never been outside of Ireland until I was twenty-two. When I *now* write about Ireland I'm doing a faintly similar thing, because I'm going back to a country which has become strange to me. Personally, I think that kind of thing is essential and disagree with that awful advice that's given to children: "Write about what you know." I'd say the opposite, in a way: "You mustn't write about what you know. You must use your imagination."

Q: Does Ireland have any advantage as a literary milieu over England, aside, say, from the kind of novelty you've mentioned?

Trevor: Yes, one enormous advantage at the moment: there is a total tax exemption for all writers and artists working in Ireland, whether they're Irish or not.

Q: Is there more opportunity to discuss one's work with others in Ireland than here? More of a tradition of enlightened patrons of the arts?

Trevor: No, not at all. That tradition has gone in Ireland, both in the north and in the south. It's a good country for foreigners to live in, but you find there aren't as many people who are involved in the arts as you would in London. There's an old-fashioned, nineteenth-century interest in portrait painting, which is very healthy, but not much more.

Q: Is it important for you to be in touch with others who are interested in writing?

Trevor: No, not at all. I write very secretly.

Q: What do you think of the work of the Arts Council?

Trevor: I would rather they gave more money to painters and sculptors, but I think any money given to anyone who's doing something is very good. I don't think they've ever given anyone an awful lot of money who shouldn't have had it.

Q: You do agree then that literature and the arts should be subsidized?

Trevor: I think what might be done is to engage the interest of large business firms and the nationalized industries and try and persuade them to arrange a labor exchange where a writer can go and accept the nastiest possible job for six months, provided he's paid enough to live for the whole year. What you want to buy is time. As it now stands, it's very hard to choose among young applicants who have done very little to deserve support. This kind of intermediary exchange function is something the Arts Council could perform very effectively.

Q: What is your feeling about the role of literary agents as middlemen?

Trevor: They take a very great load off your shoulders. They argue for you, they save you time and money. I couldn't manage without my agent.

Q: What about the book-reviewing establishment? Are you satisfied with the way your books have been treated?

Trevor: Yes, generally speaking it's satisfactory. I used to do a good deal of reviewing myself. I don't think one can complain because even if reviewers dislike a book and take great pains to say so, the more they write, the more controversy and attention they create. I don't think you can complain seriously about book reviewing.

Q: Do you feel that the leading literary reviews—the *TLS*, the *Observer*, the *New Statesman*, and so on—are politically or even personally biased, that a certain kind of writer is bound to be roasted?

Trevor: No, definitely no. There's a great honesty in England in those matters. You can't, as far as I know, "obtain" a good review, and it's most unlikely that right-wing figures are badly reviewed in the left-wing press or vice versa just because of their political views.

Q: What about a publisher like John Calder? Do you think he makes a worthwhile literary contribution?

Trevor: Yes, I do. I'm sure he takes immense risks, and I'm sure he loses a lot of money.

Q: What other publishers are interesting and important in this way? Publishing good works of fiction by relatively unknown people? Are the publishers themselves a significant factor in this? Or would talent somehow emerge in any case?

Trevor: No, I'm sure talent could get tied up with a bad publisher and could indeed be flummoxed by it. But I don't *really* think there's any publisher that I would pick out, except for bad ones which I don't really want to talk about. I don't think there's any single good one who is above all the others. If there is, it's escaped me. Calder is special because he does so many translations from the French, and those short little books which one knows aren't going to sell very well, and he takes on young English authors. It's all adventurous and it's all very good. He's also got a sort of paperback scheme which I like. And somehow one is very much on his side, because he's doing something which nobody else is doing.

Q: Who, in your view, are the promising lights of the contemporary British literary scene? If you look back at the fifties, the Angries emerge as the obvious choice. If you look now at the late sixties and forward to the seventies, is there a group to correspond to them?

Trevor: I think there are some good women writers: Elizabeth Taylor and Edna O'Brien and Olivia Manning.

Q: But is this a movement?

Trevor: No. There's no movement at all here. I see no movement of any kind in English literature at the moment.

Q: Is the kind of novel that was written by John Wain and Kingsley Amis in the fifties pretty much played out?

Trevor: I would never connect those two, though they are always connected. But both of them are too good ever to be played out. The Angries as a movement, however, I think is completely played out. It was a fashionable form almost like James Bond in many ways, and it certainly will never appeal again in the same way. There hasn't really been any movement like that since. I suppose there could have been a hippy movement, but there hasn't. All we've had is a lot of individuals going different ways.

Q: Have Amis and Wain and that group failed? Their attempt to take the popular novel and infuse some seriousness into it? Or, vice versa, to take the serious novel and infuse some popularity into it? And has their failure emphasized the split between the popular novel—the best-selling novel—and the serious novel? Is it impossible nowadays to merge serious with popular fiction?

Trevor: I don't think you can use the term "best seller" so loosely. The reasons why novels in England become best sellers are sometimes odd. Any novel about sex by, say, a woman who has written a lot of other novels and is therefore quite well known goes straight up into the best-seller category. In the same way, Graham Greene—a novelist I like tremendously well—will also go, even with short stories, into the best-seller lists in England. His last collection of stories, *May We Borrow Your Husband*, was reviewed as rather interesting sexy stuff and became a best seller. But at the same time, Fowler's *English Usage* will go into the best-seller lists, too, in England. One simply doesn't know why this happens. I've been on the best-seller lists, and my novels haven't sold particularly well. *The Love Department* was a best seller in a couple of lists and it didn't sell as well as the previous one; the same with my stories, *The Ballroom of Romance*. I think that what happens is that when a reporter rings up a bookshop and asks, "What's your best seller?" they're going to tell you the book they've got the most of, which they want to push.

Q: What do you think of the role of the universities in shaping literary taste and helping the sales of books? And what about the writer's increasing involvement with universities, as writer in residence or something like that?

Trevor: It doesn't tempt me at all. One wants to write, not to talk about it, you know. It might be pleasant to listen to the work of students and to talk about that. But if you want really to say how something should be done—at least how you think something should be done—you don't want to get hold of Dickens, but of the rejected manuscripts of a publisher, and say, "That's where it doesn't communicate; that's where it doesn't work." You can never really explain how George Eliot did it. At least it seems to me that you can't. To be a writer in residence and to begin to talk in that way would be the wrong thing for me to do. Whereas to talk to students about what they were writing would be very different, because I think one might enjoy that. And I don't think anything like that would be worth doing unless you enjoyed it. I don't think the right person to lecture about Proust would be a novelist who was writing in a very different sort of way.

Q: What do you think your audience is? Do you envision it as you write, envision some composite member of the British public whom you want to address?

Trevor: You occasionally meet your audience, and it's very pleasant, and it's an audience that seems to come from all classes and age groups and intellectual levels. But I couldn't ever visualize my readers in a general way. I'd make a terrible mistake if I ever tried to do that.

Q: You wouldn't describe your audience—those of it that you've met for example—as primarily academic?

Trevor: No, I wouldn't, not at all. I think the people who do like my books are probably great readers, more than that I can't generalize.

Q: How does the novel, in your view, compare in attractiveness with TV?

Trevor: Oh, they're completely different. I don't really see the novel being replaced, because I don't think that it's easy to take a novel and turn it into a film or a television program. And because of that, I think the novel has got a distinctive quality. Notice how few good novels have been made good films. *Great Expectations*, yes, and a few others I can think of. But generally speaking it's the bad novel that makes the good film. And it is something which isn't even a novel at all which makes the best film: something written for cinema. Going back to what I said about short stories: with short stories, you're involved with a couple of characters and tiny little situations. You write a short story, and then you look at it again, and you think, well yes, it's visual. But this is not what a novel is about at all. A novel is much more complicated and involved. Short stories have made marvelous films, like "The Fallen Idol" or "The Third Man." There are a whole lot of others which people never remember. I often meet people in film companies who read studiously and assiduously every novel and who don't read short stories. Why on earth they don't, I don't know. Even though Graham Greene has had such success with short stories, they don't go for them. But short stories are perfect for film scripts.

I believe that there's something special about reading. And I believe that there is a pleasure to be got out of reading which you don't get from anything else. And I don't think that people are likely to alter—I mean as long as they're taught to read; I don't see that they're not going to prefer books in the end to television. I was brought up on Edgar Wallace, and I couldn't stop reading that sort of book when I was a small child. I don't get the same pleasure out of television, or out of the cinema even. I love the cinema, and I'm very fond of television. But I don't get the same sort of pleasure at all. I think the novel is much more of a real thing than we've ever allowed for. That one-to-one business of the novel: you know, between two people, not between one person and a theatreful, or between one person and nine million people on television. That is what a novel is and if you like that you're going to go on liking it in spite of television or anything else.

Q: Thank you, Mr. Trevor.

John Wain

JOHN WAIN was born in 1925 in Stoke-on-Trent and was educated at the High School, Newcastle-under-Lyme, and St. John's College, Oxford. He has been married twice: to Marianne Urmston (divorced 1956) and to Eirian James; he has three children. In 1955 he abandoned an academic career at the University of Reading (begun in 1947), though he still teaches occasionally as a visiting professor at home and abroad. His first novel, *Hurry on Down* (1953), established him as one of the angrier, as well as funnier, of the Angry writers, and since then he has published several more novels, books of poetry and criticism, as well as a precocious autobiography, *Sprightly Running* (1962).

The interview took place in the garden of a pub just outside Oxford.

Q: Can a serious writer make a living from his work in England, without resorting to other, related kinds of jobs? For example, becoming a writer in residence, something Colin Wilson was writing about in a recent issue of *Encounter*?

Wain: I find that several things are happening at once. I live partly on the royalties of my past books of course. And as I get older and I have more books in print, they keep coming in, albeit very slowly, because I write the sort of book that has a tiny sale each year. And thank God, all my books virtually are in print, including things I wrote nearly twenty years ago now. So I am to some extent subsidized by my own past work. And this on the

313

whole remains very constant. It seems to me every week somebody buys a copy of each one of my books, you know, more or less. On the other hand, it is also true that the older I get the more money I need; because I have a family and so on. So my position has improved slightly, but in terms of what I need it's slightly gone down: I have less money to dispose of than I had a few years ago. Therefore, I ought to do more journalism and more broadcasting, but I have found it increasingly distasteful, because when young, one could flit from one thing to another. I find that I have to give my mind to what I'm doing. I hope that this is not just the process of aging; I hope that it is also the process of having a more deeply pondered work, you know. I hope my work is taking on a deeper note, otherwise there's no point in going on. So I have taken to the strategy now of subsidizing myself, not by the odd article which can be dashed off in a morning, but I write a book and I concentrate on the book, and I let the bills mount up. When it's finished, I definitely turn to something to make some money. Like for instance now teaching for six months in Paris. I am really not doing any writing for six months. I can't. I'm giving my time to this. But it will clear off the arrears and it will put some money in the bank. And then next autumn I'm going to Cincinnati to do a job for them at the university. I didn't mean to do two jobs in one year, but they just came in at the same time and they both seemed too good to miss, so I did them both. Which is a mistake. I wish I could have got out of it. I am spending what amounts to a whole year teaching.

Sometimes, I do a book whose main purpose is to make some money, although always one that is related to my interests. For instance I did an anthology of modern criticism of *Macbeth*. I am passionately fond of Shakespeare, but the reason for doing this book was because it was a textbook: six months' work. I don't very often do jobs that take me a day or two. I sometimes do, but not very often because the pattern of my self-subsidizing has altered. It's now officially been recognized by the government, as it were, that a serious writer cannot live. And the answer they come up with has been grants of money to individual writers, but as none of this has come my way yet, I just have to carry on and subsidize myself.

Q: Is it a good thing for writing to have poets in residence, novelists in residence?

Wain: Well, I went as a visiting professor for a month to Bristol University, and admittedly the terms of my appointment were academic: I had to lecture, but I prefer to do that. What I personally shy away from is the idea of being retained either to teach creative writing or just to sort of be a writer. I shy away from that a bit, because since I have enough interest in classical English literature to know something about it and therefore I am competent to do academic work, I would rather do that. It doesn't cross my wires so much. What I think about it is this: there is no substitute for a large, interested reading public, along with books that are reasonably cheap so that it can buy them. This is what I want, this is what I would like. Sometimes one reads with great envy about the average writer back in about 1910 who, whatever he lacked in terms of university sinecures and so on, had access to a trade in cheap books, a large reading public, one not distracted by mass media, so that people went home of an evening and read books. Now, this is what one would really like. I mean, as far as I'm concerned, there is no substitute at all for the man or woman who buys the book, takes it home, or gets it out of the library, gets it somehow, steals it, anything, takes it home, and reads it for fun. That's the relationship one wants. And all the universities in the world, and all the government bursaries, and all the everything else won't ever bring that back. There won't ever be a substitute for that. It hasn't quite gone, of course; plenty of people read. But in our time the price of books has become so fantastic that I don't expect people to be able to put down two pounds and buy a novel, not if they are going to read, as one hopes a literate person were to read, five or six novels in a month. So, ideally, what there should be is cheap books and a big reading public which will just support you.

Q: What about paperbacks?

The Writer's Place

Wain: Well, paperback editions, you know, it's largely a myth that this has revolutionized the position of the writer. The so-called paperback revolution, when you look at it, is pretty disappointing. To begin with, it's part of the economics of our time that the only thing that's worth selling is the thing that you can sell by the million. So the paperback firms which can in certain cases make very large sums only really like to handle books which will have a mass sale. So the hard-cover publisher gets more and more nervous of books which will not be immediately transferable to the paperback market, and so you get more and more pressure. [Noise of a jet passing overhead.] There's a good emblem of our time, the jet plane drowning out my words as it goes over. And the people sitting in that jet plane are reading *Life* magazine.* They're not reading books; you can't read a book in a plane.

Q: Or they're reading business reports.

Wain: Yes, if they are reading anything as intelligent even as *Life* magazine. But, really the paperback revolution has meant that books are on sale at more outlets, and that in terms of sheer gross maybe a great many books are sold, perhaps even more are sold, I don't know. But I know this: from the point of view of the writer who thinks of himself as contributing to literature, they haven't really made much difference. What they have done is to make the hardback publishers more nervous. And remember also that when a hardback book is republished in paperback, the cut that the author gets is apt to be very small. To begin with, it's cut right down the middle with the hardback publisher. So that already half of it is gone. But, you know, I am very grateful for high-level publishing, high-level paperback publishing. I wrote a book on Shakespeare which was intended to reach a large public, particularly of students and academics, and since Penguin Books brought it out, it has reached a large public and I am very pleased.

*I find it ironic and sad that, since I spoke these words, *Life* has folded. Now, the passengers are probably watching movies.

It has also made me some money, but you know it has to be the *Carpetbaggers* or something of that sort to make money, really.

Q: What do you think of John Calder who publishes first novels in paperback?

Wain: In some ways, I think that John Calder's publishing methods are very good and very refreshing. And I only wish that he were not so wedded to a certain very narrow taste which is broadly the taste of Grove Press. Because if your entire perspective on literature is to look through the spectacles of Grove Press, you do not see an awful lot that you ought to see. And in order to be published by John Calder as a young beginning writer, you have to write in the idiom of the *Evergreen Review*. And there is an awful lot wrong with the idiom of the *Evergreen Review*.

Q: Do you see anyone besides John Calder filling the need you describe: not the Grove Press emphasis, but still getting at new writers?

Wain: Oh, I think so, I think so. The publishing field is full of enterprising characters. And publishing is very adaptable I think. To take an example with my own publishers, Macmillan, who are rather old-fashioned and solid in the very best sense. They represent a tradition of immensely solid Victorian publishing, very conservative and very good. Until a few years ago, they still had genuine cloth in their cloth bindings and genuine gold in their gold lettering, long after everybody else had gone to plastics and so on. Now if they publish a volume of poetry, they automatically publish two editions to come out on the same day, a hardback and a paperback. The paperback is because the young people who read poetry, as they do in large numbers now, want the paperback, and the libraries want the hardback. So they have adapted, as it were, to the modern world in that way. Then Faber & Faber do an interesting series where they take two or three young writers and make one book out of them. And this has the

317

very good effect, by the way, of encouraging the *conte* or *nouvelle*, the story of 25,000 words which has always been a difficult length to work in economically. But I think it is a wonderful length. Some of Henry James's best stories are that length. One of my least unsatisfactory stories is about 20,000 words, but in order to get it into print at all, I had to write a lot of other short stories to go with it and publish it as *Nuncle and Other Stories*. Which was all right with me, because I write short stories anyway; but supposing I didn't?

Q: I know in *Sprightly Running* you object very much to the term "Angries," and I can see why. On the other hand, it was a handle, as it were, by which one could grab a literary generation. Is there any such convenient handle around now? Who do you think is important on the contemporary British scene? Who interests you? What kind of modern British writer do you read?

Wain: That's a question that is hardly worth asking me. I mean you weren't to know that, but I read very few writers younger than myself—for the usual reason. That is, if they are good, I am jealous and suspicious of them. But if they're bad, I don't want to read them anyway. Who wants to read the generation that is going to tread one down? But I do read some writers whom I know personally. I happen to meet them around Oxford, for instance. I know some young poets who are very good, but if I name them it would be very invidious, because there might be other poets whom I haven't read who are just as good or better. The fact is, like most practitioners of forty and over, I have given up any effort to keep up. I have no idea what is being written. There are certain writers of my own generation who mean a great deal to me. Principally, Philip Larkin. I think Philip Larkin is the only modern English writer whose work I take care to read every syllable of. But there are one or two other writers of my own generation who are always entertaining and amusing, but I have really no views on the subject. When I read, I mostly read the classics, just because I find them so interesting and illuminating, and, as I get older, they're so much more valuable to me. I don't keep up very much. I haven't read a literary magazine for years. I think that one can't attempt to keep up. I think particularly you cannot read those writers whose work is supposed to have anything in common with your own, because that's fatal. So, while I trust that there are people working away, and that there's some sort of scene, I don't consider it my duty to keep abreast of it. I do, on the other hand, think it my duty to do what I can for the art of literature. By which I mean that I think good criticism is important. I think that to encourage your supply of good critics and good reviewers and to encourage publishers to keep up standards, to help with practical things, to try to talk committees into giving money to people, anything like that, I do that. What I won't do is read everyone's output; I can't, you see.

My impression is that the sort of hippie literary scene is not very interesting. I've never found a writer of that tendency who has seemed to me to take the actual business of literature seriously enough. The ones who frankly admit that in their opinion the art of language, all the arts to do with language are finished and yet continue to be poets seem to me would be better off getting a job in the post office or something. I mean, why are they still poets? If they honestly think language is no longer interesting and that the next phase of civilization will be conveyed entirely through images and so on, well, right, let them get on with that. But to go on being poets and having things called poetry readings, I don't understand the logic of that. There must be some self-indulgent logic here which escapes me.

Q: In *Sprightly Running* again, you mention that you learned a great deal about style from C. S. Lewis, possibly from the people around him, even though you didn't share their presuppositions. Would you say there's anything like this now at Oxford or in England? Is there any opportunity for a younger writer to meet older writers to learn something from them?

Wain: I didn't learn anything about the craft of writing from that group around Lewis. What one learned from Lewis, personally, was to express oneself precisely as far as possible. One tried to

319

follow his quickness in debate which was marvelous. His wits were very quick. He could think on his feet, you know, very very quickly. This was a wonderful example and a wonderful stimulus. I didn't learn anything about how to be a writer from those people, because the ones who had any gift as imaginative writers were people whose tendency was entirely opaque to me. I could not then, and cannot now understand why people think Tolkien's work is interesting. And you know, that was their showpiece, that was the great work they had all collaborated on by encouraging him. So I can't say in those days that that particular milieu was of any use. But of course, I'm quite sure that there are points of contact. Some of them are small enough and artificial enough not even to be worth mentioning in terms of contact. For instance, there must be many people like me. You see, I live in Oxford. Sometimes it happens that a young poet or somebody with some kind of literary interest in Oxford will get in touch with me. They ring me up, or they come out to my house. And we go out and have a drink, and I talk to them and whether I'm any use to them or not, there must be many people like me. I'm not the only one. Then there's the whole institution, there's the institution of Oxford, there's the professor of poetry which is really Oxford's version of the writer in residence. Roy Fuller comes here and he gets crowds of people coming up and talking to him. Oxford life is full of informal opportunities for contact between more established writers and younger writers which don't get into the official curriculum at all. It's set up to provide endless opportunities of informal contact. I think English life is full of these opportunities. It's a small country, tightly knit, everybody lives close to everybody else. It's not institutionalized, but it's full of these opportunities. Now where young writers go in London to meet with more established writers, I don't know, because I'm not in that position. I am not in the position of being one of the London older generation or one of the London younger generation. But you can bet that it happens. Forty years ago it happened on a social level. There were hostesses who gave soirées, you know, rather like Mrs. Leo Hunter in *Pickwick*, where a young aspirant like Priestley could meet Wells and Shaw and even sometimes Conrad or Thomas Hardy. But then there was a great change. It was no longer done in that social lion way. The hostess dropped out as an important figure. The last one was Lady Ottoline Morrell, whose beer we drink because of course she's of the Oxford family of Morrell the brewer. So I feel a personal interest in having provided them with some of their fortune. But I never got any of the resulting benefits. (*laughter*) It was all over by my day. But when I was a young writer first knocking around London, the poet and critic George Fraser used to have open house once a week at his house in Chelsea. Everybody used to go along to George's and you used to take a bottle. George would provide house room and you took a bottle or anything you could afford and you went along. Now George Fraser gave up the unequal struggle in the end to make a living in London as a literary man, and he went to a university post in Leicester. And I think he still does very much the same thing in Leicester, but of course it isn't quite the same. The dragnet doesn't get so many types as it did then. But there must be a George Fraser in London now. Who he is, I don't know. It doesn't concern me anymore. But, I bet that there is plenty of that going on.

Q: One of the things that strikes me about English literary history is that somehow there seem to be spurts of good writing and then they die down again only to spurt up again.

Wain: Is it only English literary history?

Q: Yes, probably it's a general phenomenon. If you look at the spurts, they seem somehow to be connected with groups of people who come together. For example, you mentioned Lady Ottoline Morrell—Garsington—or the group you were associated with, even if loosely, around Lewis. Is it a presupposition for the production of good literature that the producers, if one wants to call them that, should be joined together? I'm thinking, for example, of your statement in *Sprightly Running* that one reason you began writing *Hurry On Down* is that you saw Amis writing a novel.

Wain: Yes, of course, young writers incite one another tremendously. And the great value of a big university like Oxford, for instance, which brings people together from all over the country and from every social class, and also brings in a lot of people from abroad, the great advantage of that is that one finds people who are interested in the same kind of thing and you encourage each other. But this is a slightly different matter from what you were saying, because after all very bad writers can be encouraged. How can I answer this? It seems to me that I believe in the existence of something that one can only call the *Zeitgeist*. One has to take over that term from the Germans. We have no other. I think there is something that one could call the *Zeitgeist* that really does work and really does produce a great impulse which seems to flow through the events of the time into the imaginative arts. And then at other times the *Zeitgeist* seems to slacken off, as it were, or to go into another direction to vitalize another aspect in the life of the nation. In English literature we have the fantastic phenomenon of the early years of the nineteenth century when Coleridge, Wordsworth, Keats, Shelley, Byron, Blake were all working. A fantastic outburst of creativity! So much so that the gigantic *Oxford History of English Literature* has to devote a whole volume to seventeen years, and even that is very crowded. After that there is a slackening, on the whole, of interest. (In France it is exactly the opposite. The first generation of French Romantic writers is less interesting than the second generation. They became interesting with the writers who wrote in the 1840s and 1850s, where on the whole we became less interesting.) What is it? The *Zeitgeist* happened to work with us. It seemed to flow through the political events of the time and directly into the images and the great symbols that these men produced. And then it seemed to ease off.

But this has certainly nothing to do with writers getting together in gangs, because some of the poorest writers that have ever been permitted have got together in gangs. And very often you see, as in the classic case of the English Romantics, they didn't know each other very well. Keats refused to meet Shelley, because he felt quite rightly that Shelley's genius might be too much for him, and it might confuse him. He wanted to develop in his own way. It's also true of the very much publicized movement of the 1930s: Auden, Spender, Day Lewis, and MacNeice. I believe it's a matter of cold fact that only once in their lives were all four of them together in a room. And actually the only ones that had anything to do with each other very much were Auden and Spender. So on the whole, I don't believe it matters much whether writers get together and cooperate. You mentioned Lady Ottoline Morrell, but frankly anybody in her circle who had any talent at all had already shown it long before her particular sun shone on them. Lawrence owed nothing to her. They came together and very often the result of their coming together was that they irritated one another. No, on the whole, I think that there is a binding principle in society which is very difficult to get at and for which one uses the word *Zeitgeist*. Just as when we say that birds find their way by instinct we mean we don't know how they find their way, so when we say the *Zeitgeist*, we mean that we don't know what it is, but it's there.

Q: Would you agree with someone like McLuhan who suggests that the *Zeitgeist* is leaving literature and moving into films and television?

Wain: Well, of course, yes. It isn't only McLuhan who says that. I mean they are now talking that up very much. It's the part of McLuhan's message that is easily adapted, and so it's rather like the part of Darwin's message being, you know, "Survival of the Fittest," which was a phrase in fact coined by Herbert Spencer, was it not? Now McLuhan is a very complex thinker, with a great personal stake in literacy. But what he has suggested is that the next phase belongs to the electronic image and so on. Well, I think this is probably quite likely. I have noticed with modern children that they will accept anything that comes to them in the form of an image. They will accept anything that can be shown to them on a screen, or on the stage, or as a photograph, or a painting. But they don't lose themselves in books the way we did. I think that there is probably a slackening. On the other hand, I see no reason why language as a great permanent human possession shouldn't reassert itself. I don't think the electronic conditions are going to make against language forever. I think, for instance, of the mid-sixteenth century when there was a great retreat from language, when all the major contributions to the arts were in painting and architecture and music. Literature was very poor. And then by the time that century ends you've got Shakespeare, Marlowe, Ben Jonson, Spenser, all working away. A tremendous resurgence came, of the word. And I am fully prepared to wait out this frost, as it were, and wait for the next great renaissance of the word. And I don't see any social reason why it shouldn't come. I don't think that these new forces are basically antilanguage. What they have done is to take the emphasis off language for the time being.

Q: Would you agree with someone like Ortega y Gasset who makes the analogy between, for example, the novel form, without any kind of narrative, and a biological species? He claims that a species has, like the novel, a certain number of possibilities; when these possibilities are exhausted, it becomes extinct. Has this happened? Or is it happening? Particularly to literary narrative?

Wain: The question here is one of time scale. Unless it is set upon and destroyed by predators as certain flightless birds were destroyed by rats in island settings—and it's possible that the novel may be destroyed by rats—but if it is not, it seems to me that it takes a species a very long time to die out and that it is impossible from outside to tell whether it is dying or merely gathering itself for another phase. The novel as written in the eighteenth century, when it had its first great success, became obsolete toward the end of the nineteenth. The novel as written toward the end of the nineteenth became obsolete sometime in the twentieth. Then at the time when I first started writing novels, which was about sixteen years ago, there was a renewal of interest in eighteenth-century fiction. And it seemed to us instinctively the *Zeitgeist* again. We didn't tell each other this, but we all independently came to the conclusion that writers like Smollett, for instance, who used farce for a serious purpose were much more interesting than anyone had ever told us they were. So we all started to write like that again, like sunflowers turning to face the sun. Nobody told us to do it. We just did it. New things arise, and there is all sorts of vitality there. So I would say that a species doesn't die out under many millennia unless it is exterminated. Now it is quite possible that the literary novel will be exterminated—in which case it will be an inside job.

Q: I notice that your own fiction is becoming more and more, how should I say?—not necessarily political but having to do with special social problems. I am thinking for example of *The Young Visitors* or *A Smaller Sky*. Is this something you are consciously moving into? Are you beginning to use the novel as a means of expressing a dissatisfaction with social or moral conditions? Do you see the novel as a means of making people aware of these problems and perhaps changing them?

Wain: Goodness me, what a lot all at once in that. When I first published a novel sixteen years ago, it attracted attention because people said that it was an expression of dissatisfaction with social and moral attitudes. So, whether or not I agreed with that—I mean if I accept that—I can't possibly accept that I have only just begun to do that. But it seems to me that the novel is certainly in this position: that the novels that attract attention almost always seem to do so because they make some effort to change the world or because it can be said of them that they make some effort. In other words, it seems to me that in the mind of the reading public, the novel is in this relationship to society: that people who read it and talk about it nearly always seem to describe it to one another as a social act, whereas you can still write a poem and have it regarded as a straight reaction to life in its purer aspects or whatever. But if you write a novel, people always seem to see in it some sort of social perspective. And it may be that they show an instinctive wisdom. It may be that the novel was very much born in the world and lives in the world. This may be so. I know that many of the writers I most admired such as Turgenev, for instance, were credited with great social influence. What can I say in answer to these specific questions? Have I recently begun to turn to it? No. Do I see myself as primarily socially reforming? No. On the other hand, a novel is a reaction to contemporary life. One thinks of a certain story, and the story seems interesting. One makes a decision to write about these characters and not some others. To tell this story and not some other. What does it come out of? It comes out of a reaction to life. And of course, if one is at all involved in the life going on about one, it is a reaction on as deep a level as one's nature has in it—to everything. I know these are clichés, but what can you say? Living as I do, primarily as an Englishman. But it's like concentric rings: I mean, the inner ring is that I'm an Englishman. The next ring is that I am a Western European. The next ring out from that is that I belong to the Western world generally. The next ring out from that is to be a human being. All these have reverberations, and I come up with a thing which I try to make as spontaneous as I can. In other words, I never, never, never have a thesis and say, now that is a thesis: I will now write a novel to illustrate it. But on the other hand, you arrive at what is almost that position by a more reliable route, which is that you think, "Oh, that would be an interesting story." Now, I don't know what specific problem you think I had in mind when I wrote *The Smaller Sky*; because that seems to me a—not to use a dangerous word—a symbolic *nouvelle* about loneliness, self-destructive loneliness. It's true that I made the man a scientist, and I think that the pressures that pressed on him might very well be such as would press on a scientist. I might have made him a poet if it comes to that. *The Young Visitors* is a departure from the straight line of my work. It's an exceptional book. I tried to deal with a Romeo and Juliet story: you know, of two young people on either side of the ideological debate who fall in love and who are dragged apart because of their commitment, which is in

326

fact a spurious commitment on either side. Now everybody told me that book was utter nonsense and rubbish and wasn't worth the paper it was written on. So I have to believe them, I suppose. I'll just try again.

Q: Would you say that book is a direct outgrowth of your experience in the Soviet Union?

Wain: Well yes, in this sense: that I was very unaware of politics. I had always been a complete political illiterate. I had never studied politics at all. And I had rather fallen for a lot of the stuff I'd read about the thaw, you know, the humanization of the Soviet Union and how much better it had got. And I went there expecting to find something like a liberal Western society. When I found a real, fully fledged totalitarian society, it shocked me so much that I said a number of tactless things which got me in a lot of trouble. But I'm glad I said them. And why the Russians were so irritated with me was exactly because I had not spent years studying these problems, exactly because I went there as a naïf and just came out with this, like the child who says the tactless thing. That's why the Soviet literary bureaucracy attacked me so furiously and for so long. But I must admit that it taught me to revalue all my political experience. It taught me what totalitarianism even with its mild face, even with its mild expression, is like. I want no part of it. And I must say that it gave me a much more critical attitude to the generation that we have in the West, who have grown up in complete protection, who have been protected from totalitarianism so that they no longer know what it means. They can even get up and shout for freedom of speech in the name of Mao Tse-tung, you know. I have the number of all those people far more than if I had never been to Russia, so it's a good thing I went, I suppose.

Q: Is one of the reasons you live in Oxford that you don't want to belong to a literary grouping in London? That you don't want to be disturbed by the odd person who knocks on your door?

Wain: Well, it isn't so much the odd person who knocks on my door. I have always found, or found for a long time—at least ten years—the atmosphere of anything that could be called a literary world very oppressive. This is quite personal. You learn to do the thing that's right for you. And certainly doing something like writing is very instinctive; without necessarily being able to give causes for it you learn not to do the thing that jars the machine. Whatever it is that produces the work is something you cannot control, you can thwart it, but you can't turn it on. You can only turn it off. And one of the things that turns it off with me is to see too much of other writers. So I never read literary papers. I never read the reviews of my own books. I never mix very much with other writers. Some writers are my friends, of course. But I don't like a literary milieu, and to live the life that some writers live in London or Paris, where they literally mix all the time with other writers, and where they are discussing the stock market quotations—I mean who's up a few points and who's down a few points—and writing articles on one another. How they still write books, even the poor books that they mostly do write, is beyond me. Because as far as I am concerned, my first advice to a writer—after that very first stage where you meet other writers, and it's all very exciting when you are twenty-one—my first advice would be: don't hang around writers.

Q: What do you think of a novelist like Joyce Cary who claimed in an interview that he did really very little reading of novels and particularly recent novels, that what he was really interested in was history, psychology, autobiography, that kind of thing? Georges Simenon, I think, was another one of these non-novel reading novelists.

Wain: Well yes, yes, I believe that. I don't think it's a criticism of the novel. I mean I don't think that it is an adverse criticism of the novel on the part of these men, who after all have invested a great deal of their lives in their belief in it. And they are prepared to take risks because they believe in the novel; I mean, they are prepared to risk poverty, neglect, and so on—risk working for years at something which turns out to be no use to them, or to anyone else. I think that when a novelist says he doesn't read novels very much, one cannot take it as a sign of lack of faith. After all, he demonstrates his faith by something much more difficult, which is writing them. On the other hand, I think it is very likely that a novelist whose own imaginative world is something that he must keep as vital as possible mostly refreshes that world not from other novels—which is, after all, rather like breathing breathed air—but from information. A writer needs information. A writer needs a great deal of information. I myself try very hard to set aside time to read serious books in the field of, say, history or politics. I try to be as well informed as my limited equipment will permit me to be. I would much rather put effort into that than to put effort into keeping up with literature. If I read a book on some classical English author who interests me, if I read a book on Shakespeare or Milton, I would much rather read a scholarly book which tells me something, even if it's not written with any imagination. If the man has found out something and he is prepared to tell me, I want that. What I don't want is his sensitive interpretation. I have had all the sensitive interpretations I want in my lifetime.

Q: Though you live in Oxford, you're off regularly to teach in Paris or America, and I can think of other writers of roughly your generation who seem to be more out of England than in it: Burgess, for instance, or Nigel Dennis. Would you say that the English writer is essentially an international writer now, in a way that, say, Dickens never was or could have been?

Wain: Yes, well of course, the experience of the individual is much less narrowly national than it used to be, obviously. And to a great extent, the whole Western world has become processed into a very similar place. We all live in much the same kind of houses, and we read the same kind of magazines, we see the same kind of programs on television, we wear the same kind of clothes, and so on. We take the same medicines and the rest of it. But if anybody were to say from that that the quality of life in one country is now exactly the same as it was in another, all I would say is that he should move around and keep his eyes open. Because moving backwards and forwards from England to France, two countries very close to one another, I am always amazed at the great difference in day-to-day texture between the French experience and the English experience. And I am sure that the experience of being a Frenchman is still really nothing very much like the experience of being an Englishman. And I am perfectly sure that to live in any country in Western Europe is not really the same as living in North America, and so on. Now, the jet plane and this and that have drawn us all closer together in some ways, but not as close together as all that. And it seems to me that there is a specifically American idiom and a specifically English idiom, and that the more one tries to be a good internationalist and not to make too much of these national things, the more one is driven back also on the fact that if one is to be truthful, one must also testify to a quite local feeling. God knows, it isn't only different living in England from living in Germany or France; it's different living in Oxford from living up in Scotland. And it seems to me that since literature deals with the particular and for some reason reaches the universal through the particular, and no other way, then it must continue to reflect its own area; and that's what I think about that.

Q: Thank you, Mr. Wain.

Angus Wilson

ANGUS WILSON was born in 1913 in Durban, South Africa, and educated at Westminster and Merton College, Oxford. During the war he served in the Foreign Office and afterwards in the British Museum, from which he resigned as deputy to the superintendent of the Reading Room in 1955. He has also taught intermittently at the University of East Anglia and abroad. His first collection of stories, *The Wrong Set* (1949), early established him as one of the most gifted satirists of the postwar period, a judgment later confirmed by his best-known novel, *Anglo-Saxon Attitudes* (1956). Aside from other novels and stories, Wilson has published several books of criticism, most recently one on Charles Dickens (1970).

The interview took place in Wilson's cottage near Bury St. Edmunds.

Q: Is there anything in Britain, do you think, that corresponds to the official or semiofficial literary groupings like the salons or the Academy in France? Could the Arts Council be in any way considered the British equivalent of the latter?

Wilson: There never has really been a literary establishment in England. I think that's the first thing one has to realize. I have just finished a book on Dickens and perhaps it's relevant to point out that Dickens in his last years collected young men, journalists like Edmund Yates and so on. There have often been rival factions connected around outstanding authors—George Eliot, for example, had her salon—but there never was really any kind of literary establishment in England. I think there have been many attempts at it, and John Gross's book gives a picture of the various attempts to create "worlds" of bookmen, but there always has been a proliferation of opposing cliques. Matthew Arnold was the only person who really ever thought of an academy, and he was the last person to realize it, I suppose.

Perhaps the critical empire of F. R. Leavis is the most powerful united force we have known; but it is far from an accepted academy. The only really serious attempt to create an English literary elite, and it has been written about so much that I think it has been exaggerated, is the Bloomsbury group. I knew a number of them quite well—not the old ones, because they were dead before I started writing—but I've always got on very well with the survivors, and there is much in me that is very sympathetic to the whole outlook of Bloomsbury. Although I've also been very satirical about aspects of their cultured, rich liberalism. But ultimately, I'm on the side of liberalism. And for those people, I would say, it was more a kind of natural getting together. I suppose anybody who comes together thinks that it is a natural getting together, but it was never a community of ideas so much as it was a community of taste. And taste was an extremely dominant thing in Bloomsbury. I think there are many ways in which you could criticize the limitations of its taste, particularly its visual taste, but taste was what dominated it. And if people wanted to criticize it, obviously it did have this class quality as well, although, you know, most of the Bloomsbury people called themselves socialists. It is unbelievable when you read Clive Bell. In *Civilization*, he tries to say that it is obviously necessary to have an artistic and intellectual elite, but that it's also necessary to be a socialist. This is going to be quite all right, because for the next fifty years there will always be people who will be glad to do the day-to-day tasks to keep this elite going. And after that there will be machines, and so we don't have to worry. Which is a very nice and easy way of looking at it.

But, to return to the point under discussion, I don't think

there's ever been any really serious attempt to create an academy in this country, and anyone, certainly, who tried to think of the Arts Council as being an academy of this kind would be very far from the point. I would think that you might get two strong bodies of opinion who dislike the Arts Council. One of these would be people of the right who dislike any sort of government subsidy for the arts, indeed who probably dislike any sort of government subsidy, period; who dislike the welfare state and regard the Arts Council as only a kind of extra part of the welfare state. Some of these might be quite cultivated people, who would argue that you had no right to impose, through taxation, any sort of cultivation upon a population which preferred to remain philistine and to use its money in philistine ways. From what I can understand of the last Conservative party conference on the arts, they do want to lay great emphasis on getting industry to supply the money rather than drawing it out of taxation.* In my own view, it's very problematical how this can be done. One of the reasons being that it's difficult enough even as it is with a treasury which can only give a grant for a year ahead, though they are now trying to arrange a three-year period. It's difficult enough under such a system to maintain a continuity of policy, for example, in theatre. How can one rely on continuing annual payments from industry? It's all right for writers, but for theatres, operas, and art galleries, I should have thought that this would be a very serious problem, but you've more experience of that, because this industrial patronage must be much more common in the arts in America. And, I think, without being critical of this Conservative policy (I'm a staunch Labour man) but without being too critical of the Conservative policy in this matter, I think that they genuinely do believe that it will help to make for more initiative if this is done by industry rather than by the taxpayer. But I think it's also the case that this would be accompanied by very large tax

*I must add that the present Conservative administration has been strong in its support of the Arts Council, as, indeed, after a short spell of vociferous demand for a return to pure free enterprise, it has supported vast areas of government activity.

concessions to industries which were willing to produce money for the arts. Maybe this is a good idea, I don't know, but the thing is two-pronged.

Q: Don't you think that this money would still be channeled through the British Arts Council?

Wilson: I've no idea about that. This would be a matter of policy. The Arts Council has been going a very long time now, and I should think it would be very difficult to start dismantling it, but I really have absolutely no knowledge of this whatsoever. I am not now suggesting, nor were the Conservatives saying, that they would stop giving money to the Arts Council or even give any less than it is presently receiving. They simply tended to lay emphasis on the necessity of getting money from industry as a better means than doing it through the government.

The Arts Council, as you know, was started by the Bloomsbury world. It was, as a matter of fact, started by Keynes. It was his child. And I would have thought, with all the faults that always attach to bureaucracies and so on, that they have done a marvelous job of work, particularly in the visual arts, in the theatre, and in opera.

But now I come to the second attack that would be leveled at it. The second attack would come from exactly the opposite end, from the younger avant-garde people and indeed they have recently produced an organization called FACOP, which calls itself Friends of the Arts Council. Their purpose is to take over the Arts Council, and their objection, of course, would be exactly the opposite: Not, as many critics on the Right would say, that it was run by "arty" people, but that it was not run by the artist; that it should be run by the artist. I think it would not be unfair to them to say, and I think they would be even willing to concede, that their concept of the artist would be of a very special and avant-garde kind in estimating those who ought to take over and run it.

Such broad criticisms aside, I should have thought that it was run very well. If you think of the sort of people who are associated with it, you find a very broad spectrum from all but the extreme right and the extreme left. And this is the best you can say for most things that work in our sort of society, I think. That's really the Arts Council. It isn't an academy in any sense. One of the great things about it is its great resistance to being one. I am, for example, one of the management of a theatre which was restored here, a Regency theatre which we restored in Bury St. Edmunds. This is to look at the affair from the opposite angle, from the point of view of the recipient. We get a subsidy from the Arts Council, and indeed we have* a company for part of the year which is also subsidized. But to suggestions from us that they should give us advice about what ought to be put on, the Arts Council is very resistant. They want us, just as they want everybody—rightly I think—I was going to say within reason, but I would almost say within unreason to do what we wish. If the standards of a thing go down *very* badly, I think after a time there might be some question, and, indeed, while I have been on the Arts Council, there have been one or two questions of this kind. But I suppose this is exactly what those extreme left people might say: "Then how do you ever get any change, or support anything new, if you never drop any old clients?" Since I've been on the Literature Panel of the Arts Council we have added to the list, for example, little presses and small magazines publishing concrete poetry and telephoto poetry and avant-garde forms of many kinds in great number, and indeed more traditional things. The range of things that we support with the small amount of money that we have is surprising. I don't know whether you've seen the list of writers that we have given grants to. During my chairmanship of this panel,† we have worked toward standardizing the kinds of grants given to writers, to avoid anomalies as far as possible. We now have only one kind of grant, and we have just made the decision to stop giving prizes as well.

---

*We had. For a small theatre it has now been proved more feasible to have mixed programs of various visiting companies.

†It is now four years since my term of office on the Arts Council ended.

The Writer's Place

We now will only give grants to three types of recipients: to writers; to publishers for the publication of books which otherwise would be very difficult to produce—there has to be proof that it would be *very* difficult, because we feel that publishers are there to take some commercial risks; and then finally to translators.

On this last matter I am very keen, because I think that translators, for all sorts of reasons, are grossly underpaid. Translation is very important, because a besetting disease of our English culture in general is its great tendency to insularity. We are not so bad as the French in this matter, but we are cut off and the more we can encourage translation, the better.

I think that if you look through those lists of writers who have benefited, you would find a very wide range of writers. We do not, of course, give money where we feel that the work is a learned work which could and would be subsidized by a university. We do not give money to writers solely on grounds of hardship. We give it on grounds of literary merit. And we do not give money, I am afraid, to writers who write frankly popular writing. This, I think, is defensible because, however competent purely popular writing is, if it needs subsidy, then it must be that it is no longer popular and has lost its main function. Help to individual writers may be of two kinds: either to allow them to give up their work entirely for a period and devote themselves to writing only. Or we may give somebody enough money to enable him not to do night work as well as day work. Or we help them perhaps to give up reviewing for a bit.

I sometimes worry about this particular assistance because reviewing is also important to literature. But I do think that if someone has creative talent, it should come before critical talent. I am enough of a creative writer to think that. In fact, I don't think it, I am sure of it. And this relief from literary journalism is one of the most vital things that has to be done. I can speak of this because I started to write as a hobby, and it grew into more than that. I was then at the British Museum, and I had to write my first novel in the four weeks of holiday that I had from work. And I felt that it was truncated. Otherwise I could only write short stories; I never acquired the capacity—some people have it, but I haven't—for writing a continuous work over long periods, with great breaks in between. But I was trying to acquire it during the last part of my time in the Museum, while writing reviews at the same time and really killing myself in the effort to do three jobs at once—of which one, my creative writing, was of course much more to me than a job.

When I resigned from the British Museum, I only had three hundred pounds in the world. I came to live in this cottage, which was then sort of derelict, and lived primitively as I never had done before, but quite luckily I wrote *Anglo-Saxon Attitudes*, which was a success, and that set me going. During that precarious time, I realized how much, if I'd gone on on that basis . . . Well, I know many young writers in that position and some of them, unlike me, with wives and children. They have to take on so much reviewing and television work and so on that they might really just as well be doing a full-time job. In fact, it is doubtful whether it would not really be better to be a schoolteacher, but then you see schoolteachers these days have to work so hard, especially if they are working in a secondary modern school in England where they may have forty pupils in the class and many of them very tough eggs. They apparently have long holidays, but in reality the holidays very seldom are what they seem on paper because there are long periods of examining and preparing and so on. There is, then, the business of doing reviewing and television work, but all of these jobs make enormous demands upon the nervous energies and I think there comes a point where it is desirable to give a chance to that person either to give up some of it or to give it up altogether for a year or two years. We have done that. The highest we ever gave was to V. S. Naipaul, I think. We gave him 3,000 pounds. We made a ruling with which I hope that my successor will agree also—and the council agreed when we presented it to them—that to give people less than 500 pounds nowadays is nonsense. And if we are giving it to them to release them from their work for a year, say, then it must not be less than

1,000 pounds. There are a few prizes still going about in this country which were organized in the twenties and thirties and they are worth about 100 pounds.* Well, this was very nice once upon a time, but now it's really meaningless except for the glory of it. So this is the basis of what we have been trying to do in the Arts Council; and it has been extended now to prose works and so on.

Even more important perhaps is to bring the writers more in touch with their public and particularly with their younger public. So we started the writers' tours. This was Julian Mitchell's idea, but we got it going. I took one group to North Wales, and Julian took one to the northwest of England, to Lancashire. There we were talking in the schools during the day and holding general meetings in the evenings. I have the feeling that it was a great success. What was exciting to me, you know, was that there are starved people in this country who want most desperately to talk to writers and to know what they are like. In the schools the response was marvelous. Now we've got going another idea for writers to visit schools individually.

These are some of the kinds of things which I think the Arts Council can do and I think they're worth doing, but they don't add up to any kind of an academy or any kind of an establishment. Perhaps the real problem at the moment is that one is fighting a battle to maintain some standards without at the same time cutting oneself off from the public altogether. I feel very strongly against all of these people who sell out to journalism and to pure trendiness. But I also feel equally strongly against all of the people—and I have a respected colleague at the university, Tony Dyson, who is one of them; and Kingsley Amis whom I respect greatly, but he's another; and indeed in a different way Dr. Leavis and perhaps even Roy Fuller—all of these people seem to be demanding some kind of strictness of standards which seems to me to go back on the idea of extended education altogether. Partly my egalitarian feelings and my feelings of dis-

*Much different now.

338

like of arrogance sway me, but also I am swayed by a different conception which is that it is no good pretending. The populace at large won't go on supplying money and support, if all good literature is something that gets remoter and remoter and remoter from them. You have got to find some kind of *modus vivendi* between these two. I only recently sent out a letter to a number of writers asking if they would be willing to go and visit schools and talk to them. One writer who shall be nameless, but who is a well-known English writer, replied that, as far as he was concerned, he had no interest in the education of the masses and in his opinion schoolteachers fell among the masses. Well, I think if you have this attitude, it is just as dangerous as indeed it is to spend your time appearing on television in parlor games and quizzes and other things, an abominable and true *trahison des clercs*.

I feel that my writing comes first, and this is why I am giving up the Arts Council now. I have done three years of it and I must now give more time to my writing. Also I am giving up the university for a year and a half. It is a very private thing for me, being a writer; what I write is very private, but it is fed by the outside world, and to some extent, I think, I must feed that outside world as well if I am going to get anything back from it. I do really believe in the social duty of the writer. And the social duty of the writer in my opinion is not really to maintain a rigid standard of values which cuts him off from the rest of the community, but to seek to bring sweetness and light into the activities of the community as far as he is able. I teach at East Anglia University here for this reason. When I joined the university at its inception, I had never done any teaching, but I've found it extremely interesting. I have taken part in running the local theatre, and so on and so on. These are activities which inevitably meant that I am some of the time—yes, well, it would not be arrogant to say—accepting and being involved with things which I regard as not as good as I would like them to be, both in performance and, more particularly, in the standard of work that

The Writer's Place

is chosen to be done. But it seems to me better that I should use my interest to try to raise the standard rather than withdraw from it altogether.

This seems to me the absolutely basic problem of the writer today. Of course, such a choice is very much the problem of a minority of writers. It's only the problem of that minority of writers who can support themselves by writing. I am lucky enough now to be one of those, though it has helped me financially to teach and so on. Primarily, however, I can support myself by writing. Therefore I can see this problem *pur et simple*, and it is up to my conscience to see what I should do about it. But of course for many writers and for most young writers, except the lucky ones like Margaret Drabble, and even for a good number of older ones, let's face it, the problem does not fall in this area at all; it is, rather, how can I write and how can I also do another job and keep myself alive? And how can I do the sort of job which will allow me the maximum amount of time for writing and will not be so socially or culturally disgusting that it will be a positively evil contribution? It's easy for a few university dons, as it seems to me, or professors, or very well-established authors like Kingsley Amis to get up and make statements about absolute purity. But I suppose he sees it in a different form. I like him very much as a person, but it seems to me that he sees it in a different form. He would be quite happy to do a book, you know, an imitation of Ian Fleming, or to be involved with films, which would seem to me to be, well, what I would call *trahison des clercs*. On the other hand, as far as the university goes, he wants it to remain an absolute elite. I suppose the answer is that I want to find some kind of middle road, while continuing to write my own work exactly as I choose to write it.

Q: Do you think that the American example of the writer alternating as the teacher of creative writing is one that should be followed in England?

Wilson: Well, I don't know what to say about that, except that I have only taught creative writing for this last term. When I was

340

asked to be associated with the University of East Anglia which
was started up six years ago as a new university within range of
where I live—well, reasonable range—I said; yes, I would be
associated, but I knew nothing about creative writing, nor did I
think it could be taught. I said that I would teach things that
interested me, if they would like me to do it; and indeed I was
included in the ordinary syllabus. I remember when I first went
there I was teaching practical criticism of a sort that I had never
done in my life, and we were analyzing passages out of Marx's
Capital and out of *Culture and Anarchy* and out of Orwell and so on,
something which was interesting to do. But then I soon liberated
myself from that. I do lectures on Richardson and his relation to
Jane Austen or to Diderot and Jacobi (I have a very great interest
in Richardson), and also lectures about Dostoevsky and Dickens,
and about the Bloomsbury group. I propose to do another one in
two years' time, when I am teaching again, about Kipling and
Wilde and Shaw; because I believe that they can be seen as three
aspects of the same thing: the aesthetic and the imperialist
movement and the Fabian movement have close connections. But
you see from this that my interests in literature are rather impure.
Still, I find all this extremely interesting.

Well, even at that I have had to say that I would only teach
one term a year instead of two. But mind you, I *am* fifty-six. If I
were younger, it might well be that I would have gone on teaching
for two terms and even three. It's partly that I hear time's chariot
behind me, and I want to give as much time to writing books as I
can, because I think rather highly of what I have written; but I still
think I could do something better. I am not the sort of modern
writer who wants to make a noise and that's the end of that. I
would like to think that I may survive, and if I do, I want to write
the best I can.

Now, creative writing I only did for this last term.* I found
that I was rather dubious about it altogether. Malcolm Bradbury,

*Since that time I taught creative writing for a whole exciting term at Iowa.
And I think now that creative writing can*not* be *taught*, but a great deal can be done
to assist and encourage it.

who organized it, has done a lot of it in America, I think, and I worked with him. I have been extremely impressed by the intelligence and the standards of the six young men who came to our seminar. We only had six with us the first term. Whether what I have been able to tell them has been of very much use, I'm not sure. I'm quite good, I think, about what it's like to be a writer, by being quite open about my own motivations so far as I understand them in connection between their style and themselves. But I would think I'm very much less good when it comes to questions of genre, because I have never been able to understand why genre should exist at all. It seems to me that the only purpose of writing is to show, as in life, that genres can be combined. And so this notion that comes up as soon as creative writing is discussed, namely of people writing impurely, is meaningless to me; because as soon as I see that somebody has attempted to join two different kinds of writing in a story, I am immediately immensely pleased and urge them to go on. Whereas, it seems to me that creative writing teachers tend to say: you've got two styles muddled here, now go and separate them out.

Q: Do you consider this a good way for a writer to earn his living?

Wilson: Well, I would not want to do it all of the time, no. There is a special reason why I wouldn't. Of course, it is a good way of feeling that you are doing something for literature. It *might* be a harmful thing. I can imagine the wrong kind of person being dogmatic in trying to stop somebody writing in the way they should write. That would be very wicked, I think. But providing one is the right kind of person, I should think it would be a socially and aesthetically valuable thing to do. But, like writing criticism, which is again one of the other ways in which writers can make their living, I think there is one grave defect and that is—but then I am a great believer in magic as far as writing goes—I do believe that you have to be a careful and extremely self-exploring person and indeed, as you have possibly seen from my writing, very interested in the seeds and nature of writing and in the nature of the writer. Nevertheless, I do believe that there is a dangerous thing about letting this sort of self-inquiry go on while you are actually conceiving a book. The only times that I have been worried at all by the university have been when I have been teaching literature and felt that something was coming into my mind during a seminar, some—oh, perhaps even from a student—some sort of criticism of my own work which I was not going to have time fully to digest, but would simply get in there and erode my self-confidence. This is a very dangerous thing to do with a magical process. This, of course, can arise equally when you're reviewing other people's books. So all these things have their grave disadvantages.

I sometimes wonder whether it isn't better to take a job of a completely different kind. Roy Fuller, who is, I have every reason to believe, a very good poet and I think a very excellent novelist, has been a very successful man in the insurance world. This has taken no doubt some doing, but it must have given him one great advantage that he remains outside the whole thing and his daily work is not ever leading him into that sort of inquiry about the creative process which I think can do harm. However, if one is going to be forced to do these things, I think perhaps it is better to teach at the university than it is to do very frequent reviewing or to be in the television world or to be in the editorial world of publishers. For the past three years, as I was telling you earlier, I have been much involved with the literary world and have found it very interesting. I am very glad that I have done it, because for years I had cut myself off from it and it has been most useful. It has brought me into touch with a lot of younger authors and I think I can help them and learn from them much more now. Nevertheless, I do believe that to live in that kind of world of constant evaluation of literary reputations is a belittling thing. It is the same thing that, in the long run, makes me dislike the whole cultural atmosphere of Rome and Paris, and, indeed, New York.

It makes for taking in each other's washing. I know the argument that is used always that this is one of the ways by which people improve, because they are subjected all the time to the fierce criticism of their intellectual equals. This may contain some truth. No doubt in me, as in all English people, there is a certain clinging to amateurism. But I do think at the same time that the world which often surrounds, for example, the giving of prizes in Rome or in Paris is really degrading for a writer and this kind of infighting and bitchery is something which you should avoid. I don't think you can ever totally avoid it if you are working closely in the world of reviewing or literary editorship or television or publishing houses, if you are a creative person yourself. Of course, I am not now saying that these are not most desirable jobs which have to be done, just as bookselling has to be done, and without which we could not exist. But I am now thinking solely of preserving the creative activity as much as one possibly can. This does not mean that I believe—whatever this means—in living in an ivory tower, far from it. Though sometimes this rather remote cottage in which I live might seem like some sort of a leafy bower. Somebody came to see me here, a very good woman writer, Christine Brook-Rose, who is our only follower of the *nouveau roman*. She came here and said, "What are you doing? Are you trying to re-create the womb?" Well, there may be an element of this, but I travel a great deal, and I go to London a great deal. I believe one should. I am going to Ceylon and to Asia for most of this winter. I do travel a lot, but, oddly enough, living in a place like this where I go to teach at the university, where I am involved in local life quite a bit and so on, there are ways in which I meet quite a variety of people whom I just never would meet if I were to be in that wholly literary world. And this I think is the most important thing for a novelist. Of course, this depends on what kind of novelist you are, but for the sort of novelist that I am—in fact, I think it applies to all novelists. Yes, even if you were only *going to be* a novelist. Look how awful it is: what a brilliant novelist Natalie Sarraute is! And yet you get her writing a novel which is about the way in which a novel is written and is discussed by a group of people and so on. What is the meaning of this Byzantinism? I am not now wishing plain man's literature or something, but there is no reason for this terrible Byzantinism.

This is what shocks and horrifies me when I talk to many continental writers, somebody like Alberto Moravia or any of those people in France. The way they use the word "bourgeois" horrifies me. Most of my best friends are bourgeois, and why shouldn't they be? What does it mean, all of this cutting yourself off from human beings? So I think I am a bit worried about those jobs which take you away from ordinary people. But how can one get a job which will give you enough time to write and not exhaust you, because writing novels is a very exhausting activity. I hesitate to say this, but poetry—I have talked to poets about this and they do admit this—that on the whole poetry is, of course, much more exhausting physically and from the nervous point of view while it lasts, but it lasts so much less long. Take a long novel like my last one, *No Laughing Matter*. I write quickly, but even so, from the moment of its first conception to completion, it took me nearly three years. My first novel took me four weeks. But even so, most of my books now take me half a year or a year. This does demand a kind of total intensity and produces an exhaustion which it is very difficult to render compatible with other jobs. When you are younger, it is easier. You have the vitality. You have the nervous energy. The most awful thing, I think, must be to know that you are a good writer and to have to write in unfavorable conditions when you are getting older or quite old, because you haven't ever had success. This doesn't happen too often because mostly such writers as I have known of that kind have had private means. But of course this type of rentier writer is now disappearing, as they are also in the world of scholarship. When I first worked in the British Museum Reading Room, when I used to be the deputy superintendent there before the war, the greater part of the scholars were nonacademic people working on private incomes. I should think that's now perhaps 1 percent.

Q: Do you think that teaching at the university, in your own experience, has tended to limit the range of characters that you might have included in your own writing otherwise?

Wilson: Well, I didn't teach there long enough, you see. I have

345

never taught there more than once a week and that for two terms in the year. Now it is only on Mondays for one term a year that I go there. I see a lot of the students, as much as I can. That has been most valuable, because as you get older, you do lose touch with younger people. I felt that the young people at the end of my last novel have a good deal of life, and other people have told me that this was so. I would like to see more of the students. Yes, I know *much* more about the younger generation from this experience. It has been very valuable. I don't see enough of my colleagues, though I see a certain amount of them. I think they would know that I feel, that I know enough about academic people already! I think if I lived in a residential university it would be death. But then I don't think I could live residentially anywhere, except in the middle of a wood like this.

I was born and brought up in a nomadic family. We moved every two or three years. Now I have lived fourteen years here. It seems unbelievable. But I have been abroad a great deal, and I go to London and stay in a flat there quite a lot. But either I must live in isolation or I must be peripatetic, I think. For a writer, I am sure this is important. Some people talk so much now, don't they, about how society is so fragmented that you can only write about small bits. Well, this may be so, I don't know. But I still valiantly try to go on to create—I say valiantly, well yes, I think it is valiant—to create a more total world, and to do this I must know as many people as I can. I am extremely aware, for example, that my world has never included the North of England and insofar as there is a strong difference between the North and the South—and there is—this difference is largely not there in my work. Many people have pointed out to me that my working class characters are either disreputable or else they belong to a rather vanishing species. I think this may be true. I don't write about the working classes from the inside. I only write about the bourgeoisie from inside. But then the bourgeoisie does these days extend over a very large area. And such aristocrats as I know would probably say that my aristocrats are a little bit dubious. But then aristocrats and working class in that old-fashioned sense are a minority in a world that is increasingly bourgeoisified. Of course, one is very well aware of *lacunae*, and anyhow one isn't a social document. I hope not, at any rate; I don't want to be a journalist. Still, you can only write about what you want to write about. I never write, practically, about "abroad," as the saying is. There were some scenes in Morocco in my last book, but only to illustrate the English people who were there. I do spend a lot of time abroad, and most of my books are written abroad, in remote parts of South Morocco, and Egypt, and all sorts of strange places. Or America, which I have traveled in a certain amount and like very much. Or Australia, which I love. This traveling is a way of allowing me to see afresh the world I do know in England, and to write about it in a wider context. My books are filled with foreigners, but they are always seen in the English context.* But then I am an English writer.

However, we came to this really from asking whether I would feel isolated if I were at the university. The answer is yes. If I were a full-time university person, I would go mad. But then I would go mad if I had to work in an editorial office or in an advertising agency . . . Of course, I wouldn't go mad. I worked for fifteen years in the British Museum and did not go mad, I think. But I got free from it and certainly would not want to go back to it. Then again, you say all that and then you suddenly think, oh yes, of course, all this is true. You need freedom, you need ease, you need, as you get older, a certain amount of relaxation so that your nervous energies are not being drawn into too many directions, and you need a lot of experience in life. But of course, fundamentally, as with the great nineteenth-century novelists or the great twentieth-century novelists, those of us who are minor twentieth-century novelists feed upon our childhood. Ultimately, it's what happened in your first twenty-one years that really matters, isn't it? I mean, the rest is the material, but the conflicts arise out of your youth, and these you go on working upon. But you do need new material to use to rework this conflict in.

*My new novel, *As If by Magic*, is laid in great part abroad, but it is still the effect of abroad on the English hero and heroine that concerns me.

The Writer's Place

Q: You mentioned earlier that you felt the two novelists you admire most were Virginia Woolf and Evelyn Waugh.

Wilson: In England and in this century, yes.

Q: Would you say that your indebtedness to them is personal as well as intellectual?

Wilson: Well, I never knew Virginia Woolf, because she died long before I started to write. You see, I did not write a word in my life until 1947, and I was not published until 1949, and she committed suicide in 1941, I think. So I never knew her. I've met her husband, who was a charming man. But maybe she was rather sharp and rather scary to be with, I don't know. My debt to her is very important. When I was young, I read her with enormous zeal. I think now that I didn't really grasp the depths at which she was writing. I always had read a lot of novels . . . I think I should explain this first: I was trained as a historian, I became a librarian, but I always had read a great number of novels, particularly nineteenth-century novels; above all, nineteenth- and eighteenth-century novels. But Virginia Woolf was one of the contemporary people I read when I was an adolescent, and Aldous Huxley too. It's sometimes said that I was influenced by Aldous Huxley. I personally hope that it's not true. If it is, it is because it's atavistic from my adolescence. But Virginia Woolf, I certainly did read then. Later I reacted very strongly against this influence. I think you would find this if you talked to Snow or to other people, that there was a reaction in the fifties against what was called "modern" literature. I think this reaction has gone very much too far. If what they meant was the restoration of the "traditional" novel, I'm entirely against it. All I ever meant and thought and all I think now on this matter is present in my criticism and in my writing, namely that we hadn't yet drained out of the nineteenth century and the eighteenth century the very extraordinary elements that were there. This is what I am interested in, the madness and newness that is to be found in Richardson, Dickens, Zola, and, above all, in Stendhal. The first

348

radio talk I ever did was an attack on Virginia Woolf. I remember this extremely well, accusing her of being cut off from society. She was living in an ivory tower, suffered from class blindness, and so on and so on. I had learned, I said, that you have always to bite the hand that feeds you, and I did. But now I have returned, and I'm going to give a lecture next year in her honor. I have been brought to her very much more by teaching her. This has been one of the values of teaching. It's taught me my great admiration for her and, I'm afraid, somewhat lessened my admiration, particularly for his early works, for Forster. But it enormously enhanced my admiration for Virginia Woolf. My last novel, *No Laughing Matter*, is immensely influenced, I think, by Virginia Woolf, by her concept in *The Waves*.

Evelyn Waugh is a different matter. Evelyn Waugh, I think, was very much influenced by Dickens. He is a social satirist of a certain kind. I was very much intrigued by him when I was young. His humor has remained with me. His politics and his outlook were entirely opposite to mine, although I think I have as great a love of traditional England as he had. But it's a different sort of traditional England. His works—their humor—do play a part in my writing, I suppose, but we both draw from Dickens. He did give me a good deal of personal encouragement in my early writing. This was very unusual in that he was not famous for giving encouragement to people, and also because he certainly very much disagreed with my political views. So I do owe him a great debt. But then this thing one has for writers has so little to do with one's social and political views. For example, the writer I admire most as a novelist in France—not as a playwright, but as a novelist—is Henri de Montherlant. But I hardly think that Montherlant's political views would be the same as mine. Indeed, when I visited him, I didn't find they were. But I think him a great humorist. I am terribly interested in the humor of writers who are sometimes thought to be "black" writers: Montherlant, Dostoevsky, Conrad. These appeal to me greatly as "dark" writers, but also for the humorous elements in them. The interplay of humor and horror in life and in books is what fascinates me. I never would be more proud than if somebody said, "I think that's the funniest and horriblest thing I've ever read." This is what I want to try to make people realize that life is: the quality of our despair is such that it's also hilarious. This is to be found, I think, in Dickens. But there is another sort of writing which is very, very rare. I would never hope to write a book of this sort and I doubt if they can be written now, because our world is not a happy enough one. But there are those odd books like the *Chartreuse de Parme*, which really are about how lovely life is, and even that has a dark ending. But that is a book I love to teach to my students, because, being used to the terrible moralism of nineteenth-century English writing, to be loosed, to be set free by that marvelous serene amoralism of the *Chartreuse de Parme* is exhilarating. But this could hardly be written now. Most books now which pretend to some kind of serenity are phony, because life isn't in the faintest degree serene.

Q: Would you say that you had other personal contacts that were of importance to you besides those with Evelyn Waugh? Writers who helped you in your career?

Wilson: Well, Cyril Connolly published my first stories in *Horizon* and I owe him a great debt for that, but my contacts with writers were very slight. I started to write very late. Therefore when I came on the scene, I was not a young writer, and the likelihood of older writers helping someone who is already middle-aged is small. No, I can't, I am afraid, say I owe very much to the actual personal behavior of older writers. They were never rude or nasty to me, but no, apart from a letter from Edith Sitwell encouraging me considerably, which I think she did with a lot of younger writers, and, I must say, very considerable encourage-ment from J. B. Priestley. Although his kind of writing is not really mine, he has been always very encouraging and has shown great interest. I don't know that otherwise I could speak of any older writers.* As I say, they have never been unfriendly. But

*In a subsequent letter, Mr. Wilson asked that Edmund Wilson and Ernest

I never had much to do with them. Just as when I was a student at the university, I never had anything to do with dons. When I started as a young writer, I was still a librarian at the Museum. I went to some literary parties; I got to know Stephen Spender quite well. We traveled in Japan together. And Alberto Moravia. But I would hesitate to say that anyone encouraged me very much. I wonder if they wanted to particularly. You know, I don't think that my kind of writing was liked so much by older writers. But Evelyn Waugh certainly did. He wrote a letter when my first story was published in *Horizon*; he wrote a particular letter to Cyril Connolly, saying, you know, this is an absolutely splendid young writer and so on. He really was marvelous. And he could be very disconcerting in a marvelous way. I remember the last time I saw him at a luncheon party . . . no, a dinner party it was. He had a big Victorian ear trumpet, an ornate ear trumpet. He was bored, I am sure, with the conversation of the dinner company and also probably with my conversation. I was talking to him about something that I am sure he did not care about at all. However, at a certain point, he took his ear trumpet and put it down and said very loudly to the whole dinner party: "What Wilson says is very interesting indeed, you know. When he says that Macmillan is our first Christian Prime Minister since Salisbury, he is quite right." It is the sort of thing that I would never think about or care about, but he did care about it and it was what he wanted to talk about. So he successfully managed to deflect us into it, and this I find very endearing. He was a great character.

John Lehmann has always been very friendly and encouraging about my work. Yes, certainly, I must say so. And I had good reviews from writers, you know, but I didn't follow them up. I will tell you whom I admired very greatly and who wrote me very friendly and helpful letters. That was old John Cowper Powys. I admired his work very greatly and I had sent him my books earlier on. He wrote me a letter, I remember, and a

Hemingway be added to the list of writers who had given him personal help and encouragement. (Ed.)

very wise letter, considering that I tend to overwrite, saying how much he liked the book but ending: "Beware, my friend, the bumblebee." Which is very true. E. M. Forster has always been encouraging. But I don't really think I have ever had, you know, a lot to do with older writers. And I am not the kind of person who does. You know, you are either the kind of person who likes to be with young people or you like to be with old people. And I have always preferred, on the whole, to be with young people. I hope I have done quite a lot to encourage younger writers. I certainly have tried to, and to meet them as much as I can. I had my twentieth anniversary of writing just this last March. We had Margaret Drabble, Melvin Bragg, Julian Mitchell, Alan Burns, and Michael Moorcock. All young writers. I don't think we had any of my contemporaries or older writers.* So this perhaps tells you about me without my having to say any more.

Q: Thank you, Mr. Wilson.

*Some were asked. Only—and I was so happy to see her—Elizabeth Bowen came.

INDEX

Index

Index

Index

Heard, Gerald, 127
Hemingway, Ernest, 26, 81, 85, 88, 90, 98, 99, 101, 277, 293, 350–351n
Henderson the Rain King, 106
Herzen, Alexander, 237
Heyer, Georgette, 76
"Hiawatha," 276
High Wind in Jamaica, 185, 186, 188, 191, 199, 201, 205, 206
Hikmet, Nâzim, 256
Hireling, The, 170
History of the Royal Society, 235
Hitler, Adolf, 3, 194, 197
Hobsbaum, Philip, 142, 145
Holiday, 285
Holland, 206
Holroyd, Stuart, 177
Holub, Miroslav, 151
Homer, 7, 197
Hope of Heaven, 28
Hopkins, Bill, 10
Horace, 6
Horizon, 350, 351
Housman, A. E., 11
Hughes, Owain, 196, 199
Hughes, Ted, 104, 140, 143, 147, 150, 153
Human Condition, The, 187, 188
Hungarian Revolution, 56
Hunter, Jim, 104
Hurry On Down, 106, 322
Hutchinson (publishing company), 82, 87
Huxley, Aldous, 6, 26, 30, 53, 127, 164, 165, 205, 348

I Like It Here, 23
Iliad, 193
Image of a Society, 124
Imperial Chemicals Corporation, 138
In Cold Blood, 86
In Hazard, 186
Ionesco, Eugene, 67
Ireland, 143, 279, 282, 283: Trevor on, 306–307
Isherwood, Christopher, 127, 287
Italy, 204, 216, 240, 247, 249

Jacobi, Friedrich Heinrich, 341
Jaffe, Rona, 245
Jamaica, 205

James, Henry, 38, 235, 236, 283, 318: Hartley on, 170–171
Japan, 351
Jerusalem the Golden, 119
Johnson, B. S., 118
Johnson, Pamela Hansford, 11, 199
Johnson, Samuel, 120
Jonathan Cape (publishing company), 87, 139, 141: Maschler on, 244–257
Jonson, Ben, 324
Journalism, 43, 80, 224, 338: Pritchett on, 280; Sansom on, 285–286
Joyce, James, 7, 30, 42, 194
Jungle, The, 213
Junkers, The, 113

Kafka, Franz, 50, 235, 247: Burns on, 53
Karl Marx University (Goethe University), 233
Keats, John, 322, 323
Kermode, Frank, 225, 230, 254
Kesey, Ken, 25
Keynes, John Maynard, 12, 334
Kipling, Rudyard, 341
Koch, Kenneth, 150
Koestler, Arthur, 14

La Rochefoucauld, Duc François de, 3
Labour party (British), 42, 229, 230
Laing, R. D., 231
Lancaster University, 150
Larkin, Philip, 129, 143, 147, 153, 318
Last Exit to Brooklyn, 70
Laurenson, Diana, 8
Lawrence, D. H., 30, 58, 89, 164, 165, 205, 211, 269, 270, 323: Burns on, 59
Le Carré, John, 37
Le monde, 242
Leavis, F. R., 105, 108, 297, 332, 338
Leavis, Q. D., 7
Leeds University, 149
Lefebvre, Georges, 231
Lehmann, John, 126, 134, 351
L'emploi du temps, 117
Lenin, Nikolai, 54, 214
Lessing, Doris, 113
Lewis, Alun, 128
Lewis, C. Day, 127, 323
Lewis, C. S., 3, 319, 321
L'express, 242

359

Index

Index

Rocks of Valpré, The, 79
Roethke, Theodore, 104
Rome, 57, 343, 344
Room of One's Own, A, 114, 115
Rosemary's Baby, 26
Ross, Alan, 125, 126
Roth, Philip, 35
Royal Literary Fund, 219, 264
Royal Opera House, 261
Royal Society of Literature, 166, 171, 235
Russia. *See* Soviet Union

Saint and Sinner, 86
Salisbury, Lord, 351
Sarraute, Natalie, 344
Sartre, Jean-Paul, 238
Saturday Westminster Gazette, 200
Scarlet Woman, The, 170
Science fiction, 28, 30: Amis on, 37; Burns on, 53
Scotland, 143, 144, 330
Scottish Arts Council, 144
Second Sex, The, 107
Second World War, 97, 202
Shackborough, Julian, 14
Shakespeare, William, 7, 32, 38, 148, 195, 226, 234, 314, 316, 324
Shaw, George Bernard, 12, 42, 100, 321, 341
Shelley, Percy Bysshe, 322, 323
Short stories. *See* Fiction
Shostakovich, Dimitrievich, 6
Shrimp and Anemone, 168
Sillitoe, Alan, 77, 247
Simenon, Georges, 101, 194, 328
Sinclair, Upton, 213
Sissman, L. E., 31
Sistine Chapel, 288
Sitwell, Edith, 350
Skidelsky, Robert, 227
Smaller Sky, A, 325, 326
Smollett, Tobias George, 325
Snodgrass, William, 152
Snow, C. P., 102–103, 348
Snowman, The, 249
Society, and the writer, 5: Amis on, 24; Burns on, 54–55, 56; Callard on, 84–85; Fuller on, 131–132; Johnson on, 218
Society of Authors, 10, 13, 86, 115:

Bonham-Carter on, 39–41, 42, 43–48
Sociology of Literature, The, 8
Sollers, Phillipe, 68
Solzhenitsyn, Alexander, 5, 47
Somerset Maugham Award, 43, 252
Sorel, Georges, 233
South America, 247
South Wales, 185, 189
Soviet Union, 83, 226, 232: writer in, 5, 19; and subsidization of the arts, 55–56; Wain on, 327
Spain, 28, 187, 279
Spanish Civil War, 130, 278, 279
Spark, Muriel, 216, 246
Spectator, 186, 295, 297, 302
Spencer, Herbert, 323
Spender, Stephen, 127, 128, 130, 133, 137, 199, 254, 279, 323, 351
Spenser, Edmund, 324
Spiegel, 242
Sprightly Running, 226, 318, 319, 321
Spring, Howard, 220
Stalin, Joseph, 6
Stand, 143
Steiner, George, 8, 250
Stendhal, 4, 6, 85, 88, 197, 348
Stevens, Wallace, 127, 138
Stevenson, Robert Louis, 207
Stone, Bernard, 140
Strachey, Lytton, 98, 164
Stravinsky, Igor, 237
SDS (Students for a Democratic Society), 233
Sunday Times, 73, 133, 250, 295, 302
Sun's Attendant, The, 249, 250
Surrealism, 59
Survival of the Fittest, The, 214
Sutherland, James, 7
Swingewood, Alan, 8
Symons, Julian, 134

Table ronde, 238
Tale of Genji, 198
Taylor, Elizabeth, 36, 309
Tel Quel group, 68
Television, and the writer: Amis on, 27, 28; Burns on, 52, 59–60; Callard on, 92; Drabble on, 111, 120; Johnson on, 212; Pritchett on, 283–284; Sansom on, 287, 293; Trevor on,

The Writer's Place